HIDING MENGELE

HOW A NAZI NETWORK HARBORED
THE ANGEL OF DEATH

BETINA ANTON

DIVERSION
BOOKS

NEW YORK

Diversion Books
A division of Diversion Publishing Corp.
www.diversionbooks.com

For more information, email info@diversionbooks.com.

First Diversion Books Edition: October 2024
Hardcover ISBN 978-1-635-76882-4
e-ISBN 978-1-635-76881-7

Design by Neuwirth & Associates, Inc.
Photo research by Gabriella Gonçalles

Printed in the United States of America
1 3 5 7 9 10 8 6 4 2

Diversion books are available at special discounts for bulk purchases in the US
by corporations, institutions, and other organizations.
For more information, please contact admin@diversionbooks.com.

TO PABLO AND HELENA

CONTENTS

HOW TO BURY A BODY
UNDER A FALSE NAME

BERTIOGA, BRAZIL. FEBRUARY 1979

I t was a beautiful afternoon, and Peter hadn't yet left the house that day. The doors and windows were closed almost all the time, even in the stifling summer air.[1] The neighbors barely knew who was inside. He was very reserved and didn't like strangers. He had arrived alone from São Paulo the day before, after a tiring bus ride through tortuous roads and a long ferry crossing. His friends Wolfram and Liselotte Bossert and their children were already waiting for him. The old man loved those kids: Andreas was twelve, and Sabine fourteen. Even so, he hesitated for a while before accepting the invitation to spend time with them in Bertioga. He said he was tired. He only agreed to go because he believed that his life was already at an end.[2] Lately, he had been irritable, nervous, and before his trip he had had a fight with Elsa, his former maid. The reason was that he liked her but it wasn't reciprocated. One more reason to relax on that hot afternoon.

---

1 "Son may have gone to Bertioga." *O Estado de S. Paulo*, June 8, 1985, p. 15.

2 "The exhumation of the enigma." *Veja*, June 12, 1985.

He decided to leave the summer house to take a swim in the sea. The whole Bossert family accompanied him to the beach. They were so close that they seemed to have blood ties. He'd known the kids since they were little, and everyone, even the adults, called him "Uncle Peter" or just "Uncle."

All five of them could speak Portuguese fluently, but always preferred to talk in German, their mother tongue. Uncle Peter was from Bavaria in southern Germany. Wolfram and Liselotte Bossert were Austrian. The two were already married when they decided to come to Brazil in 1952, attracted by botany, especially her, who had always loved the beauty of plants and venturing into nature. They also knew that there was a large community of German speakers here, which would help open doors for them in an unknown country. They had left Europe during the Cold War because they feared another armed conflict on the continent. At the time, there was a climate of uncertainty in Austria, which was still occupied by the Allied forces. Not to mention the fact that the country sat right next to the Iron Curtain, the imaginary line separating the capitalist and communist worlds. All this tension added to the fact that Liselotte and Wolfram had faced World War II just a few years earlier and believed they could not bear an experience like that again.

The Allies' nightly bombings on Graz, the city where Liselotte had lived and the second largest in Austria, left her heart "irregular," as she used to say. From that time until the end of her life, she felt that her heartbeat never returned to normal. When Adolf Hitler invaded Poland and started the war, she had been an eleven-year-old schoolgirl. The conflict shook her world. Her uncles had died fighting for the Third Reich.[3] Wolfram had also fought for the German Army, without ever rising above Scharführer, the equivalent of corporal in the military hierarchy. Uncle Peter had risen much higher, and Wolfram admired him for that: he had reached the rank of Hauptsturmführer, the equivalent of captain. Moreover, he was part of the dreaded

---

3 Personal interview with Liselotte Bossert, November 2017.

SS—or Schutzstaffel—a special force that was created to provide security for the leaders of the Nazi party and became an elite group with its own army.

However, it wasn't Uncle Peter's work in the SS or at the front that made him world-famous years later, but rather his work as a doctor in the Auschwitz death camp. Josef Mengele was his real name, something that no one could know then. That wasn't something to talk about in front of other people, especially the children, who had no idea about Uncle Peter's dark past. What mattered at that moment was getting to the sea. The beach was about a thousand feet from the house that the Bossert family rented every summer from another Austrian, Erica Vicek, who called herself a "staunch anti-Nazi." She didn't have the slightest idea of who the special guest that her tenants used to host really was.

At the end of the 1970s, Bertioga was isolated from the rest of the world, and getting there required patience. Access was via the island of Santo Amaro, in Guarujá. From there you could take a ferry across the channel. Travelers couldn't be in a hurry, as the short journey could take hours, depending on the ferry schedule. This didn't discourage many Europeans who lived in Brazil and enjoyed the coast when on vacation. In addition to the Austrians, some Germans, Swiss, Italians, Hungarians, and French had vacation homes there. It was an opportunity to relax in a pleasant and peaceful place. Cars were left unlocked, the windows and doors of the houses were open; there were no worries there, unlike life in São Paulo or in Guarujá next door, with its trendy beaches and much more expensive real estate. Many vacationers liked to take advantage of the quiet to spend hours fishing for mullet, of which there were plenty in Bertioga, as Hans Staden had described more than four hundred years earlier. The German explorer was the first person to publish a book about the beauties and dangers of that region full of indigenous people in the sixteenth century. Staden certainly spoke from experience, for he had been captured by the Tupinambás, who were cannibals, and narrowly avoided ending up in the cauldron. Another favorite pastime during those long summer seasons was card games. At least once a week, a group of Europeans of different nationalities got together to play, and even back then rumors circulated that Nazis were hiding in the area.[4]

Bertioga's main beach, Enseada, wasn't exactly the Côte d'Azur. The color of the sea was almost brown, an effect caused by the decomposition of the rich Atlantic Forest vegetation that covers the entire area. The tourists didn't mind the shade of the water, which from a distance looked dirty. The charm of the place seemed to be something else: the sea was good for swimming, unlike so many beaches on the coast of São Paulo. With a bit of luck, on some days it formed a perfect pool for children. On other days, the sea could get rough and, during vacation periods, it was not uncommon for lifeguards to report drownings. The long beach, over seven miles from end to end, with a wide strip of sand, was ideal for playing soccer, as some of the men were doing that Wednesday afternoon.

While the ball was rolling in the sand, the Bosserts and Uncle Peter went into the water. The sea currents soon began to pull, and Liselotte preferred to go to the shallows with her children. Uncle Peter swam very well, but that day Andreas saw him raising his arm, asking for help. He seemed to be drowning. Liselotte thought her friend had suffered a stroke, and Wolfram rushed to his aid. When he grabbed him, the old man was already gasping for breath. Andreas ran down the beach to get a Styrofoam float to throw to his uncle. Other people also tried to help. Two lifeguards, who were at the only post on the beach over a quarter-mile away, saw the movement and came running. Wolfram had already managed to pull Uncle Peter into waist-deep water, but he was still struggling to get out of the sea. The rescuers had to drag them both out. They performed chest compressions to try to revive Peter, who was unconscious by then, but it was too late. He was already dead.

---

4 Interview with a German descendant who spent her summers in Bertioga and witnessed Mengele's drowning on Enseada Beach. She did not want to be identified for fear of reprisals.

Someone called for an ambulance. From there, they announced the obvious: there was nothing more to be done.[5] Despair fell upon Liselotte. She hugged the body and didn't want to let go.[6] Her husband was feeling unwell because he himself had almost drowned trying to save his friend. An ambulance took Wolfram to the hospital, while Liselotte stayed on the beach with the dead man. The lifeguards made a report and called the Military Police (PM). Corporal Espedito Dias Romão, a tall, strong Black man, was in charge of the Bertioga police station that afternoon. It is ironic that he was precisely the authority to record the death of Mengele, who had said he was terrified of Black people and used to declare that "slavery should never have ended."[7]

Arriving at the beach, Corporal Dias Romão found Liselotte nervous. She told him that her uncle had died. The policeman asked for the dead man's documents, but they were at the beach house. She walked there and returned with a foreigner's ID card, which listed the name Wolfgang Gerhard, born in Leibnitz, Austria, on September 3, 1925. The document was of a fifty-three-year-old man. The age of the body lying on the beach was in fact sixty-seven, a fourteen-year difference that the young policeman didn't notice. When he received the document, he filed the police report without suspecting anything. The only thing that caught his eye was the nationality: Austrian.[8] Liselotte gave the address of her own house in São Paulo, as if the uncle had lived with her. Corporal Dias, who until then hadn't heard much about Nazism or the Holocaust, simply wrote down the details, which he then passed on to the police and the fire department. For him, it was just a bureaucratic procedure to report an accident, which he described as a "sudden illness followed by drowning." The police officer requested an official vehicle to take the body to the Forensic Medical Institute in Guarujá. While the transport had not yet arrived,

---

5 Andreas Bossert's statement to the Federal Police (PF).

6 Statement by Walter Silva, lifeguard in Bertioga, to the police.

7 "Before death, depression." *O Estado de S. Paulo*, June 11, 1985.

8 Personal interview with Espedito Dias Romão, held on January 27, 2018.

the deceased remained lying on the sand, half-naked, wearing nothing but shorts. A woman appeared with a candle and lit it next to the dead man. The mothers who were still on the beach took the children away so they wouldn't see the scene. It was late afternoon, and the vehicle was taking its time.

Corporal Dias Romão stayed with Liselotte. She kept her head down almost the whole time, never looking away from her friend. She spoke to the policeman as little as possible. To those observing the scene, it seemed like the normal behavior of a person who had just lost someone close to them. In Liselotte's case, however, it wasn't only sadness that dominated her thoughts; many practical issues were at stake. She needed to think quickly about what she was going to do. The fact that her children had gone to sleep at the house of a neighbor she hardly knew and that her husband was in the hospital worried her. And not only that: she knew the body next to her belonged to one of the world's most wanted war criminals. Would she now reveal the identity of the man she had helped to hide for so long? What would the consequences be for her and her children? She had to deal with all these questions and doubts on her own, without raising suspicion.

The first decision was to stick to the version that the dead man was Wolfgang Gerhard, as stated in the ID card. Even if she decided to reveal the truth, she wouldn't be able to prove what she was saying, because the name and the information on the document were authentic. Only the photo was false. Wolfgang's original photo had been carefully removed and in its place was a wallet-sized picture of Mengele, by then an old man with a large moustache. His real name was already well known, and he couldn't appear on an identity card without attracting attention. As far as Brazilian official documentation, neither Josef Mengele nor Uncle Peter existed; only Wolfgang Gerhard, the Austrian friend who had actually introduced the old Nazi to the Bossert family. Before returning to Austria, he gave away all the documents he had obtained while in Brazil. He figured that he would no longer need them in Europe, and that they would be very useful to help Mengele remain in the shadows without being discovered. Faced with this mess, Liselotte decided to be practical. She wanted to get it over with and chose to "follow the normal course of events," as she told the Federal Police years later.[9]

It was already dawn when the technicians began analyzing the corpse at the Forensic Medical Institute. The doctor on duty, Jaime Edson Andrade de Mendonça, found that the cause of death was "asphyxiation due to submersion in water," that is, drowning. He didn't think it was necessary to perform an autopsy or question the identity or age of the dead man. For a coroner, fourteen years don't make much difference when examining a body within that age range. What matters is the body's state of conservation; in other words, how well the deceased had taken care of their health during their lifetime. Furthermore, water makes the tissues wrinkle, another reason for the age difference to go unnoticed. Dr. Jaime made no reference to any of this. He just trusted the identification presented by Liselotte and signed the death certificate.

Exhausted, the middle-aged woman took care of every detail, as if it were someone from her family who had died. She found some clothes to dress the dead man: pants, belt, shirt, shoes, and socks. She insisted that the funeral assistant should leave the deceased's arms alongside the body. This was a request that Mengele himself had made to her. He said that he felt like a soldier, and his last wish was to be laid to rest as if standing at attention. A strange request, since the custom in Brazil was to bury the dead with their hands folded across their chests. The official was discreet and agreed to fulfill her request without questioning it.[10]

However, one question remained: What would be the body's final destination? With no one to talk to, Liselotte initially thought of cremating it. It would be convenient, because it would put an end to any trace that might reveal the deceased's true identity. But it wasn't possible, because a close relative would have to authorize the procedure.

---

[9] Liselotte Bossert's statement to the Federal Police.

[10] Id.

She then remembered that the real Wolfgang Gerhard had instructed her and her husband to have the uncle buried in Embu, on the outskirts of São Paulo, if he died in Brazil. Wolfgang had bought a grave for his mother in the Rosário Cemetery, where many Germans were buried, and there was still space in the burial plot. He wouldn't use the grave himself, because he was going back to Austria. In addition to leaving his documents for Mengele, Wolfgang also wanted to ensure his burial, because he had always felt responsible for taking care of his friend. Liselotte remembered this and had no doubt that this would be the best destination for Mengele.

The next morning, the body was released. A woman who worked at the funeral home picked up the coffin to take it to the cemetery, which was more than sixty miles away. Liselotte went along, and although it was summer, she was wearing a dark corduroy blouse. During the journey, she complained about the road, which had some impassable stretches.[11] When they finally arrived at the Rosário Cemetery, Liselotte went to the administrator and asked about the grave bought by Wolfgang Gerhard.

Gino Carita, an affectionate Italian immigrant, indicated the grave's location and asked to see the death certificate. When he read that the deceased was Gerhard himself, he wanted to open the coffin to say goodbye. Gino had met the Austrian a few years earlier when he was hired to build a small wall and make a bronze plaque with the birth and death dates of Gerhard's mother, Friederika. The Austrian returned a few times to visit the tomb and, on the last occasion, he told the administrator that he was going on a trip, but he didn't say where, and was never seen again. Before leaving, he told him that "an older relative" might be buried next to his mother. Gino couldn't believe that Wolf, as he called him, was now returning in a coffin. The Italian tried to open it, and Liselotte immediately faked a hysterical attack. She started crying and said that he couldn't do that,

---

11 Maria Helena Costa Guerra, an employee of Funerária Nova (or Noa, according to the investigation), testified to the police.

because the man had drowned and was disfigured. This was the only way she could stop him. If he had opened the coffin, the administrator would have immediately noticed the wrong man inside, and she would have been in trouble. After the minor commotion, two gravediggers dug the grave. From what one of them remembers of that day, only Liselotte accompanied the burial. Once the quick, simple, solitary act was over, she could finally go home and see her children again. Most importantly, the secret she had kept for ten years was now buried in Wolfgang Gerhard's grave.

Liselotte was sure she was doing the right thing. She didn't think her children would be able to bear the weight that would fall on the shoulders of all the family members if Uncle Peter's identity was revealed. "Keeping quiet is always better," she thought. As a Catholic, she believed that God would always help her because, in her mind, her only crime had been to help a friend whom she saw as a scientist, and not as a degenerate doctor who sent thousands to their deaths in the gas chambers of Auschwitz and who tortured innocent women and children with his experiments, without showing any remorse. Instead, the murderer died enjoying himself on the beach one summer afternoon, without ever being tried for the crimes he had committed.

1

INVESTIGATING A DANGEROUS CASE

One of my earliest childhood memories is of a teacher I had. She wasn't just any teacher, even if she looked like many others. "Tante" Liselotte had European features, was slim, and wore her hair curled in a perm, like most women in the 1980s. None of the schoolkids called her "aunt," as young schoolchildren commonly do in Brazil; only "Tante," its German equivalent. It was one of the customs of that school, a Germanic island in the heart of Santo Amaro, in São Paulo. She spoke to us kids in a mixture of Portuguese and German, which felt very familiar to me because that's how we talked at home. On cold mornings, my mother would send me to class wearing pajama pants under my clothes. As the sun rose and the fun and games made me feel warmer, it was Tante Liselotte who removed my excess layers of clothes. I remember that, whenever I didn't want to take part in an activity, I hid under her desk in our classroom. The room had huge windows through which we could see a garden. I have many other memories of those years: how we used to run freely through the grass; the little red flowers, said to hold honey inside, that I liked to squeeze; the low wooden gate and pink azalea bushes separating us from the rest of the school and the "big" students. I felt safe in that small universe.

One day, however, things changed. Someone told us that Tante Liselotte would no longer come to teach. There was no farewell. It was a sudden disruption in the middle of the semester. Another woman, I don't remember exactly who she was, would replace Tante Liselotte, and that was it. I was only six years old, and I was shocked to lose my teacher all of a sudden. Why wouldn't she come any longer? What had happened? I sensed that the adult buzz surrounding the topic had an air of seriousness about it. I didn't know exactly what it was, but from my perspective as a child I understood that something was wrong.

Only when I was an adult did I learn that Tante Liselotte, to whom our parents entrusted us every morning, had given protection to the most wanted Nazi criminal in the world at that time, Josef Mengele. For a full ten years, my teacher had hosted the fugitive in her own home in the Brooklin neighborhood, not far from the school in the South Zone of São Paulo. On weekends, she would travel on vacation with him and her family to a farm in Itapecerica da Serra and to the beach in Bertioga. She once even took him to the school gate during a "Festa Junina," the typical Brazilian festivity in the month of June, without anyone suspecting the identity of that old Nazi, dressed in a beautiful European-style overcoat and felt hat. Liselotte introduced him to the principal as a family friend, a gesture that did not raise suspicion in a school that brought together many members of the German community. Practically everyone had a relative from Germany, Austria, or Switzerland. Liselotte was also the one who buried Mengele under a false name in the Embu cemetery in 1979, so that no one would discover his identity even after his death. Thus she foiled the authorities, the Nazi hunters, and the victims who were seeking justice.

For more than six years, Liselotte had thought these events were behind her, literally buried. She went about her routine, teaching small children at the German school. However, in June 1985, the secret was unexpectedly revealed and her life was turned upside down. Our teacher not only had to leave the school abruptly, but she also became disliked in the community, received anonymous threats over the phone, and had to go several times to the Federal Police Superintendence to give statements. She was indicted for three crimes: hiding a fugitive, making a false statement in a public document, and using a false document. At least eighteen of the thirty-four years that Mengele lived in hiding following the end of World War II, he spent in Brazil, the last ten under protection of Liselotte and her husband.

During all that time she never thought seriously about handing him over to the police. Of course, if she confessed that to the Federal Police, she would have problems with the courts. Therefore, she preferred to play the victim and say that she had been afraid to tell the authorities about Mengele's presence in Brazil because of threats she had received. People linked to the Nazi doctor allegedly had told her that she shouldn't open her mouth if she wanted to protect her children. This may well be true, but it wasn't the full story. In her heart, Liselotte believed she had done nothing wrong by taking in a Nazi criminal who was wanted everywhere. In her reasoning (and in her own words), she wanted to "wholeheartedly" help a person "in trouble," a friend.

However, Mengele was certainly not a mere "friend." He was a fugitive from German justice and responsible for countless murders, according to the arrest warrant issued by the Frankfurt Court of Justice. It is true that Mengele had entered Liselotte's life under a false name, so initially she had had no way of knowing who he was. By the time she discovered his true identity, it was too late: they had become friends, and her whole family was attached to him. The bombshell revelation that the man was actually a war criminal did not damage their relationship; quite the opposite. Liselotte remained faithful to her friend until the end.

Her husband, Wolfram, told police that Mengele knew he was being sought all over the world for the crimes he had committed between May 1943 and January 1945, a period of almost a year and eight months in which he was a medical doctor at the Auschwitz concentration camp. However, contrary to what many people think, he was never the chief doctor of that huge extermination complex. That position belonged to Dr. Eduard Wirths, who was responsible for all the medical activities in the largest Nazi concentration camp. The complex was so large that it was divided into three sub-camps: Auschwitz I (the main camp, or Stammlager), Auschwitz II (Birkenau), and Auschwitz III (Monowitz). Dr. Mengele began by taking charge of the "gypsy camp."[12] When the entire Roma block was exterminated, with almost three thousand men, women, and children sent to the gas chambers, he was promoted to chief doctor of Birkenau.

One of Mengele's main duties as a "Lagerarzt," or a concentration-camp doctor, was to select the prisoners who were to die in the gas chambers and those who could still be put to work. This task was called "selection" and ran completely counter to the basic premise of the medical profession, which is to save lives, not to take them. Hermann Langbein, an Austrian prisoner who worked as Dr. Wirths's secretary, noticed that this complete inversion of values caused conflicts of conscience in some doctors, especially those who took their training seriously and weren't ardent supporters of Nazism. This was definitely not the case with Mengele. He showed up for work even on his days off and had no remorse about sending helpless people to the gas chambers. His main aim was to find twins, people with dwarfism, and people with other rare conditions, to use them as human guinea pigs in his experiments. Perhaps because of his constant participation in the selections, Mengele was nicknamed the "Angel of Death." When he appeared in the prisoners' barracks, everyone trembled with fear because they knew what his presence meant: someone would be chosen to die.

More than the selections and the striking nickname, it was the disclosure of the perverse experiments on human beings that made

---

12 The word "gypsy" is today considered pejorative and no longer acceptable in English to describe Roma and Sinti peoples. In this book, the word will only be employed within quotation marks in expressions normally used in historical situations here discussed, such as the "gypsy camp" in Auschwitz (Zigeunerlager).

Mengele known all over the world. These remained unknown to the outside world until the 1960s, after some of the doctor's surviving victims testified in public at two famous trials: that of Nazi Adolf Eichmann in Jerusalem, and in the so-called "Auschwitz trials" in Frankfurt. From then on, Mengele's experiences became better known, and in the popular imagination emerged the image of a pseudoscientist, capable of doing anything to improve the "Aryan race" so it would dominate the world.

This image has appeared in various ways in American culture. Mengele became a fictional character in Ira Levin's 1976 book, *The Boys from Brazil.* Two years later, the book was adapted into a movie of the same name, which received three Oscar nominations and featured a star cast: Gregory Peck played the character Josef Mengele, and Laurence Olivier a Nazi hunter. Later, in 1986, the American thrash metal band Slayer turned the "Angel of Death" into the lyrics of one of their songs. Decades after the liberation of Auschwitz, Mengele went from an executioner to a sinister symbol in popular culture.

Contrary to fiction and general belief, Mengele was not a crazy, solitary pseudoscientist. In reality, he had the backing of a leading research institution with enormous prestige in the Third Reich: the Kaiser Wilhelm Institute in Berlin. There he sent samples of blood and organs taken from Auschwitz prisoners, including children. The young doctor's great dream was to build a research empire and have a brilliant career after the war. Determined to achieve his goal, he took full advantage of the freedom he had in the concentration camp to commit atrocities in the name of science, protected by the racist and anti-Semitic ideology of Nazism and the idea that all prisoners were going to die sooner or later anyway. For Mengele, Auschwitz was a great deposit of human material to be used in his private research.

The list of topics he wanted to investigate was extremely long: growth disorders (such as dwarfism), methods of sterilization, bone-marrow transplants, typhus, malaria, noma (a disease that mainly affects malnourished children), body abnormalities (such as hunchback and congenital clubfoot), and heterochromia (a condition

in which the color of the iris in one eye differs from that in the other).
Not to mention research on twins, which had been on the rise since
the 1920s. It seems difficult that a single scientist would ever become
an expert on such a wide variety of subjects. As the German historian Carola Sachse wrote, it was the scientifically senseless orgy of an
excessively arrogant person. As if the various lines of research were
not enough, he also collected Jewish skeletons, human embryos, and
bodies of dead newborn babies.

The stories of Mengele's cruel and bizarre experiments have always
haunted me, even more so knowing that, when hiding from justice,
he received protection from my childhood teacher. For years I was
intrigued by what he had done and, most importantly, why. What was
behind so much evil? I remember seeing long reports on the Sunday
TV shows that talked about human experiments. They were always
shocking. It was also shocking that such a man had moved around so
freely and lived with impunity in places so close to where I live, and
that a teacher of mine had such an intimate connection to him. I've
always wondered why Tante Liselotte had protected him and what had
moved her to do it.

There are several volumes on Mengele published in Europe and the
United States, but no in-depth book about him has been written in
Brazil, the place where he spent the most time in hiding. As a journalist for over twenty years, I thought it was time to get to the bottom of
this story. I began to unravel Mengele's life through foreign books, and
then by searching for documents and people who were close to him.
Without a doubt, Tante Liselotte was a key character in this whole
story. She was the person best able to tell me what had happened
during the years Mengele was hiding in Brazil. But where could I find
her, more than thirty years after she left the school? On the internet,
her name appeared in several articles from 1985, the year Mengele's
skeleton was found in the Embu cemetery and the case became a
worldwide scandal, having received more coverage in the foreign press
than the death of Brazil's President Tancredo Neves two months earlier. After that, there was nothing else. She had disappeared.

I decided to look for the school's old staff who had known her. A former teacher, who was usually very helpful and sweet to me, didn't even reply to my message, probably because she realized what I wanted to discuss. I couldn't find any information about Tante Liselotte, and I didn't even know if she was still alive. I got in touch with the then-principal of the German school, and we sat down for a chat. "As far as I know, she's still alive, yes. I saw Liselotte maybe three or four times at the São Paulo City Council. She usually appears at the special session in honor of German-speaking immigrants," he said. It seemed that the only way to talk to her was to go to her house.

The address where Liselotte lived at the time of the Mengele case was available in various places: magazines, newspapers, official documents, and even foreign books. It remained to be seen whether it was still the same. I decided to go there. I arrived at her house on a Sunday, just before eleven in the morning. A car was parked in front of the gate. From the sidewalk, I could see through the window someone in the living room reading the newspaper. I rang the doorbell. The person on the sofa didn't even move. I was about to ring again when a woman appeared at the second-floor window. My God, it was her!

It was like seeing a fictional character in the flesh. I began by introducing myself as a former student and current journalist. She asked me what I wanted. I said I would tell her if she came down to the gate, where I was. She resisted my request for a bit but eventually gave in. Certainly, being called "Tante Liselotte" made her curious, or perhaps flattered. Downstairs, she smiled and held out her hand. Her fingers were a little crooked, revealing her advanced age. We stood facing each other, with a waist-height gate between us. I explained that I wanted to write a book about Mengele. She said she didn't talk about it with anyone, not even her own children.

"I've been offered a lot of money to do interviews, but I won't," she said with conviction.

"Why?" I asked.

"Because there's no point. Some believe it all happened one way, others don't," she replied. We continued talking about trivialities.

Suddenly, Liselotte let out a somewhat confusing confession: "They often think that everything comes out with age. It doesn't. Everything is just right." She finished the sentence without explaining what she meant, laughed, and continued speaking with her heavy accent and a Portuguese that was, at times, rather poor. "Look, it's like this, we agreed that if I stayed quiet, the Jews will leave me alone. So I stayed quiet. Because I had a family, so I don't talk about this subject," she said.

"But what Jews said that to you?" I asked.

Silence. Then: "It was Menachem Russak. He was the Nazijäger, the 'Nazi hunter.'"

Menachem Russak really existed and was in São Paulo at the time when Mengele's remains were exhumed. He was the head of the special Israeli unit in charge of hunting down Nazi war criminals.

After a short pause, she mentioned another unintelligible name, saying she was referring to a consul. "What consul would that be?" I thought.

"Did they ever threaten you?" I asked.

"No, they wouldn't do that. How can you say something like that? You shouldn't," she replied in a mocking and ironic tone. I asked if she had ever regretted helping her "friend," taking care never to mention Mengele's name directly, because I sensed that it was a kind of taboo for her.

"That's something else, because I have two children, right?" she replied.

"But what does regret have to do with your children?" I tried to understand.

"Do you know the Gesetze of the Talmud?" she asked me, once again mixing Portuguese and German. "According to the Talmud, they will chase you down to the seventh child in the family. I'm not afraid, but I can't," she added. Liselotte did not explain what she meant.

In the Talmud, the collection of Jewish books that record the discussions of the rabbis and are the main source for Jewish law, there is a quote about revenge in the seventh generation. It refers to an interpretation of Genesis in the Bible: the punishment for Cain's crime comes in the seventh generation, through his descendant Lamech, who murders him. Did Liselotte believe that she would be punished in future generations?

The conversation became more and more mysterious. My childhood teacher was scaring me. The street was empty. The person on the sofa was still there. Who could it be? Liselotte had said she wouldn't talk about the Mengele case, but all the same kept telling me some strange things. Many answers to my questions were limited to a shake of the head or a sinister smile. Then, by leaps and bounds, the conversation unfolded. Suddenly she asked: "Do you want to know something?"

"I do," I replied fearfully.

"Just from friend to friend, leave the case." My eyes widened. Why was she saying that? Was it a threat? "It's better for you," she continued. "There's a lot, a lot that nobody knows yet. I know," she said and laughed.

"Then you have to tell me," I insisted.

"No," she replied seriously. "Nothing at all, because the deal I have with them is serious. When someone says to you 'look, you've got children . . .'"

She let her words hang in the air, implying that she had been seriously threatened by the men she had mentioned earlier.

Another long silence fell between us. I grew more afraid. What was she getting at? Was she threatening me? "You'd better keep quiet about this. It's a lot of money. A lot of money," she repeated enigmatically. I was stunned and had no answers. Despite the intimidating atmosphere, we continued talking. She asked if I had a husband or children. I tried to make it seem like normal questions from an old acquaintance, but I immediately felt I was being scrutinized. I was getting more and more tense. She made veiled and direct threats, one after the other: "Look for something else that is not so dangerous to investigate. Because this case is dangerous, believe me," she said.

"But who do you think could put me in danger?" I asked, playing dumb.

Again, silence. "I'm not going to talk," she said.

I was stunned. I tried to act normal. I asked one last, light, trivial question to try to clear the air: "Do you miss school?"

She replied, "I don't miss it. But I'm happy with my life. There are a lot of people who hate me, but what am I going to do? I'm sure I didn't do anything wrong, that's all."

I wished her a good Sunday and said I'd let her know when my book was published. I walked off, turned the corner, and, once out of her sight, picked up my pace.

At that moment, I felt sure that I never wanted to talk about it again. I was afraid. When I got home, I told my sisters about the threats I had received. They laughed at me for fearing a ninety-year-old woman. I tried to remain calm, and replied only, "A ninety-year-old woman who was able to harbor Josef Mengele. I wonder who she's connected to." After asking myself this question many times, I came to the conclusion that nobody survives for more than three decades being hunted by the Mossad, the Israeli intelligence service, with an arrest warrant from the German government, and half a dozen Nazi hunters on their trail, unless they have a very well-connected network.

This network wasn't a grandiose organization like Odessa, the mythical organization to protect SS officers after the Second World War. Its existence has never been proven, and Wolfram himself said that he never received support from any Nazi group. What Mengele found in Brazil, especially in the state of São Paulo, was a network of loyal supporters, European immigrants who, in one way or another, had their lives intertwined with his. In Brazil, Mengele created his "Tropical Bavaria": a place where he could speak German and maintain his customs, beliefs, friends, and his connection to his homeland. And the best thing: in a climate that was more pleasant than Germany's. He may have felt "in trouble," as Liselotte said, but he never came close to facing the punishment deserved by those who commit war crimes and crimes against humanity.

2

REUNITING MENGELE'S TWINS

JERUSALEM. OCTOBER 1984

Josef Mengele had already been dead and buried for more than five years, but nobody knew that. Or rather, very few people were aware of it: only his friends in Brazil and his relatives in Germany, who helped him live in hiding after World War II. While the dead man had already become a pile of bones in the remote and unsuspected Embu cemetery, victims and hunters of the Nazi doctor naïvely continued the search for a living criminal. Mengele's whereabouts were a great mystery that fueled the most absurd conspiracy theories. The main suspicion was that he was living in Paraguay. There were also those who claimed to have seen him in the Bahamas, Patagonia, and Uruguay. The famous Nazi hunter Simon Wiesenthal guaranteed, with strange accuracy, that the former SS captain was at a military base in the tiny Paraguayan town of Laureles, where even the local police were not allowed to enter. Tuviah Friedman, another Nazi hunter, claimed that Mengele was the personal physician of Paraguayan dictator Alfredo Stroessner.[13] How they

---

13 "Mystery, myth. Where is Mengele?" *O Estado de S. Paulo*, March 10, 1985.

reached such certainties, we don't know. The fact is that, judging from the totally wrong guesses that reached the press, it was clear that no one had the slightest idea where Mengele was, apart from his close and loyal circle of protectors.

Even without any concrete leads, one woman was determined to find him. Eva Mozes Kor, fifty-one, a Romanian who was born in Transylvania and lived in the United States, dreamed of bringing to justice the man who had used her as a guinea pig when she was a child. "We need to find Mengele before he dies in his own bed," she said in her heavy accent during a press conference in Jerusalem in October 1984. Mozes Kor had just created the association Children of Auschwitz Nazi Deadly Lab Experiments Survivors (CANDLES), which represented the surviving twins of Mengele's experiments. As well as being the founder, she was the spokesperson for the newly created institution. She gathered journalists to announce that some survivors would be taking a two-mile walk around Auschwitz on January 27 of the following year to mark forty years since the liberation of the camp. It was to be just one event in a much larger campaign: to draw the world's attention to finding Mengele. The statement that the CANDLES association released to the press contained a frightening fact: three thousand twins had been used by Mengele in medical experiments at Auschwitz and, of that total, only 183 made it out alive. "The criminal who did this to us is still at large," she said. "Unless we do something about it, nothing will happen," she added.

Eva was convinced that the more publicity her cause attracted, the better it would be. And she was thinking big. She sent telegrams to President Ronald Reagan of the United States, and President Konstantin Tchernenko of the Union of Soviet Socialist Republics (USSR), inviting the leaders of the two greatest powers of the time to take part in the symbolic march she was organizing.[14]

Deep down, even more than bringing Mengele to trial, Mozes Kor wanted to find out what substances he had injected into her and

---

14 Survivors Appeal for Information on Nazi Fugitive (UPI), on October 13, 1984.

her twin sister, Miriam Mozes Zeiger, when they were children. Four decades after the experiments, she still had health problems caused by those injections, but she preferred not to talk about it.[15] She was more worried about her sister. Because of the experiments in Auschwitz, Miriam had developed serious kidney infections that didn't respond to antibiotics. The doctors found that her organs were atrophied, the size of those of a ten-year-old girl, the exact age the sisters had been when they served as guinea pigs in the Nazi laboratory. Unsatisfied, the doctors who analyzed Miriam begged for her files from the concentration camp to try to find out what could have caused it and, perhaps, cure her. The sisters never found either any documents or any person who could explain what had happened to them in that laboratory.

Twins Eva Mozes Kor and Miriam Mozes in Romania.
Yad Vashem Photo Archive, Jerusalem.

---

15 Interview with Eva Mozes Kor by email, conducted on August 1, 2017.

Miriam lived in Israel and Eva in the US state of Indiana, where she married, had two children, and made a career as a real estate agent. For a long time, Eva couldn't talk to anyone about her terrible experiences. Her neighbors thought she was strange, and her "weirdness" was the subject of jokes in the neighborhood ever since she chased away a bunch of kids who went trick-or-treating outside her house on Halloween. What seemed like an innocent prank reminded her of the groups of Nazi youths who used to terrorize the Jews in Porț, Romania, when she was a little girl.[16]

Eva's relationship with the past only began to change when she watched a TV series titled *Holocaust* in 1978, more than thirty years after leaving Auschwitz. The show was a resounding success, with 120 million viewers in the United States and the then-newcomer Meryl Streep in the cast. The miniseries touched on a subject that was little discussed in public at the time: the mass murder of Jews in Europe. In four episodes, *Holocaust* told the story of a Jewish family from Berlin—the Weisses—who had been prosperous and happy until the rise of Nazism, when they lost their rights due to the anti-Semitic policies of the Third Reich and ended up persecuted and destroyed. Many survivors didn't like the series because they thought the plot oversimplified very complex issues, saying it was a soap opera dealing with a serious topic. Despite the criticism, the miniseries had the merit of giving a face and a name to the suffering of the Jews and raising awareness among the general public, not only in the United States but in Germany, where the series was also a success.

The word "holocaust," which until then had only been used in restricted circles, gained popularity. The first known use of the term "holocaust" dates back to the thirteenth century. It comes from the Greek word *holokauston*, which in turn is a translation of the Hebrew word *olah*. In biblical times, olah was an offering that had to be completely consumed by fire. The use of the term holocaust, therefore, has

---

16 Eva Mozes Kor and Lisa Rojany Buccieri, *Surviving the Angel of Death: The True Story of a Mengele Twin in Auschwitz*. Vancouver: Tanglewood, 2009.

a religious meaning, which is that murdered Jews, whose bodies were burned entirely in crematoria, are considered a sacrifice to God. Over time, the word began to refer to large-scale murder or destruction.[17] Even today, there is a debate about the use of the term "holocaust." No universal agreement has been reached on its meaning: for example, whether it refers exclusively to the extermination of Jews or whether it can also be used in relation to the massacre of other peoples.[18] In Israel, there is a preference for the word "Shoah," which means "catastrophe" in Hebrew.

After the series's success, Eva realized that many people began to understand why she was different. Some people even apologized for the way they had treated her before. It was a turning point in her life, in the lives of other survivors, and also in American culture. From then on, the Holocaust gained prominence in popular books and films, such as the bestseller *Sophie's Choice*, and the 1982 movie also starring Meryl Streep, who this time won an Oscar for Best Actress. At the same time, there was a race to record in detail the accounts of concentration-camp survivors, a period that was later called the "Era of the Witness." To preserve these records, public and private archives were created in various countries.[19]

Eva, who until then hadn't touched on the subject, became a lecturer, and audiences asked her details about the Nazis' medical experiments. The problem was that she didn't know how to answer many of the questions. She then remembered that when Auschwitz had been liberated by the Red Army, she and her sister hadn't left

---

17 "Holocaust," in Merriam-Webster Dictionary. Available at: <www.merriam -webster.com/dictionary/holocaust>. Accessed on: June 3, 2020; "What Is the Origin of the Term Holocaust?" *Encyclopaedia Britannica*. Available at: <www.britannica .com/story/what-is-the-origin-of-the-term-holocaust>. Accessed on: June 3, 2020.

18 Laurence Rees, *The Holocaust: A New History*. London: Penguin, 2017.

19 Frank McDonough and John Cochrane, *The Holocaust*. London: Bloomsbury, 2008, p. 91; "The power of series against institutionalized violence." *Folha de S.Paulo*, July 21, 2019.

that hell on their own; other children had left with them. These other liberated twins could provide some useful clues, so she decided to try to find her former childhood companions who appeared in the photos and videos made by the Soviets. It was a difficult task: they were of different nationalities, spoke different languages, and were scattered all over the world. Contacting them at a time when there was no internet, let alone social networks, required Herculean willpower. Eva had had this strength since she was a child. What motivated her in this search was the thought that she could better understand what had happened to her and her sister if she collected the accounts of everyone who had gone through the same experience as them. It was a way of trying to put the pieces of that meaningless puzzle together. Eva and Miriam managed to locate 122 surviving twins from Mengele's experiments in ten different countries on four continents.[20]

In January 1985, they held the association's first international event. The American and Soviet presidents did not attend, which was to be expected. However, Eva and Miriam were firm in their resolve. They managed to take four more twins on the symbolic march to mark the fortieth anniversary of the liberation of Auschwitz. It was a small step in spreading the word about the cause. From Poland, the group traveled to Jerusalem.[21] It was there that the biggest event of the campaign to draw worldwide attention to the Mengele case was scheduled to take place. CANDLES managed to bring together eighty twins, as well as people with dwarfism, and other witnesses who could talk about the Nazi doctor's crimes. It wasn't going to be a real trial because, to that date, no government had managed to arrest Mengele, even though he was one of the world's most wanted war criminals. The lack of legal backing was not an impediment to Eva and Miriam's endeavor.

---

[20] Eva Mozes Kor and Lisa Rojany Buccieri, op. cit., p. 130.

[21] "Read about Eva's road to Forgiveness." CANDLES Holocaust Museum and Education Center. Available at: <candlesholocaustmuseum.org/our-survivors /eva-kor/her-story/her-story.html/title/read-about-eva-s-road-to-forgiveness>. Accessed on: June 8, 2020.

Mengele would be "tried" in absentia, at a public hearing. And if that event had no legal value, at least it would serve to spread the word about the crimes he had committed.

Eva Mozes Kor and Miriam Mozes Zeiger. Picture taken in Auschwitz at the same place that the liberation picture was taken [in 1945]. December 1991.

Indiana Historical Society, M1492.

3

IN SEARCH OF JUSTICE

FEBRUARY 1985

The place chosen for the hearing was symbolic: Yad Vashem, the World Holocaust Remembrance Center in Jerusalem. The name of the event, "J'Accuse" (I accuse), was also symbolic. It was a reference to the famous letter that writer Émile Zola published in the French press in 1898, addressed to the president of France, in which he defended Alfred Dreyfus. That Jewish officer had been unjustly sentenced to life imprisonment on the inhospitable Devil's Island in French Guiana. The crime attributed to Dreyfus was being a German agent and spying on the French Army, accusations that were later proven false. The campaign launched by Zola to prove the Jewish officer's innocence exposed the anti-Semitic motivations behind the accusation of espionage. The Dreyfus affair caused quite a stir in the country and became a landmark in the fight against anti-Semitism. The "J'Accuse" of the twentieth century was also part of a campaign to repair an injustice committed against Jewish people: the impunity of Josef Mengele.

The event organizers invited a panel of six renowned experts on Nazi crimes to hear the gruesome stories about the doctor's work in

Auschwitz. Prominent among them was Gideon Hausner, who had been the chief prosecutor in the trial of Adolf Eichmann in Israel. This case attracted worldwide attention in the 1960s and brought to justice the man who, during World War II, organized and coordinated the deportation of Jews to concentration camps in Eastern Europe.[22] Interestingly, Hausner and Mengele were in contact with each other years after the end of the war when both were living in hiding in Buenos Aires.

Another distinguished member of the "J'Accuse" panel was Telford Taylor, who had been the chief US prosecutor at the Nuremberg Military Tribunal during the trials of Nazi collaborators. The presence of Taylor, Hausner, and other important names added credibility and international recognition to the hearing organized by the sisters Eva and Miriam. Thirty witnesses had agreed to testify. For three days, the victims took turns in front of a packed auditorium to talk about their experiences, which were recorded and broadcast worldwide on TV, including in Brazil. Some stories had not been previously told in public and sounded unreal due to the extreme cruelty they revealed.

Joseph Kleinmann was one of the first survivors to give his testimony. He recalled a Yom Kippur night in Auschwitz in 1944. For Jews, this date, the Day of Forgiveness, is as important as Christmas is for Christians. According to his calculations, 1,200 teenagers were sent to a soccer field where, suddenly, a sensation like that of an "electric current" ran through them. It was Mengele, who had arrived on his bicycle. According to Kleinmann, the doctor looked at all those frightened boys and then stared at a thirteen-year-old. He asked his age. The boy replied "eighteen," because he certainly knew that the smallest and least able to work among them would be sent to the gas chamber. Realizing the boy was lying, the SS captain was furious and asked for a hammer, nails, and a board. He attached the piece of wood

---

22 Hannah Arendt, *Eichmann em Jerusalém: Um relato sobre a banalidade do mal*. São Paulo: Companhia das Letras, 1999, p. 176.

to a post at the height of the tallest boy present. Then he ordered everyone to line up and walk past the plank. Anyone who walked under it wasn't tall enough. Everyone realized what that meant and began to stretch up as much as possible. Kleinmann himself, only fourteen at the time, recounted that his father was standing next to him and said, "If you want to live, put some stones under your heel inside your shoe." That's what he did, but he couldn't stand on the rocks for long. To look a bit taller, he took his brother's hat, tore it to pieces, and placed them inside his shoes, which were too big for his feet; now he was able to walk. Joseph was saved that night, but about a thousand boys who didn't reach the desired height were sent to the gas chamber.[23]

Austrian doctor Ella Lingens, who worked with Mengele in Auschwitz, recalled conversations she had with him back then. Lingens was sent to the concentration camp because she and her husband had hid Jewish friends in Vienna. An informer handed both of them over to the Gestapo, the Nazi secret police.[24] Compared to the other prisoners, she had a privileged position in the camp because of her ethnic origin and profession. Lingens worked with several SS doctors in Auschwitz. At the time, the young woman attracted attention because of her blonde hair. Forty years later, with her white hair up in a bun and a soft but firm voice, she told the panelists how Mengele considered himself very "efficient" in fighting a typhus epidemic.

Mengele had explained that disinfectants to combat the lice that caused the disease were readily available in the concentration camp. However, not everything could be disinfected properly because people often hid their few belongings for fear that someone would steal them. It was precisely in these hidden items that the lice multiplied.[25] It was a

---

23 Josef Mengele's arrest order, Frankfurt am Main, January 19, 1981, p. 18.

24 "The Stories of Six Righteous Among the Nations in Auschwitz." Yah Vashem. Available at: https://www.yadvashem.org/yv/en/exhibitions/righteous-auschwitz/index.asp>. Accessed on: July 6, 2023.

25 Michael A. Grodin, Eva Mozes Kor, and Susan Benedict, op. cit.

Sisyphean task: the places that had already been disinfected would be swarming with lice again a few weeks later. Mengele realized that the disinfection process had to be done differently and decided to implement a new, more radical "cleaning" method. According to Lingens, Mengele ordered one of the Birkenau blocks, which housed between six and seven hundred prisoners, to be completely emptied. He sent the prisoners all to the gas chamber and thus was able to thoroughly disinfect the space. He then sent for the prisoners from another block and ordered them to get naked, bathe, and move into the disinfected area. Mengele continued to do this, from block to block, until every area had been disinfected and everyone was clean. The typhus was practically eradicated, but at the cost of hundreds of lives.

Witness Stephanie Heller has an identical twin and was one of Mengele's human guinea pigs when she was young. After the war, she moved to Melbourne, Australia, but agreed to travel to Jerusalem to give her testimony. Heller said that she arrived in Auschwitz with her sister Anetta when she was nineteen and already a married woman. Because they were twins, the two sisters were selected to be sent regularly to Dr. Mengele's laboratory where they were forced to take part in experiments such as having their body parts measured and X-rays taken. One day, without any explanation, each received a blood transfusion from a pair of male twins about the same age as them. The two sisters didn't know these boys and guessed that they were Polish: Stephanie and Anetta weren't sure because they didn't speak the young men's language, only Czech, which made communication difficult. Stephanie said that she and her sister had severe reactions after the transfusions: they spent two days in the concentration camp hospital suffering from severe headaches, fever, and nausea. Neither one knew what had happened to them. "We may have received the wrong blood type," she suspected. When they regained their strength, they were taken back to the prisoners' block. Someone told them that they knew what Mengele intended with those experiments. He ultimately wanted to find out if identical twins fertilized by other identical twins would become pregnant with twins. The two sisters were very frightened at the prospect of being part of that experiment. Stephanie gathered courage and asked Mengele directly that she not be required to take part in any experiments anymore. The doctor replied that she was just a number there and had no say in the matter. Luckily for her, shortly after that, the prisoners were forced to leave Auschwitz because of the imminent arrival of the Red Army, and further experiments were never carried out.[26]

One of the most striking stories was that of Vera Alexander. She, too, was nineteen when she arrived at Auschwitz in 1942. Vera said that a Nazi officer took her by motorcycle to the "gypsy" camp, where she was responsible for supervising small children between the ages of three and five. She soon realized that they were all twins. Mengele inspected the barrack and was particularly concerned about the children used in the experiments, since he wanted them to be healthy. The SS doctor brought them clean clothes, toys, chocolates, and even potties so they wouldn't have to go outside to use the bathroom on freezing nights. Vera said that these children received more food than the rest of the prisoners, and that the block they lived in was clean. One day, however, someone took away a pair of twins: Tito and Nina. A few days later, the little siblings returned with the veins in their heads and backs sewn together because they had gone through an absurd attempt to create Siamese twins. The scars were filled with pus and the children cried day and night. At that point, Vera was transferred to another location within the camp itself. When she returned to the "gypsy camp," there were no children left. Vera thinks they were all killed, although she hadn't seen any executions in the six weeks she supervised them.[27]

The audience was moved by fifty-eight-year-old Ephraim Reichenberg as he gave his testimony through a special microphone

26 Michael A. Grodin, Eva Mozes Kor, and Susan Benedict, op. cit.; "Jewish Survivor Stephanie Heller Testimony." USC Shoah Foundation. Available at: <youtube.com /watch?v=0qRp5- D0r0c>. Accessed on: July 6, 2023.

27 Michael A. Grodin, Eva Mozes Kor, and Susan Benedict, op. cit.

positioned under his chin that made his voice sound metallic, as if coming from a computer. His vocal cords had had to be removed because of the injections Mengele applied to his neck. Reichenberg wasn't a twin, but he looked a lot like his brother. When they had disembarked in Auschwitz, a prisoner had told them to pass themselves off as twins to escape the gas chamber. They were indeed very similar, except that his brother had a beautiful voice and once even sang for the Germans. Ephraim's voice, however, didn't have the same grace, and Mengele wanted to understand how it was possible for one "twin" to have a good voice and the other not. Driven by his curiosity, he conducted experiments on Ephraim's vocal cords. The experiments affected his speech throughout his life, until 1967, when his vocal cords had abnormally grown so much that they had to be completely removed. "Since that year until five months ago, I couldn't speak anymore. Then I bought this wonderful device," he said with a certain irony, referring to his microphone. "This too was invented by the Germans—and that is a pity."[28]

Another witness was identified only by his initials: O.C. He didn't want his face to be seen and gave his testimony behind a curtain, probably ashamed of what had happened to him. This survivor said that he had been given an injection in the spine that left him unconscious. A while later, he had woken up in a recovery room, where other prisoners, who also had undergone surgery, asked what had happened to him. O.C. had replied that he didn't know, as he was still under anesthesia. The other young men then told him that they all had had one of their testicles removed. An hour later, when the anesthesia had worn off, O.C. realized that they had done the same thing to him.[29]

The story of Czech Ruth Elias brought many of the hearing's attendees to tears. She experienced the worst pain a mother can

---

28 Thomas L. Friedman, "Jerusalem Listens to the Victims of Mengele." *New York Times*, February 7, 1985.

29 Ibid.

imagine at the whim of Mengele. Elias was already pregnant when she arrived at the concentration camp. Pregnancy in Auschwitz meant certain death, but she managed to conceal her condition until the last few weeks of pregnancy, thanks to her extremely thin body, her cleverness, and a stroke of luck. However, word got around the camp that there were two women in an advanced stage of pregnancy: Elias and another woman, whose first name was Berta. Mengele heard about it and summoned both women. He asked them a lot of questions and couldn't understand how he could have let two pregnant women get through the selections. According to his and Auschwitz's criteria, the two pregnant women should have been placed in line for the gas chamber as soon as they arrived at the camp. Since they hadn't, and were now about to give birth, he decided to spare them: they could give birth to their babies.[30] What he hadn't told the mothers-to-be was that he already had in mind an experiment involving the newborns.

Mengele visited the two pregnant women in the ward every day. He didn't go there just to see them. The infirmary was his territory, and there were many human guinea pigs among the patients. Elias witnessed several young women in pain after having undergone extremely cruel operations, without anyone knowing exactly what had happened to them, let alone why. For a long time, these women couldn't even speak.[31] When the dreaded day of giving birth finally arrived, a Polish midwife, who was also a prisoner in the camp, came to help Elias. In the midst of increasingly strong contractions, the woman asked her to lie down.[32]

At the hearing in Jerusalem, in front of an audience that grew increasingly quiet, Elias recalled that moment with a sad expression and an unwavering voice: "I lay on those stones, with nothing. And I

---

30 Ruth Elias, *The Triumph of Hope: From Theresienstadt and Auschwitz to Israel*. New York: Willey, 1999.

31 Ibid.

32 Ibid.

gave birth to a beautiful baby girl. No soap. No hot water. No cotton wool." She paused as if to take courage, and continued: "Nothing. In my own filth, with my baby, I walked to my cot. I didn't have a mattress, just a coverlet, which I used to cover both of us."[33] The conditions were so precarious that the midwife couldn't even sterilize the scissors she used to cut the umbilical cord. There were no diapers either.[34] The next day, Mengele arrived for his daily visit and saw that Elias had given birth. He stared at the baby for a long time and then ordered a doctor to tie the mother's breasts with a tight bandage so that she couldn't breastfeed. He wanted to know how long a newborn could survive without breastfeeding.[35] Soon Elias felt her breasts filling with milk. The baby was hungry and cried nonstop. Mengele came by every day to check the bandage and look at the child.[36]

After seven days of agony and despair, Maca Steinberg, another Czech prisoner, offered to help. She got hold of a morphine injection and gave it to Elias, telling her to inject the child with it. Steinberg explained that she couldn't do it herself because she was a doctor and had taken the Hippocratic Oath. She explained to Elias that Mengele had already told her the mother and her newborn would be sent to the gas chamber the next day. The baby, already just skin and bones, had no chance to survive, and this was the only way Elias could live, argued the Czech doctor. More than forty years later, Elias declared to the attentive audience: "I killed my own daughter." She paused again, ran her tongue over her lips, and continued. "In the morning, Mengele arrived, and I was ready to go to the gas chamber. But he didn't want me, he wanted my baby. He didn't find the baby's body in the pile of corpses in front of our block," she said with a sad and resigned expression. Thus Elias escaped the

---

33 "Judeus fazem julgamento simulado de Josef Mengele." *Jornal Nacional*, February 6, 1985.

34 Ruth Elias, op. cit.

35 Ibid.

36 Ibid.

crematorium, but was unable to escape the excruciating pain of losing her daughter.

By the end of the three-day hearing, it was clear to all the experts gathered there that there was enough evidence to convict Mengele in a real court. "There exists a body of evidence justifying the committal for trial of the SS physician Hauptsturmführer Josef Mengele for war crimes and crimes against humanity," concluded Telford Taylor, the US prosecutor. The real challenge now was to find the accused.

The day after the hearings ended, the US attorney general, William French Smith, announced that the Justice Department would open an investigation to locate Mengele. Reports that the Nazi doctor had been captured and released by the Americans shortly after World War II would also be investigated. The Office of Special Investigations (OSI) would be in charge of the unprecedented hunt, and the CIA and the Pentagon would provide all the necessary support.[37] Journalists were eager to hear about the Mengele case. US TV channels aired dozens of reports about his escape and the crimes he had committed. The victims' testimonies, as well as the questions surrounding US conduct after the war, increased the public interest in the subject. The fact that the United States had recruited hundreds of Nazi scientists in the postwar period to work on military and space projects led to the suspicion that the United States sympathized with Third Reich fugitives.

The most notable example was Wernher von Braun, creator of the V-2 rockets, which were launched over London and Antwerp near the end of World War II. The V-2 ("V" standing for Vergeltung, or "revenge" in German) was the first ballistic missile in history,

---

[37] *In the Matter of Josef Mengele: A Report to the Attorney General of the United States*: Exhibits, report of the Office of Special Investigations of the United States Department of Justice (OSI), October 1992, p. 44. Available at: <www.justice.gov/sites/default/files/criminal-hrsp/legacy/2011/06/06/10-30-92mengele-exhibits.pdf>. Accessed on: July 20, 2023.

a sophisticated weapon with extremely expensive technology for a Germany already close to defeat. It was built with slave labor in concentration camps, under such precarious conditions that more people died during its construction than in the bombing raids on the British capital. Von Braun was a mechanical engineer and an officer in the SS, an organization that the Americans themselves declared to be criminal at the Nuremberg Tribunal. But this did not prevent NACA (the predecessor of NASA) from utilizing his expertise. Von Braun's work on the V-2 and subsequent rocket projects led him and his team of German scientists to create the Saturn V rocket, which later made possible the launching of Apollo 11, the spacecraft that took the first astronauts to the moon in 1969, in an American victory in the space race against the Soviets. In the midst of the Cold War, the Soviet Union was glad to use its propaganda machine to emphasize that the United States was protecting Nazi fugitives.

Three months after the hearing in Jerusalem, the Israeli government and the World Zionist Organization offered a reward of $1 million to anyone who provided information leading to Mengele's arrest. It was yet another huge amount of money that governments, organizations, and Nazi hunters were willing to pay in exchange for information about his whereabouts. The Simon Wiesenthal Center in Los Angeles and the *Washington Times* had already put up $1 million each. The West German government offered $300,000; Wiesenthal himself $50,000; and Beate Klarsfeld, another Nazi hunter, $25,000. The total amounted to almost $3.4 million, the largest sum ever offered for the capture of a criminal.

It was a lot of money, and Liselotte, Mengele's great protector at the end of his life, knew it. Advertisements stating the amount of the reward ran in newspapers and in major magazines not only in Brazil, but all over the world. She could have become a millionaire. Even with Mengele already dead, she preferred to remain silent and go about her life discreetly. She kept a quiet routine as a teacher at the German school in São Paulo.

Liselotte certainly wanted to believe that Mengele had become for her a thing of the past. But that past threatened to resurface, sparked by the sudden worldwide interest in the Mengele case. In May 1985, authorities from the United States, Israel, and Germany met in Frankfurt and announced that they were coordinating efforts to arrest and prosecute the Nazi doctor. The pieces of the puzzle were coming together and, in less than a month, they would reach the fugitive—or, rather, what was left of him.[38]

---

[38] Henry Kamm, "Wiesenthal Lists Mengele Sightings." *New York Times*, May 15, 1985.

4

KEEPING SECRETS

Shortly after Uncle Peter's death, Liselotte and Wolfram Bossert took their children for a secret visit to the Embu cemetery.[39] Nobody knows how they explained to the two teenagers the fact that the tombstone did not bear the name of the deceased. What is certain is that they all knew that it was their uncle who lay there. This was the final farewell to the man who had been very present in the Bosserts' lives. As in every family, when someone dies, several practical issues had to be resolved urgently. That the body's real identity would be kept confidential had already been decided at the very moment Liselotte handed the false documents to the policeman on the beach. She wanted to bury the incident and go on with her life as if nothing had happened. But it wasn't possible to maintain absolute silence on the topic, and a few people had to be told right away, especially Gitta and Geza Stammer, the Hungarian immigrant couple who had been the first people to protect Mengele in Brazil.

---

39 Andreas Bossert's statement to the Federal Police.

The old Nazi lived with the Stammer family for thirteen years, practically a lifetime for a fugitive. Due to disagreements, they parted ways in early 1975 and Mengele moved alone to a house that was registered in Gitta's name.[40] The property was on Alvarenga Road, in Eldorado, on the border between São Paulo and Diadema. It was on the outskirts of the city, among small farms and humble people, that Mengele spent his last years. With his death, the house was suddenly empty. Although the Bosserts did not have a close relationship with the Stammers, they had to break the news to them—after all, the two families were accomplices, and they were the few people in Brazil who knew the true identity of Peter/Wolfgang.[41]

Two days after the funeral, Liselotte phoned Geza and told him what had happened in Bertioga. Without worrying too much, the Hungarian left all of Mengele's furniture and personal belongings to the Bosserts. The following year, he also sold the house to them.[42] The irony is that, decades later, it became clear that Mengele's personal belongings had a much greater financial value than the property itself. In 2009, Liselotte sold the house for just over $25,000. Two years later, in 2011, an ultra-Orthodox US Jewish man bought at an auction the diaries written by Mengele in Brazil for $245,000. In other words, the diaries were worth almost ten times as much as the house where Mengele had lived.[43]

On the list of people who needed to be notified of Mengele's death were also his employees. Wolfram took it upon himself to tell Frau Ines Mehlich that her services were no longer needed. Mehlich was the widow of a German and had been working as a maid in Mengele's house for the last few months. Liselotte was sure that the maid knew

---

[40] Registration No. 2762 of the 11th Real Estate Registry Office of the city of São Paulo.

[41] Gitta Stammer's statement to the Federal Police.

[42] Liselotte Bossert's statement to the Federal Police.

[43] Ofer Aderet, "Ultra-Orthodox Man Buys Diaries of Nazi Doctor Mengele for $ 245,000." *Haaretz*, July 22, 2011. Available at: <www.haaretz.com/jewish/1.5032917>. Accessed on: July 6, 2023.

nothing about her boss's past. Mengele had visited Frau Mehlich's house in the humble Jardim Consórcio neighborhood a few times, because he loved to listen to her daughter play the piano. He even told her that he thought Brazil was "a good country," but regretted the corruption in the government.[44] Soon after Frau Mehlich got the news, she told the gardener that their boss had died. Luís Rodrigues had only been fifteen when he started working at the Alvarenga house. He stayed there for almost three years and became friends with "Seu Pedro," with whom he often talked. Luís Rodrigues, in turn, told Elsa Gulpian, Mengele's former maid and unrequited crush, about the death. And so the news that "Seu Pedro" had died spread through the neighborhood by word of mouth. At that time, however, hardly anyone knew that he and Josef Mengele were the same person. Only his small circle of protectors did, and they believed that the deceased's real identity should remain a secret from everyone else.

The Bosserts had yet another mission: to send news to Germany. There would be no phone calls, as communication with the Mengele family in Günzburg, Bavaria, had always been through letters. Using a dramatic tone, Wolfram wrote to the man who served as intermediary, Hans Sedlmeier: "It is with deep sadness that I fulfill the painful duty of informing you and your relatives of the death of our mutual friend. Until his last breath, he fought heroically, just as he had done during his turbulent life."[45] Sedlmeier was Mengele's former schoolmate and became a loyal employee of the family's agricultural-machinery company. He had been a central figure in the success of Mengele's escape to South America. As they say in the Brazilian police jargon, Sedlmeier was the "homing pigeon" who crossed the Atlantic, taking cash to Mengele. He was also the person to solve any kind of problem the Nazi doctor might have, such as when the Stammers couldn't stand

---

44 Pedro Stanbei, "A última empregada: Ele gostava do Brasil." *O Estado de S. Paulo*, June 8, 1985.

45 Gerald Posner and John Ware, *Mengele: The Complete Story*. New York: Cooper Square, 2000, p. 290.

Mengele any longer and wanted to get rid of him.[46] Throughout the time he was in hiding, his relatives in Germany always knew where Josef was. And now that he was dead, Wolfram was in favor of keeping it a secret, as he stated in his letter to Sedlmeier: "Not only to avoid a personal inconvenience, but also to keep the opposing side spending money on something that is outdated." By "opposing side" he meant the Nazi hunters—or, in other words, those who wanted justice for Mengele's victims.

Wolfram also had to contact Mengele's son, Rolf, who had been estranged from the rest of the Mengele family. Wolfram wrote to him and asked him to come to São Paulo again, because his father had left him a trunk full of documents, military decorations, and diaries.[47] The latter contained pages and pages of an autobiography that Mengele had written by hand during the years he lived in Brazil. The texts focused on a character called Andreas, who was obviously himself, which shows that even in the privacy of his own diary he didn't have the courage to use his real name. Under this pseudonym, Mengele recounted his birth, his childhood, his studies during the 1930s, his hiding place in Bavaria shortly after the war, and his escape to Italy in 1949. Mengele recorded all these events with his son in mind, so that Rolf wouldn't believe the image the public portrayed of him and which he considered false. Mengele also left in his diary some "good advice" for young people who, in the 1960s, were about to finish school and had to choose a career, as was Rolf's case. Mengele's writings made it clear that the old Nazi was egocentric: he dedicated seventy-four pages to the day Andreas was born and to his baptism alone. He didn't say anything, however, about what mattered most: what he had done during World War II.

---

[46] Gitta Stammer's statement to the Federal Police.

[47] "Assustado, agressivo, vivia com medo." *O Estado de S. Paulo*, June 7, 1985, p. 26. Available at: <acervo.estadao.com.br/pagina/#!/19850607-33823-nac-0026-999-26-not>. Accessed on: July 20, 2023.

Rolf agreed to return to São Paulo to collect the things in the trunk, but he didn't arrive until December, ten months after his father's death. To avoid attracting the attention of the authorities because of his surname, he used a friend's passport. He stayed in the city for a few days and spent Christmas with the Bossert family. Liselotte and Wolfram asked Rolf not to tell anyone that Mengele was dead because such a revelation could ruin their lives. Rolf felt conflicted about what to do.[48] Before returning to Germany, he said he would never forget what the couple had done for his father and insisted on continuing to exchange letters with them.[49] One of the reasons he kept quiet at the time was to protect the Bosserts: he didn't want to expose those who had risked themselves to help his father. Of course, he was also concerned for his own family and career. Rolf was a lawyer, married, and also a father. He felt uneasy about what might happen if it became known that Mengele had died in Brazil: there would be enormous exposure in the press, which would inevitably bring up the whole story of the escape and the names of those who had covered up for him.

In Germany, it wasn't illegal to help a relative who had committed a crime. In Brazil, the law was different; furthermore, those who had protected Mengele in Brazil were not related by blood to him. Dealing with these issues wasn't easy for Rolf, who considered it an "unsolvable conflict." On one hand, he maintained that he hadn't supported his father during the years Mengele was on the run; but on the other hand, he hadn't want to betray his father and hand him over to the authorities.[50] Rolf believed that Mengele had managed to avoid arrest for so long because he led a simple life, very different from the stereotype of a Nazi officer who, in the popular imagination, lived in a mansion by the sea surrounded by German shepherds. For Rolf, his father's actual

---

48 "Rolf Mengele," *The Today Show*. NBC, June 16, 1986.

49 "Pista revela: Filho de Mengele em SP." *O Estado de S. Paulo*, June 8, 1985.

50 Inge Byham, "So entkam mein Vater. Die Geheimnisse des Josef Mengele: Seine Flucht. Seine Verstecke. Seine Jahre im Untergrund." *Bunte Illustrierte*, June 20, 1986.

living conditions in his last years were pitiful: his accommodations were miserable, his cars old, and his clothes so threadbare that no one could suspect that he had once been the all-powerful Angel of Death from Auschwitz, where he used to wear an impeccable SS uniform and decide the fate of thousands of people with a simple wave of his hand. At the end of his life he looked like a neglected old man, the best of disguises in Rolf's view.[51]

Despite being Mengele's only son, he saw his father only twice in his life, apart from when he was a baby. The first time was when Rolf was twelve years old, in March 1956, when he vacationed in the Swiss Alps with his cousin Karl-Heinz and his aunt Martha. She was the widow of Karl Jr., one of Mengele's brothers. Rolf was introduced to "Uncle Fritz" and was fascinated by the man who told stories of the adventures of the Argentine gauchos and also of the fight against the Partisans during World War II, at a time when no adult German dared to touch the subject of war. "Uncle Fritz" also gave him a little money, the first allowance of his life. It wasn't until three years later that he found out the nice man's name wasn't Fritz, and that he was actually his father. Mengele's intention on that trip was to get closer to Martha, his brother's widow, whom he married, a plan devised by patriarch Karl Mengele so as not to lose the family estate.

For years, the recently reacquainted father and son exchanged letters. At first, as a teenager living with his mother, Irene, in Germany, Rolf felt obliged to answer the letters of the man who sent him stamps from Argentina. Later, he replied out of pity, a humanitarian gesture, like someone writing to a prisoner, he thought. Rolf tried many times to forget that Mengele was his father. It was impossible. In 1977, more than twenty years after their first meeting, he decided to see him for a second time. He took it as a personal challenge to try to establish the facts of his father's life story, to determine whether everything said about him was true. He decided to spend two weeks in Brazil.

---

51 Gerald Posner and John Ware, op. cit., p. 111.

It wasn't an easy decision to go to South America knowing that he could be followed.[52] When he arrived in São Paulo for the first time, he only had one thing in his mind: the Bossert family's address. He had memorized the street name and number, so he wouldn't have to carry with him any compromising papers, in case he was approached by the police, the Mossad, or a Nazi hunter. It was on this first visit to the country that Rolf met the Bossert family in person. They talked a lot, and Wolfram offered to drive him to his father's house. They left the middle-class neighborhood of Brooklin in an old Volkswagen and drove ten miles to Eldorado. On the way, Rolf observed the landscape and was surprised. He was used to the perfect streets, avenues, and sidewalks in Germany. The farther they drove into the outskirts of São Paulo, the poorer the houses were. Alvarenga Road, where Mengele had lived, was in a terrible state. It was just a dirt road full of potholes. According to Rolf, on the left and right you could see slums for miles. When the car finally stopped in front of his father's house, Rolf's first impression was that it was no more than a shack. That was probably an exaggeration. The lot was large, ten thousand square feet, and the house itself measured almost thirteen hundred square feet. In the surrounding area, in addition to the humble houses, there were some middle-class residences, used on weekends. The Eldorado neighborhood had once seen some days of glory: its residents affirm that celebrities like singers Elis Regina and Roberto Leal had often visited a condominium a mile from where Mengele lived. The neighborhood was in a pleasant spot next to the Billings reservoir, with many remnants of lush nature, huge trees with bromeliads hanging from their branches, coconut palm trees, and a few different types of pines.

The situation in the area began to deteriorate a few years before Mengele arrived. In 1968, about a hundred families who lived in the Vergueiro favela, the largest slum in the city of São Paulo at the time, were evicted and settled in the Eldorado area. Real estate agents began

---

52 "Rolf Mengele," *The Today Show*. NBC, June 16, 1986.

circulating in the slum to sell plots of land in the Eldorado region. It seemed like a good deal: instead of being tenants, the evictees would become landowners in their own right. In this way, the favela was practically transplanted from one place to another. The residents themselves built their new homes using material from the old shacks. What no agent had told them was that the land was on a hill, far from the city center, and the living conditions were extremely precarious. Water had to be fetched from a small forest, where springs had been found. In the streets, barefoot boys, many of them naked, wandered around. There was no electricity; lighting was by candle or oil lamp. The only silver lining was the beautiful view from the top of the hill where the housing development stood, from where one could see the Billings reservoir.[53]

Indeed, for someone recently arrived from Germany like Rolf, unaccustomed to the inequalities of developing countries, that social environment was quite shocking. In the midst of this degraded scenario, he got out of Wolfram's car and for the first time as an adult saw his father face-to-face. His first sensation was one of strangeness. The old man had tears in his eyes and was shaking with emotion. Upon entering the house, Rolf noticed that it was as poor inside as it was outside. It had very little furniture: a table, two chairs, a cupboard, and a bed, which the father gave up to his son, choosing to sleep on the stone floor.

During the first few days, Rolf avoided talking about touchy subjects, such as his father's work in the Auschwitz concentration camp. The old man was excited about something else: the memoirs he had spent years writing for his son. He read a few pages to Rolf, who didn't pay much attention to it. On October 17, 1977, Mengele registered in his diary: "Cloudy, rainy, hot. After breakfast, conversations about my writing and readings. His assessment is very interesting and typical for a modern young man. More action, more events than description,

---

53 "Centenas de pessoas deixam a favela da Vergueiro e começam outra em Eldorado." *Folha de S. Paulo*, April 16, 1968.

more reflection, more tension!"[54] The differences between father and son were enormous. Mengele's mentality had stayed frozen in the 1940s and he hadn't kept up with the changes that had taken place in Germany over the following decades. The Germans of Rolf's generation had completely broken away from the ideas of the war generation.

It was clear that his son wasn't interested in his endless explanations, but wanted to hear about what he had actually done in Auschwitz. It wasn't until they had spent a few more days together that Rolf had the courage to bring up the subject of concentration camps. And, as expected, his father exploded: "How can you imagine that I could have possibly done anything like that? Don't you realize that it is all a lie, propaganda?" Mengele asked his son. Rolf decided to take a step back and go easy. "What about the selections?" he asked. Mengele admitted frankly that they existed, but made an excuse: "How could I help hundreds of thousands of people if the system itself was terribly organized? I helped many of them . . . some of them." Rolf tried to tell his father that just being in Auschwitz and not trying every day to get out was something horrible and impossible for him to accept. In fact, he could never understand how a human being could act like that. Rolf's stance wouldn't change, whether it concerned his father or not. For Rolf, his father being in Auschwitz and working for that death machine was against all ethics and morals, against understanding and human nature.[55]

54 Ulrich Völklein, *Josef Mengele: Der Artz von Auschwitz*. Göttingen: Steidl, 1999, p. 297.

55 *The Search for Mengele*. Directed by: Brian Moser. Production: Brian Moser, William Bemister, David Frost, and Roger James, 1985. Available at: <youtube.com /watch?v=I8sNiAgEKGo>. Accessed on: July 6, 2023.

5

A RISING SCIENTIST
IN NAZI GERMANY

B aron Otmar von Verschuer was the mentor every young scientist dreamed of having in 1930s Germany. His title of nobility attracted attention, but the doctor and prolific researcher really stood out as one of the pioneers in the field of twin studies, the cutting edge at the time for the advancement of genetics. By comparing identical twins, Verschuer tried to discover which characteristics of an individual were hereditary and which were determined by the environment.[56] The same methodology was used to analyze the genetic traits of different "races"—race being strictly a biological concept at the time. The issue of race, in fact, represented the central pillar of Nazi ideology and, consequently, was a hot topic in German academic circles during the Third Reich, when new research centers sprang up all over the country. In 1935, the University of Frankfurt inaugurated the Institute for Human Genetics and Racial Hygiene and invited

---

56 Carola Sachse, *Die Verbindung nach Auschwitz: Biowissenschaften und Menschenversuche an Kaiser-Wilhelm-Instituten; Dokumentation eines Symposiums.* Göttingen: Wallstein, p. 150.

Verschuer to be its director. Two years after taking up the post, the renowned scientist received a request from a colleague at the University of Munich to supervise the medical thesis of a dedicated young man: Josef Mengele. The student wanted to do his second doctorate at the pretentiously named institution headed by Verschuer. "Human genetics" is an expression still commonly used today, while "racial hygiene" (or Rassenhygiene) is a German term now widely condemned as a synonym for eugenics. The theory of eugenics largely explains the cultural milieu of that period and the environment in which Mengele trained academically.

It's important to note that it wasn't the Nazis who invented modern eugenics. This idea began in the nineteenth century with the work of the British Francis Galton, a cousin of Charles Darwin. While Darwin created the theory of the evolution of species by observing the slow process of nature, Galton believed that it was possible to accelerate evolution artificially by intervening in the mechanism of natural selection. He imagined that the selective crossing of the strongest, most intelligent, and fittest human beings could accomplish in decades what nature would take centuries to achieve.[57] In other words, Galton believed that it was possible to improve the human species through the selection of the most suitable "strains of blood" or "races," which would prevail over the less-suitable ones.[58] When Galton defended this thesis in front of the intellectual elite of Victorian society, during an evening of debates at the prestigious London School of Economics and Political Science, he could not have foreseen the terrible practical implications that it would have in the future. At the beginning of the twentieth century, eugenics became a worldwide movement, particularly in the United States. In the 1920s, more than half of the US states passed laws allowing for the "involuntary asexualization" of

[57] Siddhartha Mukherjee, *O gene: Uma história íntima*. São Paulo: Companhia das Letras, 2016, p. 64

[58] Philip K. Wilson, "Eugenics," *Encyclopædia Britannica*. Available at: <www.britannica.com/science/eugenics-genetics>. Accessed on February 5, 2021.

people considered unfit, a euphemism for forced sterilization or castration. The preferred targets were poor people with intellectual disabilities, so they would not pass on their "ills" to future generations. The forced asexualization of individuals would thus result in the cleansing of the "race" as a whole.[59] The pursuit of racial hygiene or eugenics would go even further in the following decades, reaching its apex of horror under Nazism.

At the age of nineteen, Mengele couldn't have imagined what lay ahead either. He left Günzburg, the small town where he was born in the Bavarian countryside, and headed for the state capital to attend university. He arrived at the University of Munich thinking he would study dentistry, but was soon convinced by more senior students that the best option was medicine—a decision that eventually would change the fate of thousands of people. It was also the older students who opened his eyes to Nazism. In the 1930 elections, students aged twenty and over voted heavily for the Nazi party, which became the second largest in the Reichstag, the German parliament. Due to his young age, Mengele could not yet vote and had no political affiliation. He considered himself a nationalist because of the influence of his conservative and very Catholic family, like most Bavarian families were. His only conviction as a freshman was that no one should remain indifferent in those times of great political unrest, when the country was under the threat of a Marxist-Bolshevistic takeover.

Like him, his father, businessman Karl Mengele, had felt no great passion for Nazism until then. However, the older Mengele didn't hesitate to let Adolf Hitler himself give a speech in his agricultural machinery factory during the campaign for the November 1932 elections. The largest venue for public events in Günzburg was then a 1,200-seat gymnasium, and the venue had been cramped for Hitler's first speech in the city two years earlier. For this new event, they

---

59 Vivien Spitz, *Doctors from Hell: The Horrific Account of Nazi Experiments on Humans.* Boulder: Sentient, 2005.

needed a bigger venue, as the Nazi leader had become even more popular. Karl Mengele was a pragmatic man and tried to maintain a good
relationship with everyone so that his business would run smoothly.
This was his main motivation for lending his space to Hitler, as he
wasn't exactly a deep admirer of the leader. At that point, Karl wasn't
even a member of the Nazi party, which he only joined later, also
because of his business interests.[60] There are no records of the young
Mengele returning home to see the future Führer give a speech at the
family business. What is certain is that he didn't want to follow in his
father's footsteps as a businessman, despite being the firstborn of three
sons: Josef, Karl Jr., and Alois. Mengele wanted to pursue his vocation
and walk his own path.

Medical science was by far his main interest, since clinical medicine
didn't seem to him "very scientific." Mengele then began to devote
himself to anthropology. At the time, anthropology and genetics were
part of the medical sciences and, under the influence of Positivism,
demanded from the researcher exact criteria grounded in concrete
data. It was this mathematical precision that Mengele liked most.[61]
Even before the Third Reich, Germany developed a branch called
Rassenanthropologie, or "racial anthropology," which tried to establish
what the morphological characteristics of each "race" were: skull shape,
eye color, hair color, skin color, etc. Based on anatomical descriptions
and comparisons of blood samples, the discipline aimed to find genetic
proof of the superiority of one "race" over another. Mengele pursued
this line of studies/research during his doctorate in anthropology at
the University of Munich. His thesis on the "morphology of the lower
jaw of four racial groups" concluded that it was possible to identify
one's "race" by just analyzing their jaw.[62] Professor Theodor Mollison,
then director of the Institute of Anthropology at the University of

---

[60] Sven Keller, *Günzburg und der Fall Josef Mengele: Die Heimatstadt und die Jagd nach
dem NS-Verbrecher.* Munich: R. Oldenbourg, 2003, p. 75.

[61] Ibid., pp. 81–83.

[62] Gerald Posner and John Ware, op. cit., p. 10.

Munich, supervised Mengele's work and liked the result so much that he referred his student to his renowned colleague Verschuer in Frankfurt. It was a great opportunity for Mengele's career.

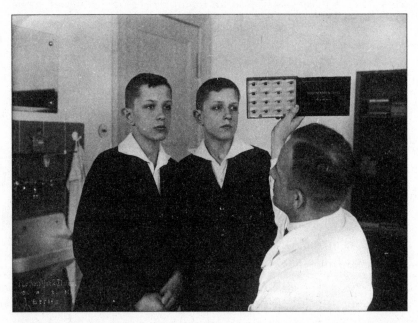

Baron Otmar von Verschuer assessing the eye color of a pair of twins.
Archives of Max Planck Society, Berlin.

By then, the young doctor, who was actually more inclined to be a scientist than to see patients, had already spent academic periods in Munich, Bonn, Vienna, and Leipzig. In January 1937, he moved to Frankfurt and joined the Nazi party in May, having developed a deep ideological affinity with the party on the issue of race. The following year, he completed his second doctorate, this time in medicine. Verschuer supervised his thesis, which investigated cleft lip as a possible genetic abnormality. Mengele traced more than five hundred relatives of seventeen children who had this condition and had been operated on at the Frankfurt University clinic.[63] His work was

---

63 Carola Sachse, op. cit., p. 209.

cited in scientific publications, with six citations in the *Handbuch der Erbbiologie des Menschen* (Handbook of Human Genetic Biology) alone, the most complete book on the subject in Nazi Germany. Until the 1960s, Mengele's thesis continued to be required reading in the field.

The future looked promising for Mengele. Verschuer chose him to be one of his assistants, and he soon became the old professor's favorite, so much so that he even asked Mengele to replace him at lectures and conferences. In addition to the academic work together, the two were responsible for drawing up evaluations for the Reichssippenamt, the Nazi office that dealt with genealogy, an important aspect of the regime's racial policy. Mengele and Verschuer used their knowledge as racial anthropologists to help the prosecution in cases of "Rassenschande" (shame to the race)—or, in other words, sexual relationships between a "German" and a "Jew."[64] In one of the cases prosecuted, the accused had a non-Jewish mother who was married to a Jew. The accused claimed not to be the fruit of this union, but of his mother's love affair with a non-Jewish man, and therefore he would not be half-Jewish, but fully Aryan. The prosecution called upon Mengele's expertise and the "scientific" data he had gathered, including family history and physical characteristics—such as the shape of the nose and ears—to affirm that the accused's father was indeed Jewish.

With Hitler coming to power in 1933, Jews began being excluded from social life through rulings and acts by the Nazi regime and the silent complicity of ordinary citizens. After the Nuremberg Laws were enacted in 1935, not only were German Jews segregated, made constant target of random attacks, and excluded from public service, but also fully excluded from society. Furthermore, they lost all political rights. In short, Jews were no longer considered German citizens (Reichsbürger).[65] Another Nuremberg law, concerning the "protection

---

64 The quotation marks are meant to highlight the absurd assumption that a Jew could not be a German.

65 Hannah Arendt, op. cit., p. 51.

of German blood and honor," prohibited sexual relations between Jews and non-Jews, on the grounds that "purity of blood was essential for the continued existence of the German people." However, there was never a scientifically drawn conclusion of what "German blood" or "Jewish blood" might be. For this reason, Germany had to define what it meant to be Jewish. Interestingly, the criterion used was fundamentally religious rather than biological. The regulation stated that "a Jew was anyone who descended from at least three grandparents who were racially full Jews," a "full Jew" being "a man or a woman who belongs to the Jewish religious community." In this way, the Nazis determined a person's "race," which for them was a biological and scientific concept, according to the religious affiliation of their grandparents.[66]

Although the Nazis clung fiercely to the notion of race as biologically defined, this idea didn't originate with Nazism. It developed slowly in Europe from the Enlightenment onward, when naturalists began to classify human beings as they had previously done with animals and plants. In the eighteenth century, the great Swedish naturalist Carl Linnaeus coined the term *Homo sapiens* to refer to our species and divided it into four "varieties": europaeus, americanus, asiaticus, and africanus. It was a first step toward categorizing humanity in biological terms. A rival naturalist, the Frenchman Georges-Louis Leclerc, Comte de Buffon, went one step further: instead of "varieties," he began to systematically use the word "races" to describe the different groups among the *Homo sapiens* species. This new terminology influenced many authors who later established new subcategories for the human species based on analyses of the physical appearance of certain groups.

Before the biological concept of "race" was established, the term had a different connotation, referring exclusively to a particular family lineage or animal species. Now understood as biology-based and as genetic inheritance, race offered Europeans a supposedly concrete and

---

66 Laurence Rees, op. cit., p. 116.

scientific justification for their feelings of superiority over other populations.[67] In the nineteenth century, European imperialism further reinforced the new concept of scientific racism, as it needed to convincingly justify the exploitation of other peoples, whether in the partition of Africa or in the new colonies in Asia and Oceania. The feeling of European superiority, however, resulted from the perception that Europe had reached a higher level of civilization than the "savages" in other parts of the world. During Nazism, this imperialist legacy combined with one of the oldest prejudices in history: anti-Semitism.

Anti-Semitism, or the hatred of Jews, is even older than the biological definition of race. It dates back to biblical times, when the Israelites were accused of killing Jesus. This accusation had the worst possible repercussions in the following centuries, as Christianity spread throughout Europe, and the continent entered the Middle Ages. During that essentially agrarian era, Jews could not own land but were allowed to practice usury, the lending of money while charging interest. Usury was one of the few occupations that Jews were allowed to have, while it was forbidden for Christians. That activity further aggravated the negative image of Jews, and they came to be regarded as cruel loan sharks, as in William Shakespeare's play *The Merchant of Venice*.

For centuries, "God's chosen people" were unwelcome to European monarchs. England expelled the Jews in the thirteenth century, and in the fifteenth century Spain and Portugal did the same. In the vibrant Venice of the sixteenth century, Jews were not expelled, but were crowded in Europe's first ghetto, living isolated from the rest of the population. The situation only improved with the rise of the Enlightenment, or Age of Reason, when the French Revolution's ideal of equality finally extended citizenship to Jews. Thus, they were able to gradually integrate into the life of the great European cities,

---

67 Nicholas Hudson, "From 'Nation' to 'Race': The Origin of Racial Classification in Eighteenth-Century Thought." *Eighteenth-Century Studies*, Johns Hopkins University Press, v. 29, n. 3, 1996.

occupy important positions in society, and revolutionize various fields of knowledge, as evidenced by the works of Karl Marx, Sigmund Freud, and Albert Einstein. Despite the social assimilation of Jews, anti-Semitism remained alive in Europe. In the corners of the Russian Empire, at the end of the nineteenth century, for example, Jews were the targets of barbaric persecution and the infamous pogroms, organized massacres of the Jewish people usually supported by the authorities themselves.

After World War I, the rage against Jews spread all over Germany, as the country searched for scapegoats to explain the defeat of the German Empire in that war. In *Mein Kampf*, the book Hitler wrote while imprisoned in Bavaria for attempting a coup ten years before coming to power, he describes in detail how his eyes were opened to the "danger of Judaism," which happened only after he moved to Vienna. During his childhood, Judaism never posed an issue for his lower-middle-class family life. However, in Vienna, the cosmopolitan capital of the former Habsburg Empire, then thriving on wealth, art, and knowledge, Hitler saw poverty up close. There he began to perceive the Jews as the source of all evil and later wrote that "the accusation against Judaism became serious" the moment he found Jewish activities in the press, art, literature, and theater. He continued: "There was a moral pestilence that was infecting the public. It was worse than the black plague."[68] Hatred of the Jews and the idea that they should be extirpated from society dominate dozens of pages of *Mein Kampf.* Furthermore, Hitler advocated ideas of eugenics, stating that the Aryan "race" was superior to all others and that the Jewish "race" was a parasite. "The strongest must dominate and must not mate with the weakest, which would sacrifice their own superior nature," he argued.[69]

Hitler's main source of inspiration for the absurd racial ideas he lays out in *Mein Kampf* was the volume *Grundriss der menschlichen*

---

[68] Adolf Hitler, *Mein Kampf.* Nova Delhi: Diamond, 2021, p. 78.

[69] Ibid., p. 338.

Erblichkeitslehre und Rassenhygiene (*The Science of Human Heredity and Racial Hygiene*), which he also read in prison. Written by three leading scientists of the time, Erwin Baur, Fritz Lenz, and Eugen Fischer, and released in 1921, it became the authoritative book on eugenics. Fischer had been the mentor of Verschuer, who in turn became Mengele's academic adviser. Mengele's academic influences show clearly how both he and Hitler were inspired by the same line of reasoning. These ideas were also behind the Third Reich's racial hygiene programs, which not only targeted Jews, but also regulated the forced sterilization of people with diseases considered to be hereditary, most of them psychiatric and neurological disorders.[70]

In 1939, at the beginning of World War II, Hitler carried eugenics to its extreme by authorizing the elimination of German citizens who were considered to be weak and led "a life unworthy of being lived." The Nazi health authorities began to encourage parents of babies and young children with physical or mental disabilities to take their children to certain "pediatric clinics." In reality, these were extermination centers where doctors administered lethal injections to the children. Later, the "euthanasia" program was extended to include adolescents and, eventually, adult patients living in care institutions and suffering from conditions such as schizophrenia, epilepsy, or dementia.

Hitler signed an authorization for doctors and their staffs to participate in these killings without the risk of future prosecution. The secret program was codenamed T4, a reference to the street where the central office in Berlin was located, Tiergartenstrasse 4. Later, six gas-chamber facilities were set up, five in Germany and one in Austria, where the victims were taken by bus or train. Upon arrival, they were sent to showers, from which not water but rather carbon monoxide came out, killing them by asphyxiation in a matter of minutes. Afterwards, the bodies were burned and the ashes given to

---

70 Heiner Fangerau and Irmgard Müller, "Das Standardwerk der Rassenhygiene von Erwin Baur, Eugen Fischer und Fritz Lenz im Urteil der Psychiatrie und Neurologie 1921–1940." *Der Nervenarzt*, v. 73, pp. 1039–46, November 2002. Available at: <www.academia.edu/25603311>. Accessed on: April 18, 2021.

relatives in an urn along with a certificate that stated a false cause of death. According to the euthanasia program's own calculations, between January 1940 and August 1941, the T4 exterminated more than 70,000 Germans with physical or mental disabilities in the gas chambers, thus ensuring the racial hygiene of the "Aryan race." If the Nazis were capable of committing such atrocities on their own people, it didn't require much for them to do a whole lot worse to those they considered to be of an "inferior race," such as Jews and Romas and Sintis. It was the prelude to the Holocaust.

WHEN THE WAR BROKE OUT, Mengele got very excited. He believed it would be the German nation's definitive fight for its very existence. He could barely wait to join the army and didn't mind leaving his wife behind, even though he had just gotten married to Irene Schönbein, a tall blonde woman six and a half years younger than him. The two met in Leipzig, while Mengele was doing his first medical residency at a children's clinic.[71] Despite his excitement about the war, he had to wait almost a year to be recruited. It wasn't until June 1940 that Mengele was called up to the Wehrmacht's Medical Replacement Battalion in Kassel, a city in central Germany. However, he didn't last a month in the unit because of a hostile instructor who seemed determined to crush his subordinates. Mengele decided to get away from him as soon as possible, and his best way out was to volunteer for the Waffen-SS, the combat unit of the SS, itself a paramilitary organization within the German Army. A year before the war, Mengele had already joined the SS, whose men were loyal to the Führer, just as the old German Army was loyal to the Kaiser (the emperor).[72]

As an expert in genetics, Mengele was assigned to be a racial examiner at the Waffen-SS office for the Consolidation of German Ethnicity in Poland, a role similar to the one he had held when he

---

71 Gerald Posner and John Ware, op. cit., pp. 11 and 16; Sven Keller, op. cit., p. 14.
72 Sven Keller, op. cit., p. 19.

worked with Verschuer in Frankfurt. His job was to evaluate ethnic German landowners and farmers in the Baltic countries to determine whether they could be repatriated to the Reich, which had expanded its territory enormously due to the conquests made during the war. The Nazis had expelled thousands of Polish farmers from their farms, forcing them to go east, and offered their land to citizens of German origin, the so-called Volksdeutsche, who had been living in countries occupied by the Nazis. Thus, 120,000 ethnic Germans from Latvia, Estonia, and Lithuania were invited to "return home" and occupy land that had previously belonged to the Poles, but was now part of the Reich.[73] Mengele was one of the examiners that determined who among those people were ethnic Germans and who weren't.

The restless young man would not spend the entire war doing this bureaucratic work in Poland. Before long, he left the Consolidation of German Ethnicity office to become a doctor for the SS troops in the Wiking division. It was as a member of this unit that he committed his greatest act of bravery, when he saved two soldiers from a burning war tank while fighting on the eastern front in Russia. His bravery was recognized with an Iron Cross First Class medal, the most important honor a German soldier could receive in battle, the very same medal Hitler had won when he fought in World War I. The Wiking division commander, supported by the doctor in charge, offered him a promotion to Hauptsturmführer, the equivalent of an SS captain. However, Mengele was wounded and had to be transferred to Berlin, where he would return to bureaucratic work in the Reichsarzt's Police and SS Department. The Reichsarzt literally means the Reich doctor. The post was held then by Dr. Ernst-Robert Grawitz, who was at the top of the SS medical hierarchy and answered directly to Heinrich Himmler, the SS boss who, in turn, answered only to Hitler himself. Grawitz played a central role in most of the crimes committed by doctors in the concentration camps. He had a group of fifteen officials

---

[73] Tony Judt, *Pós-guerra: Uma história da Europa desde 1945*. São Paulo: Objetiva, 2008, p. 36.

working with him, including a team of SS doctors, and one of his most important duties had been to find a quick method to kill the prisoners. There was no better place than the Reichsarzt if one wanted to keep informed about the medical research conducted in the Nazi concentration camps.[74]

In Berlin, Mengele was once again close to his old mentor, who had just been assigned an important post in the German capital. Verschuer was the new director of the Kaiser Wilhelm Institute for Anthropology, Human Heredity, and Eugenics in the Dahlem district of the capital. This was one of several institutes under the umbrella of the Kaiser Wilhelm Society, created during the German Empire to promote various scientific fields in the country, alongside the universities. At the beginning of the twentieth century, the Society became a symbol of cutting-edge research in the country and welcomed world-renowned scientists such as Albert Einstein, who had developed the theory of relativity, and Max Planck, considered the father of quantum physics.

The Institute of Anthropology was inaugurated in 1927, and its first director was Eugen Fischer, one of the three authors of the aforementioned *Grundriss der menschlichen Erblichkeitslehre*. The basis of Fischer's research had been carried out in 1908, during a trip to German South West Africa, a former German colony and now the country of Namibia. There he studied the offspring of Dutch men and native women of the ethnic group called Hottentots in colonial times and now known as Khoisan. The anthropologist concluded that "Black blood" was inferior to white and warned that the races should not mix because, according to him, this would mean the death of European culture. Fischer went on to create the first courses on racial anthropology taught to doctors in the SS, and his abhorrent ideas had a direct impact on the Nuremberg Laws and the sterilization of Germans considered undesirable.

Mengele as an assistant
at the University Institute
for Hereditary Biology
and Racial Hygiene in
Frankfurt, 1939 or 1940.

*Archives of the Max
Planck Society, Berlin.*

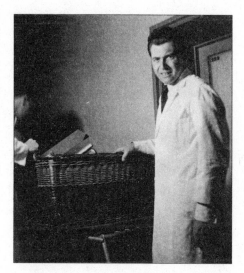

Mengele with Nazi
geneticist Hans Grebe.

*Archives of the Max
Planck Society, Berlin.*

Verschuer was Fischer's student and also his favorite to replace him at the Kaiser Wilhelm Institute. When Fischer reached the age limit for the position of director, he nominated Verschuer to take his place. The scientist accepted the invitation and moved to Berlin in 1942, taking with him a huge database on twins that he had created during his time in Frankfurt. His database was used in various areas of research at the institute, such as hereditary pathology, immunogenetics, serology, blood groups, and even hereditary psychology. More than two hundred doctorate theses on twin research were published in Germany during Nazism, which clearly suggests how popular Verschuer's methodology became and the influence it exerted on Mengele.[75]

After he left the institute, Fischer kept in touch with Verschuer. In a letter from January 1943, Verschuer told him that his assistant Mengele had just flown back from Salsk, on the Russian front, and had been transferred to an SS office in Berlin, but would be able to do some work for the Kaiser Wilhelm Institute as well.[76] Verschuer took the opportunity to invite Mengele to work at the Kaiser Wilhelm Institute, where the young man would mainly help with the preparation of reports on race and parenthood.[77] This gave Mengele the chance to get to know some colleagues and the research difficulties they faced during the war, such as the lack of twins available for studies.[78] One colleague said that Mengele had been asking to be transferred to Auschwitz, because he believed there were great research possibilities there. His chance came at the end of April 1943, when Benno Adolph, the doctor at the Roma camp in Auschwitz, came down with scarlet fever and had to be removed. Mengele took his place, and his new position seemed like the perfect opportunity for him to gain access to thousands of people of different "races" and to use them as guinea pigs in medical experiments at his own discretion.

---

[75] Ibid., p. 206.

[76] Sven Keller, op. cit., p. 23.

[77] Carola Sachse, op. cit., p. 151.

[78] Ibid., p. 230.

6

THE KINDLY UNCLE

AUSCHWITZ-BIRKENAU. MAY 1943

Mengele was ordered to report to the commandant of Auschwitz as soon as he arrived from Berlin, on May 30, 1943. His immediate superior, however, was not the commandant, but Dr. Eduard Wirths, who was responsible for the entire medical services of the huge complex. This included the pharmacy, the dentists, and all the SS doctors. In fact, Auschwitz had at least thirty of them working there during the war. Some of these medical professionals treated the German troops, while others took care of the inmates. The latter doctors, called Lagerarzt, selected prisoners recently arrived from all over Europe who were suitable for work, and sent the others to the gas chambers.[79] A decree signed by Heinrich Himmler determined that only doctors trained in anthropology could make the selections and supervise the extermination of Jews, Roma, and other "enemies" of the Reich. Mengele's résumé perfectly qualified him for this role.[80]

---

79 Sven Keller, op. cit., pp. 29–30.

80 Benno Müller-Hill, *Murderous Science: Elimination by Scientific Selection of Jews, Gypsies, and Others, Germany 1933–1945*. New York: Oxford University Press, 1988, p. 19.

The largest Nazi concentration camp was colossal in size, and each SS doctor was responsible for a section of it, in addition to working in the infirmaries and on the train-arrival ramps. Right from the start, Mengele was in charge of the BIIe section, the "gypsy camp" in Birkenau.[81] The Roma had arrived three months before him. The sad story of their deportation to the concentration camp began before the war, when German scientists traveled all over the Reich to examine and register them. The examiners looked at eyes and noses, researched family relationships and baptismal certificates—most of them were Catholic—and finally wrote racial reports.[82] This process, considered scientific, was well known to doctors trained in anthropology, such as Mengele. On the basis of these studies, psychologist and psychiatrist Robert Ritter, the leading Nazi authority on the "gypsy question," concluded that more than 90 percent of those who considered themselves Roma had mixed blood, were asocial individuals, and, according to him, useless, and therefore should be isolated from the rest of society.[83] The Nazis were determined to cleanse the Aryan "race" of all contamination from other "races" deemed inferior and to halt miscegenation. Consequently, all registered Roma in the Reich and occupied territories were confined to ghettos, the same fate imposed on the Jews. The final blow came in December 1942: Himmler ordered all people with "Gypsy blood" to be sent to the Auschwitz-Birkenau extermination camp. Two months later, almost twenty-three thousand men, women, and children were plucked from various corners of Europe, the majority coming from Germany, Austria, Poland, and the protectorate of Bohemia and Moravia in Czechoslovakia. There were also

---

81 The Archives of the Auschwitz-Birkenau State Museum contain two original "*Record Books of the Gypsies*," who were placed in the so-called *Family Camp* (*Zigeunerlager*) in the Birkenau section BIIe. https://www.auschwitz.org/en/museum/about-the-available-data/sinti-and-roma/.

82 United States Holocaust Memorial Museum.

83 Benno Müller-Hill, op. cit., p. 14.

Women and children on the Birkenau arrival platform. The Jews were removed from the deportation trains and then faced a selection process. Most of them were sent immediately to their deaths, while others were sent to slave labor.

Yad Vashem Photo Archive, Jerusalem.

smaller groups from other countries, such as France, the Netherlands, and Belgium. Of all the Sinti and Roma deported from across the European continent, nearly 1,700 were murdered as soon as they set foot in Auschwitz.

Unlike the other prisoners, Roma families were allowed to stay together in the huge barracks that lined the camp. Experience had shown that trying to separate them, especially the children, led to resistance and unrest, even though many families had already been torn apart by persecution policies before arriving at Auschwitz. Some Roma were also allowed to keep their own clothes, a privilege not afforded to other prisoners. The latter had had to get rid of all their belongings, and had their hair shaved off as soon as they disembarked. The "special" treatment the Roma received was due simply to the low supply of prisoner uniforms in the camp.[84] Once in Auschwitz, all the Roma had an identification number tattooed on their arms, just like the other prisoners. The difference was that their numbers were preceded by the letter "Z" for Zigeuner, or "gypsy" in German. They also had to wear a black triangle on their clothes, which designated inmates who were considered asocial, such as prostitutes in the women's camp. The color of the triangle indicated the reason for their imprisonment: political prisoners wore a red triangle, and "professional" criminals, such as thieves and murderers, a green one; Jews were given two yellow triangles, which formed the star of David.[85]

The "asocial" symbol reinforced the Roma stereotypes already imprinted in the public imagination long before Nazism from a long history of prejudice. In the nineteenth century, such prejudice was confirmed by science and therefore seemed irrefutable. The father of criminal anthropology, the Italian psychiatrist Cesare Lombroso, created a biological concept to define the born criminal: *Homo delinquens*. Lombroso elaborated on this concept in his classic 1876 book, *Criminal Man*. In his work of over five hundred pages, Lombroso mentioned Roma only five times, but made it clear that he considered them to be born criminals. This sparse mention of the Roma nevertheless planted a seed in the public, and from it stemmed the idea that this minority group suffered from a biologically based tendency to criminality.[86] The Roma are an ancient people originating in a territory that is now part of India. They emigrated from that region in the fourteenth century and spread to various parts of Europe, but for centuries maintained their traditions and their own language, Romani, derived from an

---

84 Roni Stauber and Raphael Vago, *The Roma: A Minority in Europe*. Budapest: Central European University Press, 2007, p. 90.

85 Hermann Langbein, *People in Auschwitz*. Chapell Hill: University of North Carolina Press, 2005, p. 12.

86 Roni Stauber and Raphael Vago, op. cit., p. 44.

older language similar to Sanskrit. Additionally, there are subgroups among the Roma, such as the Sinti minority, who settled mainly in German-speaking countries. Many of these Roma experienced a difficult dilemma during Nazism because, although they saw themselves as Germans, they also wanted to maintain their Roma identity.

In Birkenau, prisoners who survived the selections were forced to work to exhaustion, but the Roma seemed to be the exception to the rule. Some were called in to finish work on the BIIe sector, which was still under construction, but a large proportion of the Roma had no regular tasks—which further reinforced the stereotype that they were "asocial."

In the overcrowded barracks, the families lived in miserable conditions, and epidemic outbreaks proliferated, especially of typhoid and diarrhea, and the mortality rate was extremely high. The situation worsened in the summer of 1943, shortly after Mengele's arrival. At that time, an extremely rare disease called noma, caused by malnutrition, poor oral hygiene, and unsanitary environments, broke out among the children in the "gypsy camp."[87] The noma infection eats away the tissues of the face and roof of the mouth, leaving horrible physical consequences among the survivors, who become disfigured.[88] Without medical attention, the disease leads to death in a short time. Even worse, no one knew the exact cause of this highly infectious disease.

The newly arrived Dr. Mengele was convinced that he could discover the origin and cure for noma. To do this, he isolated all the infected children in barrack number 22, located in the infirmary of the "gypsy camp." He chose a prisoner to take care of it: Dr. Berthold Epstein, an internationally renowned Czech pediatrician who had been a professor at the University of Prague before being deported to

---

[87] "Sinti and Roma (Gypsies) in Auschwitz." Auschwitz-Birkenau State Museum. Available at: <auschwitz.org/en/history/categories-of-prisoners/sinti-and-roma-in-auschwitz>. Accessed on: June 1, 2021.

[88] María García-Moro et al., "La enfermedad de Noma/cancrum oris: Una enfermedad olvidada." *Revista Española de Quimioterapia*, v. 28, n. 5, pp. 225–34, 2015. Available at: <seq.es/seq/0214-3429/28/5/moro.pdf>. Accessed on: July 10, 2023.

Auschwitz for being a Jew. The doctor had been working in Monowitz, one of the three main camps, where IG Farben had set up a synthetic oil and rubber factory. This powerful company, which took advantage of slave labor, was a conglomerate of the largest chemical industries in Germany, including those known today as Basf, Hoechst, and Bayer.[89] Mengele spared the pediatrician from manual labor in the factory and told him that he would certainly never leave the camp alive, but he could make his life more bearable by writing a scientific article for him. Epstein knew Mengele was right, for most of the prisoners who worked at IG Farben died within three or four months because of exhaustion.[90] Mengele chose another Czech Jew, dermatologist Rudolf Vitek, to be assistant. Under Mengele's direct supervision, these two prisoner-specialists had the mission of investigating what was causing noma. Dr. Epstein accepted the proposal and decided to write about the disease, in addition to helping the patients.

Forty-five Roma children participated in the study, which lasted almost a year, from August 1943 to June 1944. Mengele ensured that they received more food and medicine than the others. He also photographed the patients when they first arrived and then after their treatment. One case became a source of pride for the team. A girl named Zdenka Ruzyczka, about ten years old, had a puncture wound in her cheek so severe that it was possible to see her teeth even when her mouth was closed. Once healed, her skin closed up and a scar formed on the spot.[91] However, not all the participants in the study were as lucky as she was. Mengele had some children with noma killed and their corpses sent to the SS Hygiene Institute in Rajsko, a village less than six miles from the camp. The Institute assistants—who were prisoners but also scientists, some of them highly regarded in their

---

89 "iG Farben," *Encyclopædia Britannica*. Available at: <www.britannica.com/topic /IG-Farben>. Accessed on: July 10, 2023.

90 Nikolaus Wachsmann, *KL: A History of the Nazi Concentration Camps*. Boston: Little, Brown, 2015.

91 Hermann Langbein, op. cit., p. 338.

The young Josef Mengele.

Criminal Museum of the Teaching
Directorate of the National Police
Academy / Museu Criminal da
Diretoria de Ensino da Academia
Nacional de Policia.

fields—had to analyze the tissues under microscopes.[92] Mengele could have simply sent tissue samples for histopathological examinations, but he preferred to send the whole bodies, a more complete material for study. At Rajsko, the bodies were decapitated and the heads placed in glass jars with formaldehyde to be sent to the SS Medical Academy in Graz, Austria, which had been established to train the next generation of SS doctors. What remained of the small bodies at the Institute was sent to be burned at the crematorium III in Birkenau. Despite these unnecessary deaths, no one was ever able to discover the exact cause of the disease.

The noma research was only the first of numerous experiments Mengele conducted at the camp. He was especially interested in twins, available in large numbers in the "gypsy camp." Ironically, before

---

[92] Helena Kubica, "Dr. Mengele und seine Verbrechen im Konzentrationslager Auschwitz-Birkenau." *Hefte von Auschwitz*, v. 20, pp. 378–79, 1997.

arriving at Auschwitz, Mengele had never published any studies on twins, even though that was his mentor Otmar von Verschuer's specialty. In fact, Verschuer was considered the leading authority of twin studies in Germany. Mengele had experience in family research, at the time another area for the study of genetics, and which he had used in his doctorate in Frankfurt. The truth is that, in peacetime, it was difficult to find mothers willing to let their twin children take part in medical research that could cause pain or health consequences. Suddenly, Auschwitz opened up for Mengele a great opportunity to venture into this research field without any legal or moral restrictions.

Mengele's first experiments on twins in Auschwitz were carried out on Roma children. He ordered them all to be gathered in a single barrack, number 31. Once again, Mengele was concerned about the diet of his guinea pigs and had them fed on soups with meat broth, milk, butter, bread, jam, and even chocolate. Such food variety was a real feast compared to what the other prisoners in the camp normally received: Ersatzkaffee, a kind of dirty water, for breakfast; a thin soup for lunch; and a piece of black bread for dinner. Not surprisingly, the inmates' bodies soon turned cadaverous, and the prisoners just a shadow of their former selves. Mengele also gave the Roma children toys and sweets stolen from Jewish children who had been sent straight to the gas chambers upon arrival at Auschwitz. Mengele would go into the Roma children's barrack with his pockets full of candy and give each child a piece.[93] As a result, the children began to trust him and to call him their "kindly uncle."[94]

The man must have seemed like a real angel to those people in a situation of complete helplessness. He had a kindergarten built in barracks 29 and 31, which were in relatively better condition than the others, and decorated with colorful drawings of scenes from fairy tales, an absolute antithesis to the reality of the concentration camp. Between eight o'clock in the morning and two in the afternoon,

[93] Hermann Langbein, op. cit., p. 339.
[94] Helena Kubica, op. cit., p. 381.

not only his pet twins, but all children up to the age of six could attend that improvised nursery school in the middle of the Nazi extermination complex. The prisoners themselves ran the school, like the German Helene Hannemann, who had five children and was married to a Roma man. Her whole family lived in the BIIe sector in Birkenau. Two Polish women and a Jewish woman from Estonia helped Helene with her work. In addition to the kindergarten rooms, a children's playground was created in an area behind barrack 31, with a sandpit, a merry-go-round, swings, and gymnastics equipment. At first, the prisoners were surprised by what Dr. Mengele was doing, but they soon understood that it was all for appearance. High-ranking SS men and civilians often visited the kindergarten and photographed and filmed the children playing.[95] In addition, Mengele used the place to recruit his little guinea pigs. The selected ones were taken from barrack 31 to his workroom behind barrack 32, also in the "gypsy camp." The laboratory occupied part of the bathrooms and was therefore known as the "sauna." It was there that he carried out his anthropometric studies on the twins at his disposal.

SEPTEMBER 1943

Theresienstadt was a small fortress town forty miles from Prague. It was named after Empress Maria Theresa, who had had military barracks built there during the Habsburg Empire. Surrounded by a wall and a deep moat, the site was perfect, in the Nazis' view, for isolating the more privileged, older, and wealthier Jews. It would be an attempt at a model ghetto, which could be exhibited to the world. Gentile citizens were expelled and soldiers posted at the only exit from the citadel. At its peak, sixty thousand Jews were crammed into Theresienstadt, where only thirteen thousand civilians and military personnel had lived before.[96] The Red Cross even inspected the ghetto in June 1943, but found nothing wrong

---

95 Ibid.

96 Ruth Elias, op. cit.

because the Nazis had disguised the citadel's real living conditions, like the children's playground in Auschwitz. They hid the extreme hunger and high mortality and launched a campaign to "revitalize" the city: they washed the streets and even installed gardens. It was a beautiful staging. Soon after the Red Cross inspectors left, one of the largest mass deportation operations to Auschwitz began. The Nazis feared that the overcrowding of Theresienstadt could lead to an explosion of typhus cases, and they also wanted to avoid another explosive situation like the Warsaw ghetto uprising. A first group of five thousand people was deported in September 1943, and more transports left in the following months. In total, more than seventeen thousand Jews from the ghetto were settled in the new family camp in the BIIb sector in Birkenau.

As soon as they arrived, they didn't have to go through the selection process: everyone was going to live, even if only for a few more months. For only the second time in the history of Auschwitz, families were able to stay together. In the BIIb sector, there were two rows of wooden barracks, which were also called blocks. The women stayed in the ones on the right and the men on the left, and they all shared the same bathrooms. Their sleeping arrangements consisted of large three-tiered wooden bunk beds, without any mattresses. As the camp was overcrowded, five prisoners had to squeeze into each three-tiered bunk. Barbed-wire electric fences and watchtowers prevented prisoners from escaping. If any of them approached the fence, they were immediately shot. Many preferred to die like that rather than endure such a harsh life.[97] Just like the "gypsy camp," the Theresienstadt Jewish camp offered terrible living conditions. Diarrhea was common, and there was no toilet paper. Desperate hunger was constant. Some prisoners were completely disconnected from others and even from themselves, turning into walking skeletons with bulging eyes. They were referred to as the "Muselmänner." The singular form of the word, "Muselmän," referred to anyone who had reached extreme emaciation, exhaustion, and apathy, and had little chance of survival.

---

[97] Ibid.

Ruth Elias, a young Czech woman, who decades later gave her testimony in Jerusalem about the atrocities committed by Mengele, arrived on one of the trains from Theresienstadt. She was already seven months pregnant when Mengele entered her block with a group of guards to carry out a selection of prisoners for his experiments.

Ruth Elias.
United States Holocaust Memorial Museum

"Take off your clothes," they ordered. A long line of women formed and, one by one, they were forced to walk naked in front of Mengele. With an impassive face, Mengele looked the prisoners up and down and then indicated which row they should go to. Elias noticed that young women were being sent to one side and older women, the sick, and mothers with children to the other. She became desperate. How could she save her life? She quickly asked some girls who were still healthy to go in front of her. Surrounded by them, she walked by unnoticed and was not sent to the gas chamber. Elias would always remember what she saw that day: daughters being separated from their mothers, or one sister from another, and all the women crying in despair.[98] Ruth was lucky to escape. When any doctor or the SS guards found out a Jewish prisoner already registered for work in the camp was pregnant, they would send her to the gas chamber, either before or after giving birth, and the newborn was also killed. Dina Gottliebová was twenty-one, the same age as Elias; both were Czech and lived in the Theresienstadt family camp. One day, a German Jew called Fredy Hirsch, who looked after the children's block, asked Gottliebová to paint something on the wall. The young woman was a talented artist, and Fredy believed that she could help cheer up the children. The vast majority of Jewish children were coldly sent to their deaths as soon as they arrived at Auschwitz, but those who came from the Theresienstadt ghetto were allowed to live a little longer. With a lot of effort and without many resources, Fredy started a school in one of the blocks. Gottliebová painted a scene from *Snow White* that she had seen at the movies before being arrested. Jews were forbidden to go to the cinema, but she saw the movie a few times as an act of rebellion. One day, an SS guard named Lucas saw the drawing of Snow White and told Mengele about it. The doctor ordered him to summon Gottliebová. Lucas went to the Theresienstadt camp and drove Gottliebová to the "gypsy camp." When they met Mengele, the guard introduced her: "This is the painter I told you about." Mengele

---

98 Ruth Elias, op. cit.

had been trying to photograph the Roma, with unsatisfactory results. "Do you think you can paint as accurately as a photograph and get the colors right? Because in photos the colors don't come out right; they look too garish," said Mengele. Dina replied that she would try. Lucas took her back to the Theresienstadt family camp, and, as soon as she arrived, the young artist started looking for her mother to say goodbye: she was sure they would send her to the gas chamber. However, time passed and nothing happened to Gottliebová.

Rumors began to spread that the Jews of Theresienstadt would be sent to another labor camp. Many people didn't believe it and pulled their lower eyelid down with the tip of their index finger in a common gesture of distrust: it was obvious to them that they were all going to be sent to the gas chamber. In February 1944, Dina was called to the infirmary. Dr. Hellmann, who was also a prisoner, told her that she would be included on Mengele's list, which meant that her life would be spared. Dina became very nervous and asked, "What about my mother?" Hellmann tried to calm her down, saying that Mengele didn't have much time for such things, but Dina was emphatic: "I'm not staying here without my mother." The young woman threatened to throw herself against the electric fence. It was a big gamble on her part, but Mengele ordered someone to look for the mother and put the two of them at the top of a list of twenty-seven prisoners. This list also included ten pairs of twins, Dr. Hellmann, and his two nurses.

MARCH 1944

On the night of March 8, trucks took people from the Theresienstadt camp to the gas chambers. According to various reports, the prisoners walked in singing the Czechoslovakian anthem and the Hatikva, a song that speaks of the Jewish people's hope to live free and sovereign, and which later became the anthem of Israel. All the remaining Jews from the first group of five thousand that had left Theresienstadt in September 1943 were killed that night, except for those on Mengele's list. After the war, Mengele wrote that he had in fact helped to save lives at Auschwitz, perhaps referring to the aforementioned list. Nevertheless, he failed to mention that all the listed people were of some use to him, just as he omitted the fact that he personally sent thousands of human beings to the gas chambers.

A few days after the killing, an SS man showed up to take Dina to the "gypsy camp" again. Mengele gave the young Czech woman one of the two rooms in his laboratory to do the paintings he needed so he would have faithful records of the complexions of the Roma prisoners he had been studying.

IN THAT SAME MONTH, MENGELE had other things on his mind besides the extermination of prisoners. On the 16th, his first and only son, Rolf, was born in Freiburg, Germany. The baby had been conceived in Auschwitz itself, when his wife, Irene, visited the concentration camp. Dina noticed that her boss was very excited, jumping for joy, in stark contrast to his normal, extremely reserved demeanor. Saying he didn't smoke, Mengele gave her two packets of cigarettes, a small fortune in the camp, where a single cigarette was a valuable bargaining chip. He had never been so friendly with her. After the birth of their son, Mengele stayed in touch with his wife in Freiburg through letters. A month after Rolf was born, he wrote to tell her some news.

> Every now and then, a little ray of light appears in my gloomy daily routine in this concentration camp business. This afternoon, at 4pm, I was sent to the commandant's office and awarded a medal (War Merit Cross, Second Class with Swords). Although it's not a rare honor, and although I already have more valuable decorations, I was touched by the recognition of my work and dedication. My work sometimes puts my health and even my life at risk, so I was very grateful. (You can see, my dear Butzele, that the medals are arriving slowly, one after the other, to stay on this hero's chest!) I was supposed to receive it on 20.04.1944, the Führer's birthday, but I wasn't here, because I was at home with you. Dr. Thilo received the same honor; we now call it the

"typhus medal." When I got back, they were already waiting for me with three bottles of wine and a bottle of champagne. I was with a group of nice people (Fischer, Frank, Mulsow, and their wives) and we enjoyed everything we had. During our meeting, I made a toast to Rolf and his lovely mother.

One page of a letter written by Josef Mengele to his wife, Irene, on April 26, 1944, while Mengele was stationed in the Auschwitz concentration camp. He drew his Iron Cross First Class medal in the background. *Spungen Holocaust Postal Collection.*

Mengele shared a few more details of his routine in the camp and signed the letter affectionately: Papili.[99]

The "typhus medal" mentioned in the letter refers to the radical method Mengele created to combat epidemics in the camp. Decades later, the Austrian doctor Ella Lingens, who worked with Mengele, gave a detailed account of this incident at the 1985 symbolic trial in Jerusalem. As Dr. Lingens reported, hundreds of women were sent to the gas chamber just so a single block could be disinfected. This same method was used in other sections of Auschwitz to eradicate outbreaks of other diseases, such as scarlet fever and measles. The "typhus medal" was just the first distinction in a career that would go a long way in Auschwitz.

---

[99] "The Mengele Letters." CANDLES Holocaust Museum and Education Center. Available at: <candlesholocaustmuseum.org/educational-resources/mengele-letters .html>. Accessed on: July 6, 2022.

7

APPETITE FOR RESEARCH

AUSCHWITZ-BIRKENAU. MAY 1944

Mengele stood like an eagle watching his prey. He was thirty-three years old and looked rather striking. He liked to wear his hair slicked back and wore an immaculate SS uniform with a gold rosette pinned to the lapel.[100] His boots were always well polished, even in such a sordid place. His smile showed a gap between his two front teeth that was impossible to miss. Even so, the young Mengele was so attractive that he could have been a movie star, as many former female prisoners later described him. He had been working in the camp for a year. Anyone who glanced at his armband realized immediately that he was a doctor as he stood on the ramp. The trains brought Jews from all over Europe: from the territories of the Reich itself, from Poland, France, the Netherlands, Belgium, Italy, Romania, Hungary, and other countries that the Germans had occupied or whose governments were allied with the Nazis.

---

100 Miklós Nyiszli, *Auschwitz: A Doctor's Eyewitness Account*. London: Penguin, 2012, pp. 2 and 61.

Jews await selection on the ramp at Auschwitz-Birkenau.
Yad Vashem Photo Archive, Jerusalem.

In stock cars originally made to transport cattle, entire families were squeezed together more tightly than if they *were* animals, with no room to lie down or even sit. The doors were locked from the outside so no one could get out. Like sardines in a can, men, women, and children traveled for days without knowing their destination. There were no toilets on board, and for the entire journey each stock car received two buckets: one with water and the other to be used as a latrine. The stench was unbearable, and there were only small windows located high up and covered with barbed wire. Through these small spaces, passengers begged those outside the train for something to drink. The thirst was relentless. Once, at one of the stops between Romania and Auschwitz, a guard agreed to give them some water in exchange for five gold watches. It was an absurd and disproportionate demand, but the Romanian Jews trapped in the wagon didn't hesitate to quickly collect what had been demanded.

After taking the watches, in a gesture of pure sadism, the guard threw the bucket of water on the ground and no one was able to drink anything apart from a few drops.[101] Another train carrying Jews deported from the Greek island of Corfu, where there was one of the oldest Jewish communities in Europe, spent twenty-seven days without food or water. When the train arrived at the death camp, the doors opened and no one obeyed the order to get off: half the passengers were dead, the other half in comas.[102] The situation was so precarious and degrading that it seemed like nothing could be worse than that journey. In fact, that was just the beginning, and much worse awaited the passengers. Auschwitz was indeed a factory of death.

The smoke coming out of the crematoria chimneys could be seen at least twelve miles away, a sign of what was to come. The train stopped at the platform and the doors were opened with a thunderous noise. The guards' dogs barked and, like a Tower of Babel in the midst of hell, orders were given in German, a language that many didn't even understand. Someone finally began to translate: everyone had to disembark and put their luggage on the ground next to the train. Disembarking meant stepping over the bodies of those who had died along the way, whether strangers or relatives. Outside, the smell of burning human flesh filled the air.[103]

The Nazis planned very efficiently. The masses discharged from the wagons were quickly divided into two large groups: men on one side, women and children under the age of thirteen on the other.[104] The crowd then moved slowly forward in a line, until they approached an SS doctor. That day, Mengele was working yet another shift on the selection of prisoners. He smiled at times, which lent him a

---

101 Eva Mozes Kor and Lisa Rojany Buccieri, op. cit., p. 22.
102 Miklós Nyiszli, op. cit., p. 75.
103 Hermann Langbein, op. cit., p. 449.
104 Miklós Nyiszli, op. cit., p. 3.

youthful expression. In an almost gentle voice, he asked if anyone was ill. If so, the person was told to move to the left, thus joining the elderly, children, and mothers with small babies. He examined each person in the blink of an eye and, in that split second, decided with a flick of his index finger which way they should go. Nobody knew at the time that going to the left meant dying immediately in the gas chambers, and going to the right meant living a little longer to work exhaustingly.

Auschwitz was at the center of the entire Nazi concentration-camp system; no other camp had so many staff or prisoners,[105] and none killed so many people. Everything was much harsher there. Unlike the Treblinka, Belzec, Sobibor, and Chelmno camps, where very few people survived to tell the tale, Auschwitz functioned not only as an extermination camp but as a concentration camp, which meant that it housed prisoners for forced labor. From the Nazis' logistical point of view, Auschwitz had two great advantages: it was both close to a railway hub and away from prying eyes. It was on the outskirts of a Polish town called Oświęcim. In the early months of World War II, the Nazis incorporated the town—as well as all of western Poland—into the Third Reich and gave it its German name: Auschwitz. Wooden houses and barracks belonging to the Polish Army were used as the prison camp.

The first train carrying deportees arrived in Auschwitz in June 1940. It brought 728 Poles from a prison near Krakow who were accused of committing "anti-German activities."[106] For almost two years, Poles represented the vast majority of prisoners at Auschwitz. There were some Jews among them, but they weren't the most significant group yet, because practically the entire Jewish community in occupied Poland remained in ghettos. After the Germans invaded the Soviet Union in June 1941, another category began to arrive in

---

105 Nikolaus Wachsmann, op. cit.

106 Ibid.

large numbers: Soviet prisoners of war. By October of that year, they numbered ten thousand men. They were put to work and became very useful in fulfilling Himmler's determination: to prepare Auschwitz for the "final solution" to the "Jewish question."[107] It was a euphemism used by the Nazis to refer to the mass extermination of Jews. As a matter of fact, the Germans never used direct expressions to talk about murder: they preferred euphemistic terms like "special treatment." At the behest of the Nazi chief, the residents of the village of Brzezinka, located two miles from the main camp, were expelled. The Soviet prisoners demolished the village houses, leveled the ground, and drained the marshy land.[108] They built access roads and 250 barracks destined to house 200,000 prisoners. The village's Polish name was replaced with a German one: Birkenau. Four crematoria were also built, each with fifteen ovens. A single gas chamber could hold about three thousand people at a time. This meant that thousands of people could be exterminated on a single day.

The first group of Jews deported from Europe arrived at Auschwitz in the spring of 1942. Intent on avoiding riots or other incidents while leading their victims to the gas chamber, the SS kept their real intentions secret. Inside the first room, SS guards ordered everyone to get naked—men, women, children—claiming that they were going to take a shower after the long train journey. If there was no resistance from the unarmed and exhausted civilians, there was certainly a lot of embarrassment. Especially on the part of Orthodox Jews, who wouldn't go unclothed even in front of their own spouses, let alone strangers. But there was no choice. In order to avoid panic, the Nazis' deception went so far as to post notices on the walls asking new arrivals to memorize the number of the hook on which they had hung their clothes, as if they were really going to return from their "bath." A work unit made up of prisoners, called the Sonderkommando, took part in

107 Hermann Langbein, op. cit., p. 20.
108 Memorial and Museum of Auschwitz-Birkenau.

the operation and was in charge of the dirty job of later disposing of the bodies.

Once all the prisoners were naked inside the gas chamber, the SS and the Sonderkommando men were told to leave and the doors were closed. A Red Cross ambulance brought Zyklon-B, a pesticide that was initially used in concentration camps to fumigate vermin-infested sites. A Nazi health officer put on a gas mask, lifted the lids of the short concrete tubes that protruded from the ground every hundred feet outside the building, and poured in the pesticide granules. When those granules came into contact with the air, the Zyklon-B turned into gas, which burst out of the perforation of the supposed showers and, within a few seconds, filled the entire chamber.[109] Desperately, people would climb on top of each other in an attempt to escape the gas. Within five minutes, everyone inside the room was dead. About twenty minutes later, fans were turned on to disperse the gas. The doors were then opened and the Sonderkommando began the hard work. The Sonderkommando men collected the victims' clothes and shoes. They also aimed water hoses at the bodies that had piled on top of each other as high as the ceiling. It was not uncommon for Jewish members of the Sonderkommando to recognize their own relatives among the corpses.

Another Sonderkommando commando was created especially for pulling out the gold teeth of the dead. Mengele called for prisoners capable of performing dental surgery, and many dentists volunteered in good faith, believing that they would be able to practice their profession in the concentration camp. In reality, the job was to pull out the gold teeth of the dead and put them in buckets full of acid that would dissolve any remaining flesh. When the bodies were no longer of any value, members of the Sonderkommando carried them to elevators that led to the incinerator. Trucks collected the ashes and dumped them in the Vistula River, just over a mile away.[110] It was such

---

109 Nikolaus Wachsmann, op. cit.

110 Miklós Nyiszli, op.cit., pp. 28–32.

a horrendous process that even Himmler felt nauseous when he first witnessed mass extermination in a gas chamber.[111]

In May 1944, the war entered its final phase. The Allies were preparing for the landing at Normandy in northern France, the largest-ever military operation by land, water, and air combined. Meanwhile, instead of focusing all their attention on the battlefront, the Nazis chose to begin the most intense period of extermination at Auschwitz. In two months, 430,000 Jews were deported from Hungary after Hitler's troops occupied the country. The Führer ordered the invasion because he was afraid that the Hungarians, Germany's former allies, would follow the Italians' example and abandon the Axis. Of every ten people arriving on the trains from Hungary, between seven and nine went straight to the gas chambers.[112]

EDITH EGER'S FAMILY HAD JUST arrived among a group of Jews deported from Kassa, a city that was part of Hungary during World War II. Music played, something completely incongruous in such a bewildering setting, where nothing was ever explained, and everyone just followed orders without even blinking. Her father, Lajos, a talented tailor, was filled with hope when he saw a sign in German at the entrance to the camp that read: "Arbeit macht frei": "Work sets you free."

"You see? It can't be such a terrible place," he said. "We will just work for a while until the war is over."[113]

As soon as he said that, the family was separated. The father was placed in the men's line and waved to his wife and two daughters, who followed the women's line together. When they were at the front of the line, Mengele stared at Ilona, the mother. Her face was

---

111 Hermann Langbein, op.cit., p. 282.

112 Laurence Rees, op. cit., p. 442.

113 Edith Eva Eger, *A bailarina de Auschwitz*. Rio de Janeiro: Sextante, 2019, p. 49.

smooth-skinned, but her hair had already turned gray. She stood between her two teenage daughters, who were trying to protect her. The SS doctor sent Ilona to the left, where the people deemed unfit to work gathered. Edith, the youngest daughter, tried to follow her mother, but Mengele did not let her. He held Edith by the shoulder and said, cynically, "You'll see your mother soon. She's just going to take a bath." Edith obeyed and followed her sister, Magda, to the right, not knowing that this would be the last time they would see her.[114] A little while later, Edith asked a prisoner who had been in the camp for a long time when she would be allowed to see her mother again. Coldly, the woman pointed to the smoke rising from one of the chimneys and said: "Your mother is burning in there. You'd better start talking about her in the past tense."[115] That's when Eddie, as she was called by those close to her, understood that she would no longer see her father either.

After another day of sending many people to the gas chambers, Mengele walked around the barracks in search of entertainment. Like in a performance of the theater of the absurd, a world-class female violinist was playing in the death camp that evening. The doctor entered one of the women's barracks with his assistants and met Eddie again. From the teenager's posture and physique, he must have deduced that she was a dancer; in fact, not only was she a ballerina, but she was also a gymnast. Mengele approached her and ordered: "Dance for me." The girl agreed without rebelling. She knew that her life depended on it. The musicians played the opening of the "Blue Danube" waltz and, with her eyes closed, Eddie performed the ballet steps as if she were at the Budapest Opera. As she did her best to please the man who had sent her mother and father to the crematorium hours before, she heard him discussing with his assistants who would be the next women selected for the gas chambers.

---

114 Ibid., p. 50.
115 Ibid., p. 51.

Eddie prayed. She felt that her actions at that moment were to please Mengele and, thus, save her life. At the end of the performance, he threw her a piece of bread to show that he had enjoyed it. Even though she was starving, Eddie generously shared it with her sister and other prisoners, who never forgot the gesture. On the Death March, months later, when the camp was liberated and she could no longer walk in the freezing cold, those same prisoners carried her and saved her life.

Mengele spared Eddie, but he took away her parents. For decades, the memory of his cynicism haunted her thoughts. As an adult living in the United States, she still saw that man's face in everyday moments, such as at the fish market when she heard the salesman call her name.[116] For most of her life, Eddie's mind returned to the same images: herself, her mother, and her sister arm in arm in line at the camp; Mengele's gap-toothed smile. A doubt haunted her: If she had said that her mother was her sister, would she have been able to save her? The truth is, probably not. There is no record of the exact number of victims he selected, but it is certainly in the thousands, as documented by the arrest warrant issued by the German courts in 1981 on the basis of several witnesses' accounts. For Mengele, Eddie's mother was just one of the thousands he sent to the gas chambers during his almost twenty months in Auschwitz, especially in the spring of 1944, the camp's deadliest period. In the same month that Eddie arrived at Auschwitz, Isu and Charlotte Grossman were deported from Slovakia with their twin daughters, Vera and Olga. They were a very wealthy Jewish family but had lost everything to finance their escape from the Nazis for more than three years. They hid in the forest while they were hunted down like animals. When the money ran out, the people who had protected them were the same ones who denounced them, and the family of four was forced onto a cattle train to Auschwitz. Their arrival was like any other: they had to jump over the bodies of those who

---

116 Ibid., p. 154.

had died during the journey. In the midst of the chaos—screaming, beating, crying, and dogs barking—they heard an order in German: "Zwillinge raus!"—"Twins out!" Charlotte went into shock. She didn't know what to do, afraid that her little girls would be taken away from her. A female Polish prisoner, who was collecting the belongings left by those who had just arrived, approached her and said quietly, "Are those your twins? Run out quickly with them if you want to stay alive." On disembarking, Isu, who was about twenty years older than Charlotte and well into his fifties, was forced to separate from the rest of the family, and they never saw him again.[117] The mother took her two daughters and introduced herself to an SS guard: "These are my twins." Immediately, the three were taken to see Mengele.

The doctor was making yet another selection on the ramp. He was wearing white gloves and holding a whip. That image impressed Vera, who was only six years old. The meticulously clean clothes and the gap between his front teeth also caught her eye. In her innocence, she thought, ironically, that Mengele's face resembled that of a Roma, since he had brown hair and brown eyes and looked quite different from the stereotype of the blond "Aryan" man. The guard told Mengele that he had brought a mother and her twin daughters for him. "It can't be!" the doctor shouted as he saw the woman's blue eyes and fair skin, a classic example of an "Aryan," while the two girls had much darker features. "Where did you find these 'gypsy' children?" he asked. Charlotte ignored her fear and replied emphatically: "They're not 'gypsies.' I'm a Jew from Slovakia and these are my daughters." "Good," said Mengele, and ordered the three to be taken to the twins' block.

This was one of the few times that a mother was allowed to accompany her own children in Mengele's medical experiments. The large, freezing block was located in the women's camp in Birkenau.[118] It was

117 Michael A. Grodin, Eva Mozes Kor, and Susan Benedict, op. cit., pp. 40–41.
118 Carola Sachse, op. cit., pp. 77–78, 103.

home to around 350 pairs of twins, mostly girls aged between two and sixteen, almost all of them Jews of various nationalities, but mainly Hungarians and Czechs. From the age of four until sixteen, the male twins were placed in another block, where more than a hundred people lived. Within a year, Mengele had set up his own private section where all the prisoners were twins, readily available for his experiments. His mentor, Otmar von Verschuer, had taken eight years to achieve a similar number in Berlin when he began this type of research in 1927. Not only was Mengele able to gather so many twins in Auschwitz in a short period of time, but he also didn't have to worry about costs or bureaucratic barriers, and, above all, about securing the consent of individuals to conduct his research.[119]

The first experiment with his new "guinea pigs" involved putting them in a wooden cage lined with straw. The space was so small that Vera and Olga couldn't move, stand, or sit; they could only crouch with their heads resting on their leg. Charlotte and her daughters stayed in that cage for almost two weeks and were given food through the bars. Mengele came by every day to give them spinal injections, which left the children numb. Vera felt sick all the time, and her sister, Olga, felt dizzy; she even fainted.[120] One of the injections caused large blisters on Vera's body, and she had no idea what was happening. Without giving any explanation as to what he was doing, Mengele injected the girl with another substance, which made the blisters disappear. He was happy with the result and proudly told his SS colleagues about the experiment.[121]

The Nazi doctor wanted every limb of Vera's and Olga's bodies to be rigorously measured and recorded. It was an exhausting job that required a lot of time he didn't have. That's why, in addition to using the large number of human test subjects available in Auschwitz,

---

119 Carola Sachse, op. cit., pp. 235–36.
120 Michael A. Grodin, Eva Mozes Kor, and Susan Benedict, op. cit., p. 42.
121 Carola Sachse, op. cit., p. 79.

Mengele also took advantage of the numerous highly educated prisoners who had attended renowned European universities and were now available to work for him for free. These prisoners were often grateful "for the opportunity" to work, since it kept them alive. One of them was Countess Martina Puzyna, who was sent to Auschwitz for being part of the Polish Resistance, an underground movement fighting against the German occupation of Poland. She was arrested in March 1943, deported five months later, and was selected for hard labor upon her arrival at the camp. The hard work she was assigned there soon caused her to get weak; she contracted typhus and ended up in the hospital, which in Auschwitz was practically a death sentence. Mengele visited the patients regularly to identify which ones had a poor prognosis and could be killed right away—another one of his duties as a camp doctor. He examined Puzyna quickly and was about to leave her bedside when another doctor commented that she was an anthropologist. Mengele turned to her and asked what her academic background was. In a faint voice, the woman told him that she had been an assistant to Professor Jan Czekanowski, a famous anthropologist who had developed a system for classifying European races. Mengele was impressed by the forty-two-year-old woman's academic and aristocratic background and ordered her to come to his office.

Too weak to walk, Puzyna needed the help of two prisoners to get to the office. As in a job interview, Mengele asked her what she had done since arriving at Auschwitz. He laughed when the countess told him that her job was to carry heavy rocks. The two soon got into a conversation about anthropology, comparative research with twins, and the correct ways to take measurements. In the end, he ordered that the countess be given an additional ration of food and, although she remained a prisoner, her status was now that of a doctor. Dr. Puzyna was given a room specially equipped with all the necessary tools: Swiss calipers, compasses, rulers, etc. Two assistants were also assigned to work with her. One had been an anthropology student and would help with the measurements; the other, a younger woman, would write down the data.

The prisoners Mengele sent to Puzyna had to wait for hours in an unheated room in Poland's cold weather, completely naked and helpless. Many of them were children. Meanwhile, Dr. Puzyna tirelessly measured the width and length of the eyes and nose, the distances between them, the ears, the jaws, and every imaginable detail.[122] Little Vera and Olga underwent these thorough examinations. Without clothes, freezing, the two of them waited long hours to be measured, have X-rays taken, blood tests carried out, and prints of their palms and soles made. Dina Gottliebová, the young Czech artist recruited by Mengele, drew portraits of their bodies.

The objective was to compare the twin girls to identify what was genetic inheritance and what was the result of environmental conditions. This nineteenth-century concept by the Briton Francis Galton was revived years later in Germany and boomed in the 1920s, after the publication of physician Hermann Werner Siemens's work. Siemens established the methodological foundations for twin research, which were later expanded by Verschuer, Mengele's mentor. In the 1930s, German scientists considered twin research to be the ideal way to learn about human heredity and to study both genetic diseases and "racial biology," a trendy "science" at the time.

The first step in that type of study was to establish which twins were identical and which were fraternal. The basic assumption was as follows: since the differences between fraternal twins are caused by genetic inheritance *and* by external conditions, whereas the differences between identical twins arise exclusively from environmental influences, a comparison of both categories of twins could determine how influential hereditary factors are, in contrast to environmental

---

122 Yehuda Koren and Eliat Negev, *In Our Hearts We Were Giants: The Remarkable Story of the Lilliput Troupe: A Dwarf Family's Survival of the Holocaust.* New York: Carroll & Graf, 2004, pp. 108–9.

conditions. Distinguishing between the types of twins was not so simple, because until then it required analysis of the placenta and the amniotic sac. The breakthrough came with a new method based on the observation of anatomical and psychological characteristics. Verschuer formulated a questionnaire that addressed fifteen hereditary traits including, among other things, blood group, Rh factor found on red blood cells, palm print, eye color (graded in sixteen different shades), and ear shape (divided into nineteen sub-shapes). Therefore, when Mengele forced children to expose themselves naked in the cold for hours, he was only trying to determine whether they were identical or fraternal twins.[123]

The anthropometric tests were grueling, but the most traumatic experience Vera would undergo was yet to come. At some point, she was locked alone in a room where wall shelves displayed, inside glass containers, human organs and body parts such as ears, noses, and even the penis of a small boy. Vera felt that someone was watching her. When she turned around, she suddenly noticed another shelf, full of preserved eyes of all colors: blue, green, brown—all staring at her. Vera fell to the floor, horrified. Even though she was a very young child, she had already understood that those eyes had been taken from other prisoners. Would she be next? Her whole body began to tremble, until Mengele entered the room and lifted the girl off the floor, placed her on a stretcher, and put some drops in her eyes. When he had finished, he shouted: "Get out!" Vera ran to her mother, who was waiting for her.[124]

This experiment was an attempt to change the color of the irises of children and babies using chemical substances. The experiments caused redness, swelling, and suppuration in the eyes. Dr. Ella Lingens, who worked with Mengele, said that a newborn baby named Dagmar died after receiving injections to turn her eyes blue. Romualda Ciesielska, a prisoner in charge of the children's block in Birkenau, said that Mengele

---

123 Carola Sachse, op. cit., pp. 201–3.

124 Ibid., pp. 79–80.

had chosen thirty-six minors for that experiment. They suffered a lot of pain, and one of them almost went blind.[125]

Since the 1930s, it had been believed that hormones or enzymes could play a role in the development of eye pigmentation. The assumption was that the gene would be activated by a mediating substance and consequently stimulate the production of pigment. Mengele's experiments investigated the influence of external factors on the genetic determination of eye pigmentation. This research was especially important during the Nazi period because the structure and color of the iris were used in the aforementioned racial reports and could decide whether a person had Aryan or Jewish ancestry. Mengele didn't do such work on his own, but was in direct communication with Berlin.

Mengele started a collection of Romas' eyes as soon as he arrived in Auschwitz. Each eyeball was placed in a numbered jar and later sent to the Kaiser Wilhelm Institute. The recipient of the material was research biologist Karin Magnussen, whom Mengele had met on his visits to the Institute during the war. At a few meetings, the two talked about scientific work and the difficulties of research in Berlin. Mengele was not qualified in the histology or biochemistry of the eye. The only specialist in this field at the Kaiser Wilhelm Institute was Magnussen, and thus she was the one who determined which substances Mengele should use to experiment on the children. In Berlin, Magnussen tested the effectiveness of various hormones and pharmacologically active substances on the development of eye pigmentation in rabbits. No one knows exactly what Mengele dripped into the children's eyes, but it seems fairly obvious that it was the same substances that Magnussen used on the animals. After the war, researchers managed to identify one of these substances: adrenaline, the stress hormone. Mengele revealed this information to a Polish prisoner, Dr. Rudolf Diem, claiming that it would change the color of the iris.

---

[125] Ibid., p. 247.

At the Kaiser Wilhelm Institute, Dr. Magnussen was conducting a study on heterochromia, a condition that causes a person to have differently colored eyes. An employee of the Institute who worked in criminal biology identified a Roma family in which this condition occurred frequently, including in twins. Later, in the spring of 1943, Magnussen even photographed these twins,[126] but after they were deported to Auschwitz she was denied access to them. Only with Mengele's help was she eventually able to establish their family genealogy and elucidate the genetic heritage that determined the color of each person's eyes. Magnussen then asked him—should anyone in that Roma family die—to send her the autopsy report and the deceased's eyes. The prisoner Iancu Vexler, a medical doctor of Romanian origin, worked in the "gypsy camp." Mengele told him that seven or eight members of the same Roma family (last name Mechau) had heterochromia and that, if they died, he should carefully remove their eyes, store them, and send them for research in Berlin. Curiously, eight members of the Mechau family died in the space of a few months, and Dr. Vexler followed Mengele's orders. It was clear that the Mechau family members had been murdered so their eyeballs could be removed. All the biotic material was sent to the Kaiser Wilhelm Institute, as Magnussen had requested.[127]

TEN-YEAR-OLD SISTERS EVA AND MIRIAM Mozes were holding their mother's hands on the arrival platform in May 1944. There was a smell of burning chicken feathers in the air. As soon as they got off the train from Porț, Transylvania, their father and two older sisters disappeared in the confusion. The same routine scene took place: people shouting, dogs barking, and guards giving orders. "Zwillinge, Zwillinge!"—"Twins, twins!"—shouted a man from the SS. Seeing Eva and Miriam in

---

126 Ibid., pp. 242–43.
127 Ibid., pp. 240–45; Helena Kubica, op.cit.

Children survivors of Auschwitz, wearing adult-size prisoner jackets, stand behind a barbed wire fence. Among those pictured are twins Miriam Mozes and Eva Mozes wearing knitted hats.

United States Holocaust Memorial Museum, courtesy of Belarusian State Archive of Documentary Film and Photography.

identical burgundy dresses, he asked their mother if they were twins. The woman replied with a question: "Is that good?" The guard said yes. She then stated categorically: "They're twins." Without a word, the man snatched the two girls from her hands. She didn't even have a chance to say goodbye. The mother disappeared into the crowd, and they never saw each other again.

Eva and Miriam joined thirteen other pairs of twins who arrived on the same train as they did.[128] The children were accommodated in a barrack in Birkenau. During the night, Eva and Miriam needed to go to the toilet, and left the block in freezing cold weather. The toilet was just a latrine consisting of holes in the floor. Vomit and feces lay everywhere. Amidst that filth, they saw three naked bodies of dead children. Eva had never seen a corpse before, and at that moment she

---

128 Eva Mozes Kor and Lisa Rojany Buccieri, op. cit., pp. 27–29.

understood that death could happen at any time. Quietly, she promised herself that she would do everything in her power to ensure that she and her sister didn't end up like those dead children in the latrine.[129] The next day, they were taken to the experiment block. Other pairs of twins were also there, boys and girls, all naked, while prison doctors took measurements. The two went to the laboratory three times a week to have blood taken. Eva thought: "How much blood can I lose and still stay alive?"

One day they injected a substance into Eva's arm without telling her what it was. In the evening, she had a high fever, her head hurt, her skin burned, and her whole body shook. Eva didn't want to be taken to the infirmary, because she knew there was no turning back. She had realized also that if one twin died, the other would "disappear" without explanation. But in her present health condition, she had no choice: Eva was separated from Miriam and taken to the clinic. After examining her, and unaware that Eva understood the language, Mengele said in German to the other doctors: "What a shame. She's so young and has only two weeks left." He knew exactly what was wrong with the girl; after all, it had been caused by the injection he had administered. Eva was very ill, but she was determined to survive and kept telling herself, "I'll get better." Two weeks later, as if by a miracle, Eva really did get better. Throughout her life, she never found out what exactly had been done to her.[130] Miriam also went through a strange experience: she was injected with an unknown substance, without any explanation. In her case, however, the complications only emerged in adulthood, leading to her premature death.

Mengele sent blood samples from more than two hundred Auschwitz prisoners to the Kaiser Wilhelm Institute. Some of them were twins; most were children. Each sample was accompanied by a

---

129 Ibid., pp. 34–36.
130 Ibid., pp. 53, 65–66.

complete anthropological identification that had to include race and relationship to other people who had also "donated" blood. As had happened to the heads of dead Roma children, this biotic material was first sent to Rajsko, where the blood was studied. The samples were then sent to Berlin.[131] For Mengele, it was irrelevant that those large amounts of blood were collected by puncturing malnourished children, which most often resulted in anemia; yet, it could have been much worse. According to prisoner Hani Schick, the mother of one-year-old twins, on Mengele's orders her children had to have so much blood drawn that they died soon after.[132] In any case, it wasn't only children who were forced to have blood drawn repeatedly.

IT WAS PAST MIDNIGHT ON May 19, 1944, when Mengele was hastily summoned to the train platform. The soldiers were guarding a group of Orthodox Jews who had just arrived from Hungary. The order was that no one was to touch new arrivals until Mengele saw them. There were twelve members of the same family: three women and two children were of normal height, but the rest had dwarfism. For a genetics expert who studied kinship relations, the Ovitzes were quite a find. Mengele exclaimed: "I have work for twenty years!" He spared them all from the gas chamber and made sure they weren't trampled by the other prisoners. In the Theresienstadt family camp in Birkenau, he arranged for them to be accommodated in the fourth room of the camp, which was previously reserved for the Block Älter, the prisoner responsible for maintaining order in the barrack. The Ovitz family also received blankets, sheets, and even pillows. They were able to keep their clothes and didn't have to have their hair cut. Mengele provided a sink for them to bathe in, as well as a potty taken from a child who had been sent to the gas chamber, so that they wouldn't have to use

131 Carola Sachse, op. cit., p. 232.
132 Helena Kubica, op. cit., p. 397.

the disgusting communal latrine. He didn't want his new test subjects anywhere near the other prisoners, to prevent them from contracting any diseases.

Every day, the seven people with dwarfism took hours scrubbing themselves, grooming, and brushing their hair, before being taken to meet Mengele in the "gypsy camp's" laboratory. Every few days, the doctors would draw blood from them with large syringes and in enormous quantities. They weren't allowed to eat on the night before each procedure, and they would get so weak that they often fainted. None of this stopped Mengele's appetite for research.[133] What he didn't suspect was that he was being deceived. The seven who had dwarfism were in fact related, but when they arrived at Auschwitz, the Ovitz family had with them members of their household who were not blood relatives. Mengele had no idea that this was the case, and he could not understand why some in the group were of normal height and others of short stature.

MIKLÓS NYISZLI ALSO ARRIVED IN Auschwitz in the deadly month of May 1944. He was Hungarian but had studied medicine at the University of Breslau in Germany and therefore spoke German fluently. Together with his wife and teenage daughter, he had traveled on a train from Hungary. And as it happened daily, Mengele was on the platform to make his selection. That day, he hoped to find among the large group of new arrivals an assistant for a special task, and thus asked all the doctors to step forward. Nyiszli came forward, along with about fifty other people. Mengele asked who had studied at a university in Germany, who had knowledge of pathology, and who had practiced forensic medicine. And he warned anyone who was considering volunteering: "Be very careful. You have to be up to the task. Because if you're not . . ." Nyiszli wasn't afraid of the veiled threat. His résumé

---

133 Yehuda Koren and Eliat Negev, op. cit., p. 83.

met all the requirements perfectly. Being an experienced pathologist, he stepped forward and answered all the Nazi doctor's questions with ease. For the rest of the year, Nyiszli would be one of the main witnesses to Mengele's macabre work at Auschwitz.[134]

---

[134] Miklós Nyiszli, op. cit., p. 4.

8

MENGELE'S PROMOTION

A very unusual heat wave swept through Auschwitz that summer. In the "gypsy camp," naked children ran around and played, while their parents, wearing colorful, cheerful clothes, sat on the ground in small groups and talked.[135] They didn't know it, but the date of their deaths had already been set: August 2, 1944. The SS commander had actually ordered their extermination three months earlier, in May, but the plan had to be postponed because of the Romas' resistance. Men and women armed with knives, iron pipes, and metal objects refused to obey the order to leave the barracks, despite being surrounded by more than fifty guards and having no real chance against the SS. Although unequal in force, and practically symbolic, the small rebellion was victorious, at least temporarily. The Germans preferred to retreat, for fear that a riot would spread to other parts of Auschwitz. Additionally, they must have taken into account that, among the Roma, there was a significant number of Wehrmacht veterans. A few days after this first

---

[135] Miklós Nyiszli, op. cit., p. 12.

attempt at extermination, the SS transferred more than 1,500 Roma to the Buchenwald concentration camp, 82 to Flössenburg, and 144 to Ravensbrück, where previously there had been only female prisoners. Just under 3,000 Roma remained in Birkenau.[136]

Dina Gottliebová, the Czech artist who worked for Mengele, was told that there would be no more portraits of the Roma prisoners. Her last task would be to portray the doctor himself, using only pencil and paper. He posed for the young painter, who felt the pressure of pleasing the Nazi officer, as she was constantly fearful that she would no longer be needed and, consequently, eliminated with a simple gesture of his hand. When she finished the drawing, Gottliebová realized that Mengele was bothered by the size of his neck in her drawing: he thought it was too short. She lengthened it a little. Then he asked her if she had noticed anything on his left ear that only his wife knew about. "The button on the ear?"—"Knopf im Ohr?"—she asked back, referring to the famous German Steiff stuffed animals, which had a silver button attached to their ears to prove their authenticity. Mengele chuckled and answered yes.

A WEEK OR TWO LATER, on Himmler's orders, all prisoners were forbidden to leave the Birkenau barracks. The quarantine lasted until the SS men finally managed to get all the Roma to line up and leave their barracks. To do this, the guards handed out bread with salami, the old Nazi tactic of deceiving their victims about their true intent. Many Roma believed, or wanted to believe, that the Nazis' whole objective was just to transfer them to another camp, as had happened three months earlier. After all, who feeds those destined to die?[137] In any case, some resisted the offer of food. Gottliebová heard voices and screams. A

---

136 "Sixty-First Anniversary of the Liquidation of the Gypsy Camp in Birkenau." Auschwitz-Birkenau State Museum, August 1, 2015. Available at: <https://www.auschwitz.org/en/museum/news/sixty-first-anniversary-of-the-liquidation-of-the-gypsy-camp-in-birkenau,427.html>. Accessed on: July 12, 2023.

137 Miklós Nyiszli, op. cit., p. 93.

boy was shouting in German: "I'm only seventeen, let me live! Mom, I'm only seventeen!" Gottliebová tried to go back to sleep. She didn't expect to survive either, and thought her death was only a matter of time.[138] That night, the Roma were exterminated.

From the beginning, Mengele had opposed the extermination of the "gypsy camp" and tried to persuade his superiors to change their minds. It wasn't compassion, but rather scientific interest.[139] He had conducted three types of research in the Roma barracks: on the origin and treatment of noma; on the causes of multiple births; and on the causes of dwarfism and gigantism. Dr. Epstein, the renowned pediatrician from the University of Prague rescued by Mengele from forced labor at Monowitz, ran the experiments. Mengele visited the barracks every day and took an active part in every stage of the experiments.[140] When the order came to kill everyone in the "gypsy camp," he was reluctant to lose all his "research material." Since he had no choice, Mengele decided to collaborate with his superiors and led the night of terror. Taking advantage of the trust that some children had placed in him, he managed to draw them out of their hiding places by offering sweets and candies, as he usually did. The camp was almost empty when two boys were found. Mengele gave them a lift in his car, as he had done on other occasions, except that now their destination was the gas chamber.[141] Exactly 2,897 men, women, and children were killed on that date. Crematoria I and II operated throughout the night, spewing ominous smoke into the sky. The next day, dawn broke over a deadly silent "gypsy camp."

After the killings, only twenty-four bodies had not been turned to ash. Twelve pairs of twins were laid on the concrete floor of the morgue

---

138 Dina Gottliebová-Babbitt interview to Hilary Adah Helstein. Visual History Archive, USC Shoah Foundation, September, 26 1998. Available at: <vha.usc.edu /testimony/46122>. Accessed on: July 12, 2023.

139 Yehuda Koren and Eliat Negev, op. cit., p. 103.

140 Miklós Nyiszli, op. cit., p. 13.

141 Yehuda Koren and Eliat Negev, op. cit., pp. 103–4.

in a macabre gathering of siblings of various ages: from newborn babies to sixteen-year-old teenagers. Before they went to the gas chamber, Mengele marked the letters Z and S on each of their chests with a special chalk. The older ones believed that the letters would spare them from death. The letters stood for "Zur Sektion" (dissection) and served as a warning to the Sonderkommando that these bodies should not be burned. Dr. Nyiszli carried out the pathological study of the twelve pairs of twins with the greatest possible care. He then passed on all the details to Mengele and even argued with him on some points. Mengele trusted the pathologist's work so much that he could even forget for a few moments that the Hungarian doctor was just a prisoner whose life wasn't worth a penny in Auschwitz. In the excitement of a heated discussion on medical topics, Mengele even offered the other man a cigarette.[142]

Performing autopsies on twins who died simultaneously was unthinkable anywhere else. "Where, under normal circumstances, would anyone come across twins dying at the same time and in the same place?" Nyiszli wondered. In Auschwitz there were hundreds of pairs of twins. He understood the reasons Mengele gave the selected twins and people with dwarfism extra food and better hygiene conditions: so that they would not contaminate one another or die from the inhumane conditions of the camp. The purpose of—and justification for—such privileged treatment, Nyiszli realized, was that the twins had to die together and in good health. Once dead, they would end up on his desk for a comparative autopsy, which he would rigorously carry out and then present its conclusions to Mengele.[143] After three months working in Auschwitz, Nyiszli had a clear sense that this was not a scientific institute. The studies on a supposedly superior race, on the origins of the birth of twins, on the assumed degeneration of people

---

142 Miklós Nyiszli, op. cit., p. 97.

143 Ibid., pp. 34–35.

with disabilities, which would prove the inferiority of the Jews—all this was false pseudoscience, Nyiszli concluded.[144]

EIGHT DAYS AFTER THE ROMA massacre, Irene Mengele arrived in Auschwitz to visit her husband and celebrate their fifth wedding anniversary. Little Rolf, eight months old, had stayed with his paternal grandparents in Bavaria. The first three weeks that she spent with Josef were idyllic. As it was very hot in August, the two of them spent their days bathing in the river Sola. Together they picked blackberries, with which Irene enjoyed making jam. There was no need to worry about housework, because Jehovah's Witness prisoners were available for that.[145] In fact, they were chosen to work in the Auschwitz commandant's house precisely because of their strict religiosity, which prevented them from stealing. Irene noticed that the entire area of the large complex was surrounded by barbed wire, but she justified it in her mind, thinking that it was necessary for a large camp of political prisoners and prisoners of war. At that time, she had never admitted to herself that a death industry was operating there.

In addition to the romantic days with Irene, Mengele had some good professional news. The head of the medical service for the entire Auschwitz complex, Dr. Eduard Wirths, had decided to promote him. In a report dated August 19, 1944, Wirths wrote about Mengele:

> During his period as Auschwitz concentration camp doctor, he put his knowledge to practical and theoretical use, while combating serious epidemics. With prudence, perseverance, and energy, he fulfilled all the tasks given to him, often under very difficult conditions, to the complete satisfaction of his superiors, showing himself capable of dealing with every situation. Furthermore, as an anthropologist, he has zealously used his little free time to advance his studies. Using scientific material available to him because of his official position, he

---

144 Ibid., p. 76.

145 Gerald Posner and John Ware, op. cit., p. 54.

has made a valuable contribution to anthropology in his work. His performance can therefore be considered excellent.[146]

Mengele was promoted from doctor in charge of the "gypsy camp" to chief doctor of the entire Birkenau (Auschwitz II) concentration camp.[147] It was quite a promotion, even though Mengele remained subordinate to Wirths.

Eduard Wirths (center), the chief doctor at Auschwitz, with Vinzenz Schöttl, commander of Auschwitz III-Monowitz (left), and Rudolf Höss, commander of Auschwitz-Birkenau (right).

United States Holocaust Memorial Museum Collection, Gift of Peter Wirths.

Dr. Wirths often complained to his secretary, the Austrian prisoner Hermann Langbein, that he couldn't reconcile the murders required of him with his conscience as a medical doctor, which caused him a lot of suffering. He asked several times to be transferred, but was never granted his request.[148] In the spring of 1943, coincidentally the time Mengele arrived at the camp, Wirths convinced his superiors that

---

146 Ibid., pp. 52–53.

147 Helena Kubica, op. cit., p. 421.

148 Hermann Langbein, op. cit., p. 367.

the SS doctors should make the selections on the train-arrival ramp. He took this initiative because he realized that the SS officers who carried out this task were usually too strict and selected prisoners still able to work who could be saved from the gas chambers. In a letter to his brother, Wirths acknowledged the horror of the task: "I had to burden the doctors subordinate to me with this terrible reality." Wirths himself made a point of doing his shifts on the ramp because, even though he didn't like it, he felt he had to set an "example" for his subordinates.[149]

In one of several conversations with his assistant, Wirths revealed that he was not a Nazi, but a doctor. He had studied medicine in Würzburg, Bavaria, in the 1930s. In order to continue his academic career, he needed a certificate of "political reliability." He had been designated "unreliable" because he supported the Social Democratic Party (SPD), and he understood that he needed to change his profile in order not to be expelled from the university. For this reason, he applied to join the SA, the Sturmabteilung, a paramilitary group within the Nazi party. However, he wasn't admitted to the SA. As he wanted to continue studying, he then decided to join the more elitist SS.

At that time, if you wanted to advance in your career, you had to be part of a Nazi organization. During World War II, Wirths worked at the front in Lapland, then in the Dachau concentration camp outside Munich, and finally took on the position of chief doctor at Auschwitz due to his medical skills. When he accepted the post, he was told that his only task would be to protect the SS men in the camp from typhus. Then, when he came across the widespread system of mass extermination, he went to the commandant of Auschwitz, Rudolf Höss, who confirmed that this was indeed an extermination camp and that any medical help to the prisoners was useless. The grim reality of his position led Wirths to the brink of suicide. In a letter to his father, he asked for advice on what to do and was told to

---

149 Ibid., p. 374.

stay on the job and help as best he could. Wirths was able to put an end to the practice of administering phenol injections into the chests of sick patients to kill them instantly. He also controlled some epidemics and gave work to prisoners who were doctors. Although he stood out from the rest of the SS men, Wirths was far from a saint: he allowed the doctors to use the "human material" from Auschwitz for experiments, and conducted experiments on prisoners himself as, for example, when he wanted to test a new drug against typhus. Since there were no other patients suffering from the illness in the camp, Wirths purposely had four healthy Jews infected. The result: two of them died.[150]

Three SS officers socialize on the grounds of the SS retreat of Solahütte, outside Auschwitz, July 1944. From left to right: Richard Baer (commandant of Auschwitz), Mengele, and Rudolf Höss (the former Auschwitz commandant).

United States Holocaust Memorial Museum Collection, Gift of an Anonymous Donor.

---

150 Ibid., pp. 376–80.

According to the Third Reich regulations, testing on humans was not forbidden. What was prohibited by a 1933 law was the use of animals in surgeries or treatments that could cause pain or injury.[151] Experiments on humans *were* allowed during the Nazi period and could be categorized into three types. The first category consisted of military experiments to help the army at the front. The Germans wanted to understand, for example, how long a paratrooper could survive in freezing water. The second consisted of experiments to prove the Nazi ideology of the superiority of the Aryan "race" and, consequently, the debasement of races considered inferior—which is where most of Mengele's research fit in. And the third encompassed experiments for a new population policy, to be applied mainly in Eastern Europe.[152] This last type included experiments to sterilize women. Himmler wanted the Reich doctors to find a method that was cheap and quick and could be used on a large scale on "enemy" populations such as the Poles, Russians, and Jews. Ever since *Mein Kampf*, Hitler had made it very clear that he wanted to exterminate not only the Jewish community, but also the Slavs, in order to create Lebensraum, living space, for the German population in Eastern Europe. His thinking was that if the women of enemy peoples were sterilized *en masse*, their working capacity could still be exploited by the Germans, while the risk of reproduction would be eliminated.

Sterilization experiments were carried out in Auschwitz from March 1941 until January 1945, when the camp was liberated.[153] Dr. Carl Clauberg, who sterilized thousands of young Jewish and Roma prisoners, developed a method that involved injecting an irritating solution into the uterus. This was carried out during "routine" gynecological examinations, so that the women's reproductive capacity was affected without their realizing what had been done. Another doctor, Dr. Horst Schumann, tried a method based on X-rays applied to the

---

151 Vivien Spitz, op. cit., p. 62.

152 Carola Sachse, op. cit., p. 123.

153 Vivien Spitz, op. cit., p. 191.

victims' genitals. At least one hundred Polish, Russian, and French women—all of them young, beautiful, and healthy—were selected for this experiment. However, almost all of those who took part in the procedure had to be exterminated because they were unable to work due to the severe burns caused by the X-rays.[154] Mengele was definitely not the only doctor to conduct experiments on prisoners at Auschwitz. However, Langbein, who, being Dr. Wirths's secretary, for bureaucratic reasons had access to the work of all the doctors in the camp, observed what made Mengele stand out from all the other doctors: he was a workaholic.

ANNA SUSSMANN ARRIVED AT AUSCHWITZ pregnant in August 1944 and managed to hide her condition throughout her pregnancy, most likely because she was undernourished. At that time, the camp administration learned that many women were concealing their pregnancies. In order to get those expecting to come forward, and to avoid having to examine every woman, the SS announced that pregnant women would be given one quarter of a liter of milk a day. A Polish doctor, who had become Sussmann's friend, advised her not to say anything about her condition. This was difficult for Sussmann, because prisoners usually only received two cups of soup a day to share among six people. After some hesitation, one pregnant woman decided to come forward and indeed received the promised amount of milk. Others followed her example and reported their pregnancies too. After a while, they were all taken away and never seen again.

Sussmann preferred to keep a low profile. She continued to do her hard work in the camp, which led to a premature birth, as was to be expected. She began to feel contractions during the morning roll call, when the prisoners had to stand for hours on end, often under the worst weather conditions, be it rain, snow, or scorching heat. Sussmann managed to disguise the fact that she was in labor and

---

154 Ibid., p. 194.

only when roll call was finally over did she go into the barrack and hide under some blankets. She tried her best to contain the pain of a natural birth, but she couldn't take it. She screamed as she gave birth to a baby boy. Mengele heard the noise and found her. Without hesitating, he picked up the baby and threw him directly into the fire, burning the newborn alive, even before Sussmann's body expelled the placenta.[155]

To avoid such barbaric scenes, gynecologist Gisella Perl, a prisoner who worked for Mengele, decided that she would perform abortions on all pregnant women in Auschwitz. The practice went completely against her own religious faith but, since known pregnant women were sent directly to the gas chamber or died soon after giving birth, she considered abortions morally best to give a childless woman a better chance to live. Dr. Perl had to act secretly, because her life was at risk, too, should she be caught. She worked for Mengele at the hospital during the day and secretly went into the barracks at night to help the women.[156]

At first, like other prisoners, Perl was naïve enough to believe that the SS really did offer advantages to pregnant women who came forward, such as extra food or better accommodation in another camp. One day, however, she witnessed SS men and women beating and whipping pregnant women, who were also being attacked by dogs. When the women fainted, they were thrown into the crematorium while still alive. Perl watched the scene motionless, unable to utter a word or even scream. Horror turned to revolt, and at that very moment she decided that she would use her expertise as a gynecologist to save all the pregnant women in the camp. She ran from block to block to tell others what she had seen and to warn that no woman should ever report that she was expecting a baby.

---

155 Hermann Langbein, op. cit., p. 337.
156 Gisella Perl, op. cit., p. 8.

Dr. Perl began to deliver babies secretly in the dark corners of the camp—in toilets, on the ground, in filth, without a drop of water. Afterwards, she would bandage the mother's belly and then send the woman back to work to avoid suspicion. Babies were sacrificed and buried in the dead of night, as were aborted fetuses. When necessary, Perl managed to get some of the women to the hospital—which, in her opinion, was practically useless, since it had no medicines or proper instruments, just a few rusty tools. Perl diagnosed the mothers with "pneumonia," a disease that was considered "safe" and wasn't cause to send the prisoner to the gas chamber.[157]

Every afternoon, Mengele paid a quick visit to the hospital where Dr. Perl worked. It was a dreaded moment, because he poured all his sadism into the doctors and nurses who were prisoners. He could beat them, whip them, kick them with his heavy boots, or send them to the crematorium—in short, he could do whatever he wanted. One night, a group of nine prisoners who worked in the hospital thought he wouldn't be coming because it was already late. They managed to light a fire to cook some potatoes, a feast for those starving. A car pulled up outside the hospital; it was Mengele. He stared at the group, baring his teeth like a wolf's fangs. The women were paralyzed with fear. After a few seconds of silence, he lunged at them like a wild beast, kicked the stove, knocked over the potatoes, and turned over an operating table. "This is how I imagined a Jewish hospital. You filthy whores . . . you disgusting Jewish pigs!" he roared in a fury. Dr. Perl quickly tried to think of something to appease Mengele's wrath. She approached him, carrying a fetus in a jar, and stammered, "Herr Hauptsturmführer, perhaps you would be interested in this specimen, it is seldom possible to remove one in a single piece." He stopped shouting, grabbed the jar, and sneered, satisfied. "Great . . . beautiful. . . . We'll send it to Berlin,"

---

[157] Ibid., p. 57.

he ordered. Then he turned around and walked away, as if nothing had happened.[158]

Finally, a few days later, an order arrived that no pregnancy would be punishable by death, but the fetus would have to be removed and handed over to Mengele. Dr. Perl breathed a sigh of relief. She had the official authorization to do what she had already been doing, but now without risking her life and in better conditions than on the filthy floor of the barracks.[159] Mengele began to collect human fetuses as yet another line of research he pursued at Auschwitz.[160]

IN THAT LONG MONTH OF August 1944, some men from the Sonder-kommando accomplished a remarkable feat. A civil worker smuggled a camera into the concentration camp, hidden on the bottom of a bucket. The camera ended up in the hands of a Greek Jew named Alex who, despite the enormous risk of being caught, entered a gas chamber and hurriedly took four photos without even looking through the view-finder. The most shocking image Alex captured was that of a pile of naked bodies in an open-air incineration pit in front of Crematorium V. He then returned the camera to the bucket, which stealthily made its way to Helena Dantón, an employee in the SS canteen. She hid the photographic film inside a tube of toothpaste, left the camp, and delivered the material to the Polish resistance in Krakow with a note written by two political prisoners:

> Urgent. . . . We send you photographs from Birkenau showing pris-
> oners sent to the gas chamber. One photo shows one of the open fires
> where corpses are burned, since the crematorium is not enough to burn
> them all. In front of the bonfire lie corpses waiting to be thrown into
> the fire. Another photograph shows a place in the woods where the

---

158 Ibid., p. 80.

159 Ibid., p. 52.

160 Carola Sachse, op. cit., p. 238.

detainees undress to supposedly shower. They are then sent to the gas chamber.[161]

This enormous act of courage recorded in irrefutable images the horror described by so many survivors, scenes that are difficult to imagine by anyone who was not an eyewitness at the Nazi extermination machine. No one saw the workings of this machine as closely as the men of the Sonderkommando, who smelled the corpses, felt the weight of the murders on their shoulders, and carried the dead in their arms. The first group was selected in July 1942 from among Jews who had come from Slovakia. Twelve teams followed, one after

Sonderkommando photographs of open-air incineration pit burning corpses in Aushwitz II-Birkenau in the summer of 1944.

The Archive of The State Museum Auschwitz-Birkenau in Oswiecim (negativ n 281 & 280).

---

[161] Didi-Huberman, *Imagens apesar de tudo*. São Paulo: Ed. 34, 2020, p. 31.

another. The members of the Sonderkommando were not allowed to leave the crematorium area and lived completely isolated from all the other prisoners in the camp, in absolute secrecy. After a few months, when they had learned too much about the workings of mass extermination, they, too, were killed—the novices' initiation was precisely to burn the corpses of their predecessors. Dr. Nyiszli, in addition to performing autopsies for Mengele, was the doctor responsible for caring for the men who worked in the four crematoria: 120 from the SS and around 860 from the Sonderkommando.[162] He lived among those marked to die and the living dead, as he put it. In the short time they had to live, these men had many privileges over the other prisoners. They could keep their own clothes and had access to the best-quality food, drinks, cigarettes, and medicine—all arriving in the luggage belonging to Jews from the various corners of Europe. Some new arrivals at Auschwitz had not had all their possessions taken away by anti-Semitic persecution and carried a lot of valuables in their suitcases.

OCTOBER 6, 1944

Mengele walked out of the autopsy room at nine o'clock in the morning, leaving an order for Nyiszli to dissect the body of a Russian officer that lay on the table. It would have taken the pathologist forty minutes at the most to complete the task, had this not been his last day. Nothing was certain, but Nyiszli felt that death was imminent. Since he couldn't work, he decided to take a walk. He heard some men whispering in the corners, and it soon became clear that they had hatched a plan. Nyiszli learned that they were going to attempt a mass escape that night and that they had the right weapons: a hundred boxes of explosives smuggled in from an ammunition factory where Polish Jews worked, as well as five machine guns and twenty hand grenades. The signal to attack would be given with a

---

162 Miklós Nyiszli, op. cit., p. 21.

flashlight. They would only have to deal with three SS guards at each crematorium.

After learning of the plan, Nyiszli thought it best to return to work and complete the autopsy with the help of his assistants before Mengele returned. They had been working for twenty minutes when a tremendous explosion shook the walls. Then machine guns started firing. They didn't understand what had happened, as the plan was for a night escape. Through the window, Nyiszli saw the arrival of between eighty and a hundred Nazi trucks. Half of one troop jumped out of a truck and moved into battle position. The men of the Sonderkommando had taken control of the crematorium and were firing on the SS guards.[163] The Nazis had brought fifty well-trained dogs and set them loose on the prisoners, but, for some reason, the dogs refused to attack. The battle raged for about ten minutes. Soon the machine guns stopped firing and the SS invaded the crematorium from all sides. A group entered the autopsy room and beat Nyiszli and his assistants before taking them out to the courtyard . The guards forced everyone to lie face down on the ground, and anyone who dared raise their head would be shot in the back of the head.

After about twenty or thirty minutes waiting for the SS bullet, Nyiszli heard a car engine: it was Mengele. An officer shouted: "Doctors, on your feet!." The four of them got up and approached Mengele.

"What part did you play in all this?" he asked.

"None," replied Nyiszli, "unless obeying the Hauptsturmführer's orders can be considered a crime. We were dissecting the Russian officer's body when the incident occurred. The explosion disrupted our autopsy," said Nyiszli.

Mengele looked at his bloody shirt and ordered, "Go wash up and get on with your work." The four men had taken about twenty steps when they again heard the sound of machine guns. Nyiszli didn't dare look back, but slowed his pace. It was the end of that

---

163 Ibid., pp. 110–15.

Sonderkommando. Their bodies were cremated by thirty new men, hastily recruited for the new team. The revolt of the Sonderkommando was a milestone in the history of Auschwitz. Although they didn't achieve the goal of a mass escape, and 853 men died, the prisoners inflicted a high number of casualties on the SS: seventy in total, including officers. And, most importantly, news of the riot reached the outside world.[164]

A month later, early in the morning, an SS officer entered Nyiszli's room and confidentially informed him that his superiors had decided that, as of that day, November 17, 1944, no more prisoners would be killed at Auschwitz. The pathologist found the information suspicious and thought it was another SS trick to deceive the prisoners. Later that morning, however, a train with five wagons arrived, carrying five hundred ill people. For the first time during the period Nyiszli had been there, the sick were not exterminated within an hour of arriving at the camp. On the contrary, this time they were sent to rest in hospital beds. Nyiszli realized that something was changing in Auschwitz. A mixture of relief and panic gripped the Hungarian doctor; he feared that the extermination of all witnesses of the past heinous crimes committed in that hellhole was imminent.[165]

That month, the SS demolished Birkenau's four crematoria and gas chambers. The last crematorium to remain standing was number V, which was only imploded later, on January 26, shortly before the camp was liberated.[166] Wirths wrote a letter to his wife at the end of November, telling her the news: "You can imagine, my dear, how good it is for me not to have to do this horrible work anymore." The mass deportations of Jews were also coming to an end. None of this meant that the Nazis had given up on the "final solution"; rather, they wanted to avoid a repeat of what had happened in another extermination camp, Majdanek, where the Soviets found gas chambers

164 Ibid., p. 120.
165 Ibid., pp. 137–38.
166 Nikolaus Wachsmann, op. cit.

practically intact. Parts of the Birkenau crematoria were dismantled and sent to an ultra-secret location near the Mauthausen concentration camp in Austria. The SS intended to rebuild the former crematorium complex there, but it never happened. Prisoners were already being relocated to other Nazi concentration camps farther west, away from the approaching Red Army.[167] The families of SS officers abandoned their luxury homes in Auschwitz. Commandant Rudolf Höss's wife left at the beginning of November and took her children with her. The Nazis who stayed behind were increasingly apprehensive about the imminent arrival of the Soviets.

---

[167] Ibid.

9

THE LIBERATION OF AUSCHWITZ

AUSCHWITZ-BIRKENAU. JANUARY 1945

The war was about to see the beginning of another year, but this one promised to be different. The end of the Third Reich was near. Hitler's New Year's radio speech was so monotonous, and its tone contrasted so much with the excitement of his previous public addresses, that many Germans thought it had been recorded in advance or was fake. In yet another of his delusions, the Führer told the soldiers that Germany was now engaged in a merciless fight for its very existence, against an international Jewish conspiracy whose objective was the extermination of the German people.[168] The situation was indeed irreversible for the Reich, but it obviously had nothing to do with the Jews. At that point, the fall of the Eastern front along the Vistula River was only a matter of time. From the Baltic to the Adriatic, the Soviet Union had mobilized almost seven million men, who were advancing rapidly westward on several fronts. Hitler was especially worried about Budapest, which the Soviets had surrounded the day

---

168 Laurence Rees, op. cit., p. 463.

after Christmas. The Führer wouldn't allow the German troops positioned there to give up a European capital and insisted that they defend the city to the bitter end. The result was horrendous carnage and great suffering for the civilian population.[169] Descriptions of the Red Army's passage through the towns and cities of Eastern Europe are reminiscent of narratives about barbarian invasions: the generalized rape of women, children, and the elderly; looting; and arson. No wonder the city inhabitants tried to flee as fast as they could before these new barbarians arrived.

In Auschwitz, the landscape was completely white, covered by snow as far as the eye could see. The SS men who hadn't deserted were almost always drunk. Rumors circulated that Mengele had already left the concentration camp—which was no longer called that, but rather a "labor camp," as if the name change could erase the horrors that had been perpetrated there. "Raus! Raus!" shouted the guards trying to get everyone out of the barracks. "We're taking you away for your own protection!" they kept saying. On January 17, against that icy backdrop, rows of prisoners set off on foot toward other concentration camps still under Reich rule. On the Death Marches, as they later became known, anyone who didn't have the strength to walk was shot and abandoned along the way. More and more bodies covered the roads as prisoners walked. During the long hours of marching, Dina Gottliebová, the Czech artist, kept looking at her mother's feet to make sure the older woman stayed close to her. It was Dina's twenty-second birthday,[170] and she and her mother ate snow to quench their unbearable thirst. After three days of walking without food, the two women were put back on a cattle wagon. Crowded together into the same space, young Ukrainian and German women pushed and were hostile to the Jewish women. Just like when they had been taken

169 Antony Beevor, *A Segunda Guerra Mundial*. Rio de Janeiro: Record, 2015, pp. 1187–88.

170 "Jewish Survivor Dina Gottliebová-Babbitt Testimony Part 2." USC Shoah Foundation. Available at: <www.youtube.com/watch?v=e85gLhT5c2A>. Accessed on: July 10, 2023.

to Auschwitz, again they all traveled like sardines in a can, to the Ravensbrück concentration camp. Despite the suffering and hunger, more intense than ever, there was a feeling in the air that it was all coming to an end, that the Third Reich was falling apart.

On the night of January 17, Dr. Nyiszli was still in Auschwitz and decided to go to bed early. Around midnight, he woke up to the sound of explosions and machine guns. Nyiszli ran to call his companions. They quickly put on warm clothes and got ready for the march, stuffing cans of food, medicine, and cigarettes into their pockets. It was around fourteen degrees Fahrenheit, if not colder. The guards' rooms, where the archives of the Birkenau camp were kept, had been set on fire. Nyiszli came across some three thousand prisoners in front of the camp gate, who were waiting for an order to leave. Without hesitation, he blended into the crowd, as other members of the Sonderkommando had already done, to avoid the danger of being killed by the SS for knowing too much. At around 1:00 a.m., he saw the last Nazis leave the camp. The lights were turned off and Birkenau was plunged into darkness. Nyiszli's group left, escorted by SS men. A few miles down the road, Soviet troops on the lookout mistook the rows of prisoners for soldiers and started firing machine guns. Nyiszli and other prisoners hid in a trench on the side of the road and managed to save themselves, despite the crossfire. When everything calmed down, they resumed their walk.[171] Between January 17 and 21, around fifty-six thousand prisoners left Auschwitz and its sub-camps toward the west. At least nine thousand died on the way, but most likely the number was as high as fifteen thousand.[172]

The twins Eva and Miriam Mozes, who had been Mengele's guinea pigs, remained in Auschwitz. When they heard that thousands of prisoners were leaving, Eva told Miriam that she wasn't going on any

---

171 Miklós Nyiszli, op. cit., pp. 149–50.

172 "The Final Evacuation and Liquidation of the Camp." Auschwitz-Birkenau State Museum. Available at: <www.auschwitz.org/en/history/evacuation/the-final -evacuation-and-liquidation-of-the-camp>. Accessed on: November 4, 2021.

of the marches. Although still a child, she thought that the Nazis hadn't been particularly nice to the prisoners while they were winning the war. Therefore, they wouldn't be any more tolerant when they were losing it. With this in mind, the two ten-year-old girls decided to stay, as did other twins. Luckily for them, no guards came back to check that the barracks were really empty. The children wandered around the camp looking for food and warm clothes to wear. Eva found a pair of shoes in "Canada," the famous storage room where personal effects stolen from the Jews were kept. One day, she went out to get some bread and heard the engine of a jeep: four Nazis had returned to the camp and were machine-gunning whoever was left. Eva fainted and fell to the ground, which probably saved her life. When she got up, there were several bodies around her.[173]

The sick were also left behind in the hospitals and infirmaries of Auschwitz. The Nazis decided that those who were too weak to walk should be executed, but the order to exterminate them was not followed to the letter. The Germans preferred to save their own skin and flee, rather than wait for the Red Army. In the end, the sick were luckier than those forced to leave Auschwitz on foot. Primo Levi, the Italian chemist who became one of the main witnesses to later write about what had happened in Auschwitz, could hardly celebrate the Germans' escape: "If I had my normal sensibility now, this would be an extremely exciting moment."[174]

The Soviets were very close. They took over Krakow with ease, since the city had already been abandoned. The same was not true of the liberation of Oświęcim, where the battalion commanded by Ukrainian Major Anatoly Shapiro faced stiff resistance from the Nazis. Half of the nine hundred men in his battalion died in the fighting. The Germans also laid land mines along the way to make access to Auschwitz more difficult. On January 27, Major Shapiro, ironically a Jew, was the first person to open the gate below the infamous "Arbeit macht frei" sign.

---

173 Eva Mozes Kor and Lisa Rojany Buccieri, op. cit.

174 Primo Levi, *É isto um homem?*. Rio de Janeiro: Rocco, 2013, p. 223.

Inside, the military found seven thousand people. Most were nothing but skin and bones; many didn't even have shoes in the freezing cold of the Polish winter. They were the living dead who had barely reacted to the liberation of the camp. One or two who still had the strength to speak asked if it was true that they were being liberated. The Red Cross staff immediately started making chicken and vegetable soups, but many prisoners couldn't eat because their stomachs had atrophied so much.[175]

Ten days passed between the departure of the Death Marches and the arrival of the Red Army. Among the prisoners left behind, there were around five hundred children and teenagers under the age of fifteen. Most were exhausted and suffered from a lack of vitamins, and many had tuberculosis. All of them were at least ten pounds underweight, some as much as forty.[176] Among them were Eva and Miriam Mozes. The twin sisters appear in some well-known images of the liberation of Auschwitz in which children show their tattooed arms to the camera. The Soviet Army sent a medical team to treat the survivors, and officers interviewed some inmates. The prisoners told them about the gas chambers and the medical experiments. The information was sent to the Red Army's propaganda chief, and a short article appeared in the Soviet military newspaper. There was no outcry at the time denouncing the horrors unveiled at Auschwitz, probably because the Communist Party insisted that the Jews did not represent a special category, and only the suffering of the Soviet people should be highlighted.[177]

175 "60 years after liberation: 'I was skin and bones': Soldiers remember Auschwitz." Jewish Telegraphic Agency. Available at: <www.jta.org/archive/60-years-after-liberation-it-was-skin-and-bones-soldiers-remember-auschwitz>. Accessed on: November 2, 2021.

176 "The Fate of the Children." Auschwitz-Birkenau State Museum. Available at: <www.auschwitz.org/en/history/fate-of-children/the-fate-of-the-children>. Accessed on: July 12, 2023.

177 Antony Beevor, op. cit., pp. 1210–11.

This film was taken by a Soviet military film crew upon liberating Auschwitz in January 1945. Among the children showing numbers on their arms is Eva Mozes Kor.

RG-60,0038, Accessed at United States Holocaust Memorial Museum, courtesy of National Archives & Records Administration.

THE RUMORS CIRCULATING IN THE camp were right: Mengele had left and had taken with him all the notes relating to his experiments. To this day, they have yet to be found. What records of his work still remain are found in very few documents in the Auschwitz-Birkenau Memorial Museum. The information available today is mainly based on the accounts of the human test subjects who survived the experiments, the witnesses of the selections, and the professionals who served as his assistants and therefore closely followed Mengele's work.[178] With the evacuation of Auschwitz, Mengele was assigned to another concentration camp, Gross-Rosen, in southwestern Poland. It was home

---

178 Carola Sachse, op. cit.

Bl. 17	Kinder ohne Eltern.			Oswięcim, 9. II. 1945.	
				wyrażenie Kalowe (castus)	
L.№	Name	Vorname	geboren am	Nationalität	
1	Hellstein	Fella	8 Jahre	Polen	109
2	Zelewski	Samuel	12 "	"	
3	Zelewski	Leib	11 "	"	
4	Appelbaum	Hilek	9 "	"	
5	Appelbaum	Adolf	9 "	"	
6	Rosenzweig	Israel	13 "	"	
7	Schlesinger	Pawel	7 "	Č.S.R.	
8	Schlesinger	Robert	11 "	"	
9	Winter	Otto	11 "	"	
10	Winter	Erika	14 "	"	
11	Weinheber	Bertha	14 "	"	
12	Moses	Miriam	12 "	Ungarn	
13	Moses	Eva	12 "	"	
14	Klein	Anna	12 "	"	
15	Klein	Judith	12 "	"	
16	Salomon	Rosalia	9 "	Ungarn	
17	Salomon	Sarolta	9 "	"	
18	Eckstein	Vera	9 "	"	
19	Eckstein	Ilona	9 "	"	
20	Bleier	Ernö	9 "	"	
21	Bleier	Edith	9 "	"	
22	Malek	Jakob	4 "	"	
23	Malek	Elias	4 "	"	
24	Malek	Judith	14 "	"	
25	Schlesinger	Sidonie	14 "	"	
26	Sauer	Sary	14 "	"	
27	Sauer	Margit	14 "	"	
28	Neumann	Gabriel	8 "	Č.S.R.	

List of names of twin children, the victims of Mengele's experiments, who were liberated in Auschwitz by the Red Army on January 27, 1945.

The Archive of The State Museum Auschwitz-Birkenau in Oswiecim.

to a vast industrial complex of German companies that also used the slave labor of prisoners. There was a network of at least ninety-seven sub-camps. The best known of these is Brünnlitz, which went down in history because of its connection to businessman Oskar Schindler, who created his famous list with the names of more than a thousand Jews whom he selected to work in his factory and, in this way, saved from death.[179] Mengele couldn't stay long in Gross-Rosen because the Red Army soon arrived once again and liberated the camp, on February 13, 1945. At that time, the greatest fear of German officers, especially the SS, was falling into Soviet hands.

In the last days of the war, Mengele arrived at a military hospital in Saaz, in Sudetenland. The region in the former Czechoslovakia became known worldwide in 1938 for having been occupied by Hitler under the pretext of protecting the German-speaking population living there. Now the situation was quite different: the so-called ethnic Germans were being expelled en masse. In the first of a series of master strokes, Mengele showed up at the hospital wearing the uniform of a German Army officer, not that of the SS, to which he actually belonged. Luckily for him, the head of the field hospital, Dr. Otto-Hans Kahler, was an old friend of his who before the war had also worked with Otmar von Verschuer. Kahler asked the unit commander for permission for Mengele to join them.[180] The commander consented, and Mengele camped with the unit in a forest in Sudetenland, a mountain range that formed a natural border between the former Czechoslovakia and Germany. Formally, the area was supposed to be under the responsibility of the United States, but no Allied country had arrived there yet; it was a no-man's-land. With the Soviets at their back and the Americans at their front, the German soldiers remained trapped in that forest for six weeks.

---

179 "Gross-Rosen." United States Holocaust Memorial Museum. Available at: <encyclopedia.ushmm.org/content/en/article/gross-rosen>. Accessed on: July 12, 2023.

180 *In the Matter of Josef Mengele: A Report to the Attorney General of the United States,* op. cit., pp. 26–27.

BAVARIA, AMERICAN SECTOR. JUNE 1945

The war in Europe ended on May 8, 1945, with Germany's unconditional surrender, after the Soviets had dropped forty thousand tons
of bombs on Berlin in just two weeks, reducing the German capital
to a pile of rubble. The situation all across the continent was chaotic. In Germany alone, twenty million people had nowhere to live.
Throughout Western Europe, transportation and communication systems had been rendered inoperable.[181] Against this backdrop, just over
a month after the official end of the conflict, in mid-June, the military
hospital where Mengele had spent the last few weeks received orders
to move to the American sector, because the Red Army was about to
occupy Sudetenland. The medical unit's vehicles formed a convoy and
drove together to Bavaria. Almost out of fuel, they were stopped by
the Americans and the personnel taken to a POW camp near the town
of Schauenstein. It could have been the end of the line for Mengele,
had someone found out who he was. Right from the start, the former SS captain understood this and started using false names. When
registering at the prison camp, he said his name was Josef Memling,
using the surname of a fifteenth-century German painter. Nobody
noticed the joke except for Kahler, who was very fond of art. Kahler
told Mengele that it was not dignified or honorable for a German officer to use a false name, and thus he should use his real one.

The victorious Allied countries had divided Germany into four
sectors, and each great power occupied one of them. The United
States, which was left with part of the center and the south, faced
a complicated situation. They had more than three million prisoners of war under their responsibility, very few supplies, and an enormous displaced population.[182] In these challenging circumstances, the
Americans were in a hurry to release as many people as possible. At

---

181 Tony Judt, op. cit., pp. 30–31.

182 *In the Matter of Josef Mengele: A Report to the Attorney General of the United States*,
op. cit., p. 37.

the same time, they worried about mistakenly releasing those who had actively collaborated with Nazis. That June, then, the US Army authorized what had already been happening in practice for some time: German prisoners could be released—with the exception of those who fell into the category of "automatic prison." This meant SS men, Nazi party members above a certain rank in the military hierarchy, and war criminals. By that rule alone, Mengele should have been arrested. Luckily for him, however, no one there knew that he fit practically every one of those categories. Additionally, the United Nations War Crimes Commission released lists of wanted criminals, and Mengele's name appeared on list number 8, published in May. Additionally, the Polish authorities were after him, since Auschwitz was in Poland. There were many reasons for Mengele's arrest and many groups looking for him. The problem was that, in the postwar chaos, list number 8 didn't reach the places it should have: the large camps that housed German prisoners.

Sorting out the soldiers from the various defeated countries was not an exciting task for most American soldiers. Until a few weeks earlier, the two sides—Germany and the Allies—had been facing each other in fierce battles. Now the soldiers, who didn't speak German and were itching to get home, had to deal with this bureaucratic job. But they couldn't complain; they should have been happy to be staying a little longer in Germany, since occupation work was a kind of reward for the best-rated soldiers. The alternative was to be sent to the Pacific Theater of Operations, where the war against Japan was still in full swing.

In the end, German officials took over most of the process of prisoner release at Schauenstein. But no one there thought of consulting the lists of wanted war criminals; they were only concerned to not release members of the SS. These were identified either by personal documents or by a unique mark members of this elite Nazi group had tattooed under their left arm: their blood type. At the Schutzstaffel's training centers, members would take a blood test and be tattooed by a doctor. However, those who had joined the SS before the war might not have this tattoo. This was Mengele's case. Without that mark, it was easier to evade the Allies. That's not to say that the Germans didn't recognize each other. They had a code word—Odessa—that they used to identify themselves as former SS members.[183]

After six weeks in Schauenstein, Mengele, Kahler, and another doctor known to them, the neurologist Fritz Ulmann, were transferred to another camp a little farther south in Bavaria, in the town of Helmbrechts. There, the order of the day was to release the prisoners of war as soon as possible. At long tables, the Americans analyzed each German soldier's case. In the initial screening, everyone had to take off their shirts and raise their arms so that the Americans could inspect whether anyone had an SS tattoo. Those who didn't were released, unless there was something suspicious in their documents. If there was any doubt, an American officer questioned the prisoner with the help of an interpreter. If the issue was not resolved, the prisoner's documents were sent for analysis by a higher authority.

Mengele passed the screening, and two weeks later the long-awaited day arrived: he and his two medical colleagues were released and given a discharge certificate. Mengele gave his real name, but it's unlikely he did so because of Kahler's moralistic reprimand; after all, he was more concerned with saving his own skin than with honor or dignity. American army trucks took those who had been released to a point inside the American occupation zone, where Mengele and Ulmann boarded a vehicle bound for Munich. Mengele got off first, in Ingolstadt, near his parents' town, Günzburg. He had the discharge document with his own name on it and, by another stroke of luck, he also got a copy of Ulmann's release, since he had received two. This document would prove very useful to Mengele as he endeavored to keep his identity secret in the next steps of his escape.

In August 1945, the United States dropped the atomic bombs on Hiroshima and Nagasaki, forcing Japan to surrender. On September 2,

---

183 Bettina Stangneth, *Eichmann Before Jerusalem: The Unexamined Life of a Mass Murderer.* Nova York: Vintage, 2015, p. 89.

the Japanese signed their unconditional surrender and World War II finally came to an end. At that point, one thing Mengele mostly wanted to avoid was going home. Throughout most of the conflict, Günzburg had managed to escape destruction, but toward the end of the war it suffered three major bombing raids by the Allies. The first target was a factory belonging to Messerschmitt, the German warplane company. Two other attacks destroyed the railway station and damaged public services. The main problem for Mengele was not the physical damage, but the fact that the Americans had taken over the city after Germany's surrender. The US troops wouldn't leave until the early 1950s, and their first action was to purge all Nazis from the city administration. The occupying forces also changed street names, disarmed the local police, changed the curriculum in schools, and stationed an infantry regiment in Günzburg, which made Mengele's hometown a risky place for a former SS officer.

The US authorities used the "automatic arrest" mechanism to arrest Mengele's father, Karl, for having been a municipal economic adviser. His younger brother Alois had not yet returned home because he had been taken prisoner of war in Yugoslavia. Karl Jr., the middle brother, had been discharged from military service, for the Nazis considered his work in the agricultural-machinery company essential to the war effort. When the Americans took over the town, Karl Jr. became the target of a long process of denazification and thought it best to leave the firm in the care of Hans Sedlmeier, the family's loyal employee, who later would be a key figure in Mengele's escape to Latin America. In the end, the Americans didn't carry out an intensive search for Mengele in Günzburg, because they were convinced he wasn't there. They even questioned his wife, Irene, who had moved with her son, Rolf, and mother-in-law, Wally, to Autenried, a village nearby. Apparently the US forces were after Mengele simply because he was a potential suspect, and not because they had received an actual order to arrest him. Going home was definitely out of the question for the former SS captain.

OCTOBER 1945

Mengele did not return home, but did not go far either. He asked for work at a farm in the village of Mangolding, in the district of Rosenheim, also in Bavaria. The farm owners were a couple, Maria and Georg Fischer, to whom Mengele introduced himself as Fritz Ulmann. Mengele invented a believable story for the couple: that he had just returned from the Soviet-occupied sector after an unsuccessful search for his wife, who had been sent to central Germany during the war. Maria and Georg saw no problem in giving him a job and took Mengele in for almost three years without knowing who he was. It was an almost perfect hideout for a while. Even in hiding, Mengele found a way to meet up with his brother Karl Jr. They talked in the middle of the road, six miles from the farm, and he updated Mengele on the situation of the firm, his relatives, and the town. A while later, Mengele was also able to see his wife. Irene told him everything that had happened since they had last seen each other in Auschwitz, including that she had been interrogated by the US military. She suggested that he leave Germany because it would be impossible to live a normal life there. It became clear then that their marriage was over, for Irene wanted to lead a normal life, not live in hiding.

Mengele became increasingly entangled in a web of lies. For example, he had to fill out a questionnaire prepared by the Allied forces to identify Germans who were "liable for war crimes." Sixteen million people all over Germany answered the questions, and there was no way Mengele could avoid doing the same.[184] But that wasn't a problem for him; on the contrary, he relished the stories he made up and even helped other farm employees with their answers. The questionnaire was one of many measures the Allies implemented in an effort to eradicate Nazism from Germany, a considerable challenge to say the least. When the war ended in Europe, there were eight million Nazis in the country; it wasn't possible to arrest or put every single one on trial.

---

184 Tony Judt, op. cit., p. 70.

The Allies chose to carry out a process of denazification of German society, which included compulsory visits to concentration camps so that civilians could see for themselves the atrocities the Nazis had committed. In addition, the Allies renovated library collections and controlled the printing of newspapers. Mengele didn't feel completely safe in that environment. What certainly made him lose sleep was the news that the authorities had arrested a war criminal in Rosenheim, the town where Mengele lived, and sent him to Belgium. The same could happen to him if he was discovered, and he could be extradited to Poland. There, the authorities would try the SS members who had worked in Auschwitz. Moreover, two months earlier, the Allies had begun to try the Nazi leaders at Nuremberg.

10

THE NUREMBERG TRIALS

I f the German state of Bavaria was the cradle of Nazism, the city of Nuremberg could have been its official postcard. It was in Nuremberg where the Nazi party organized its grandiose rallies that attracted thousands of supporters in the years before the war. At those events, the most emblematic image was that of Hitler with his arm raised, saluting the uniformed "Aryan" masses, who responded fanatically with "Heil Hitler." It was as if the Führer embodied a demigod in the center of the Zeppelin Field tribune (grandstand). The place was reminiscent of the Pergamon altar—an ancient Greek building dedicated to none other than Zeus, the greatest god on Mount Olympus. The Nazi tribune, framed by giant red flags with intimidating black swastikas, had the feel of a festival where the public was often led into a collective catharsis. The spectacle was meticulously planned so that Nazism would have a profound popular appeal while appearing to be the great restorer of civilization. The rallies caused an enormous impact on the spectators, who watched the event live or in Leni Riefenstahl's film *Triumph of the Will*, the ideal example of Nazi propaganda. Nuremberg was also known as the city where, in 1935, the Nazi leadership announced the implementation of laws that officially excluded Jews from German society, stripping them of their citizenship, and forbidding them to marry non-Jews. These were the famous "Nuremberg Laws." In this city so symbolic for Nazism, the Allies decided to set another example when the war ended: that of international justice.

Initially, putting the Nazi top echelon on trial was not such an obvious choice. Prime Minister Winston Churchill, who led the British war effort when all seemed lost, preferred a firing squad to a tribunal. US president Franklin D. Roosevelt also hesitated over the best way to deal with the Nazis. But Harry Truman, who took over the presidency upon Roosevelt's death, had no doubts: there must be a trial. The fact that he himself had been a judge before becoming president certainly influenced his decision. The day after Roosevelt's death, in April 1945, Truman heard a speech by Robert Jackson, a US Supreme Court associate justice, that impressed him. Jackson stated that you shouldn't try a man if you don't want to see him free, should his guilt remain unproven, and concluded that the world had no respect for courts created only to condemn. Truman invited Jackson to head the prosecution of the first international war tribunal in history. He accepted the challenge because he believed that civilization would not survive another world war and because he wanted to send a message to belligerent leaders: if they provoked a conflict, they would face serious consequences in the international courts.[185]

The trial began in November 1945, with four judges from the victorious countries—the United States, the United Kingdom, France, and the Soviet Union. A brand-new simultaneous translation system allowed the trial to take place in four different languages. German was also used, even though there was no German judge, one of the many issues for which the tribunal was criticized. The Nazi top echelon was

---

185 Norbert Ehrenfreund, *The Nuremberg Legacy: How the Nazi War Crimes Trials Changed the Course of History*. New York: Palgrave Macmillan, 2007, pp. 10–11.

accused of four crimes: conspiracy to wage aggressive war, waging aggressive war, war crimes, and crimes against humanity. The latter included the torture and extermination of millions of people on the basis of "race"; these actions later became known worldwide as the Holocaust.

Medical Case Trial at the Nuremberg Tribunal, 1946.

United States Holocaust Memorial Museum, courtesy of Hedwig Wachenheimer Epstein. Source Record ID: Collections: 1994.A.117.

It is well known that Hitler and major Nazi leaders committed suicide before any trial could have taken place. Führer Adolf Hitler, along with his loyal propaganda minister, Joseph Goebbels, died in the bunker in which they were hiding during the last days before the fall of Berlin. Heinrich Himmler, the head of the SS, took his own life after being captured by the British. Hermann Göring, commander of the Luftwaffe and second in command, was actually sentenced to hang in Nuremberg; but the night before he was to be hanged he swallowed a cyanide pill. Additionally, Martin Bormann, Hitler's private secretary, went missing and was tried in absentia. Only decades later was it discovered that, in fact, he had already been dead at the time of his trial. As a result, the docket at the Nuremberg

Military Tribunal was missing several of the expected defendants, yet twenty-two high-ranking Nazis were tried and twelve of them sentenced to hanging.[186] The tribunal also classified four institutions as criminal: the top echelon of the Nazi party; the Security Service (SD); the Gestapo, which was the Nazi secret police; and the SS, to which Mengele belonged. That decision by the tribunal meant that the mere fact that a person belonged to any of these organizations had already constituted a crime.

OCTOBER 1946

The war had been over for more than a year when the United States decided to carry out twelve more trials in Nuremberg. After the Allies had tried the top echelon, the Americans took to the docket the professionals who enabled the wheels of Nazism to turn: doctors, judges, industrialists, police commanders, military officers, civil servants, and diplomats.

However, the United States had to pursue this endeavor alone, because the Cold War was already beginning to manifest itself, with the Soviet Union now defending different interests from the former Allies. In the United Kingdom, Winston Churchill had been defeated as prime minister in a July 1945 election, and the other nations had no money to pay for the tribunal. Within that unsettling political context, four US judges began to work at the Palace of Justice in Nuremberg.

The first of the twelve trials was precisely that of the medical professionals. Mengele had plenty of reasons to be concerned, for he had committed exactly the same crimes for which the United States had indicted twenty doctors and three health officials. There were four charges: conspiracy; war crime; crime against humanity; and belonging to a criminal organization, in Mengele's case the SS. The main accused was Karl Brandt, Hitler's personal doctor and the one responsible for implementing the T4 program. This program called for the

---

186 Norbert Ehrenfreund, op. cit., pp. 87–89, 149.

secret extermination of Germans with physical and mental disabilities and was essentially the seed stage of the Holocaust. Several doctors who had been important scientists, surgeons, heads of clinics, hospitals, or universities in Germany were also present at the trial because they had practiced medical experiments in Auschwitz, Dachau, Buchenwald, Ravensbrück, Sachsenhausen, and other concentration camps. Regardless of legislation, whether international or national, all these doctors had violated the Hippocratic Oath and its fundamental principle for the ethical practice of medicine: "First and foremost, do no harm"—*primum non nocere.*

General Telford Taylor, who had been a member of Jackson's team, was the main prosecutor. In December 1946, when the trial of the Nazi doctors finally began, he made the opening statement:

> The defendants in this case are accused of murder, torture, and other atrocities committed in the name of medical science. The victims of these crimes number in the hundreds of thousands, but only a handful are still alive. Some of the survivors will appear before this tribunal. . . . For their killers, these people were not individuals. They came in droves and were treated worse than animals.[187]

Taylor stated that all the defendants had committed war crimes by taking part in medical experiments between September 1939 and April 1945. The defendants "played a central role, collaborated, ordered, supported, or gave approval" to experiments that used human beings as guinea pigs. Such experiments were carried out without the consent of the victims, who included both civilians and military personnel from the armies at war with Germany.

The prosecutor then began to briefly describe some of the experiments. The first example was high-altitude tests conducted with

---

187 "The Doctors Trial: The Medical Case of the Subsequent Nuremberg Proceedings." United States Holocaust Memorial Museum. Available at: <encyclopedia.ushmm.org/content/en/article/the-doctors-trial-the-medical-case-of-the-subsequent-nuremberg-proceedings>. Accessed on: July 12, 2023.

prisoners placed in low-pressure chambers that reproduced atmospheric conditions of up to 68,000 feet—twice as high as contemporary commercial airplanes fly. As a result, many people died or suffered serious injuries. The prosecutor also reported on experiments to test human resistance to cold. Prisoners were placed naked in tanks of icy water for up to three hours at a time, or left naked outdoors in subzero temperatures, which caused many of them to die. Taylor claimed, too, that the doctors had infected more than a thousand people with malaria. Such experiments on the infectious disease not only resulted in many deaths, but also caused the survivors a lot of pain and left some of them with permanent sequelae.

In another, even crueler, experiment, the Nazis purposely wounded prisoners and then injected the open wounds with streptococci and bacteria that cause gangrene and tetanus. Wood splinters and shards of glass were then placed on the wounds. Taylor reported that the victims obviously died in great pain. Some Nazi doctors also tried to perform transplants to regenerate bones, muscles, and nerves, as if the human guinea pigs were dolls that could be reassembled, completely ignoring the suffering involved in this type of procedure. The US prosecutor said that body parts were removed under intense pain and agony, and those who survived faced permanent disability. In yet another experiment, he continued, inmates were given no food for days, only salt water.

In the forced-sterilization experiments, such as those that took place in Auschwitz, thousands of women were sterilized with X-rays, drugs, or through surgery. In the typhus experiments, more than 90 percent of the people intentionally infected died. Some experiments used various types of poison mixed into prisoners' food, without the victims' knowledge; and after they died, their bodies were studied at autopsies. Taylor concluded his summary of the horrors perpetrated by the Nazis relating one more type of experiment, which involved incendiary bombs. The Nazis burned their prisoners with the phosphorus extracted from explosives, causing excruciating pain to the victims.[188]

---

188 Vivien Spitz, op. cit., pp. 44–45. 5 Ibid., p. 296. 153

Dr. Brandt and other doctors argued that they had only acted as scientists doing research under the orders of the Nazi leaders. But that argument did not convince the judges. Although in European penal systems no crime has been committed unless a prior law defines it, in Nuremberg the principle of humanity took precedence and overruled the postulate *nullum crimen, nulla poena sine praevia lege.* In other words, it was clear to the magistrates that an exception to the principle of legality was required, in view of the exceptional gravity of the crimes committed. The judges also understood that the defendants bore individual responsibility for those outrageous crimes and thus must be punished for them.

On August 20, 1947, the sentences were handed down. Seven defendants were sentenced to death by hanging, including Brandt. Seven others were acquitted, and the rest received prison sentences.[189] It was a powerful image to see a medical doctor on the gallows, considering that he was a man supposedly dedicated to science and reason but condemned for crimes carried out during the twisted exercise of his profession. In short, he had committed the ultimate betrayal of his Hippocratic Oath. That shocking scene, however, contained a very clear message: from that point on in history, doctors could no longer use their professional status to justify doing to their patients whatever they saw fit. That reasoning was the origin of the Nuremberg Code, which establishes ten basic ethical principles that every doctor must follow. The first point states that any experiment on human beings must have the informed consent of the patient.[190] This was an important legacy of the trial.

More than three hundred Nazi doctors committed crimes while practicing their profession, but only twenty were tried at Nuremberg.[191] This does not mean that all the others came out as unscathed as Mengele. American, British, and French courts tried lower-ranking

---

189 Ibid., p. 296.
190 Norbert Ehrenfreund, op. cit., p. 149.
191 Vivien Spitz, op. cit., p. 50.

Nazis in their respective occupation zones, although how many of them were doctors is not precisely known. In total, more than five thousand Germans were convicted of war crimes or crimes against humanity; from these, almost eight hundred received the death penalty. The Allied forces also extradited Nazis to other countries, mainly Poland and France, to be tried by the courts of the places where they had committed their crimes.[192] This happened to Dr. Erwin von Helmersen, a former colleague of Mengele's. The two had very similar backgrounds, as both had been SS doctors, had worked at Auschwitz-Birkenau, and had been arrested by the Americans at the end of the war. However, there was a striking difference between them: Helmersen was deported to Poland, sentenced to death by a court in Krakow, and executed in April 1949.[193] Mengele, who had been his boss in the "gypsy camp," lived in hiding unscathed on the Bavarian farm. This begs the important question: How did Mengele manage to evade the occupying forces and escape justice in the post-war period? One initial answer is that Mengele was not actively sought after the war, despite his name appearing on two lists. Added at the request of the Polish authorities, his was the 240th name in List 8. Mengele was also on the list of the Central Registry of War Criminals and Security Suspects (CROWCASS), an Allied organization that coordinated efforts to find those who had committed crimes during World War II.[194] The truth is that the US authorities who were part of the occupying forces in Günzburg were unable to find him on their first attempt and gave up the search. Moreover, the Americans initially didn't even have a clear picture of the crimes he had committed.[195]

The survivors, however, knew in detail of his conduct in Auschwitz and were ready to denounce him. The opportunity arose in December

---

192 Tony Judt, op. cit., p. 67.

193 Carola Sachse, op. cit., pp. 228–29.

194 *In the Matter of Josef Mengele: A Report to the Attorney General of the United States*, op. cit., p. 41.

195 Ibid., p. 61.

1946, when the Austrian newspaper *Der Neue Weg* published a story claiming that Mengele had been arrested in Germany. Although false, the news spread like wildfire through dry grass. The newspaper asked for information about the activities of "one of the greatest war criminals" and requested that any reports be sent to a committee of former concentration-camp inmates in Vienna. The Hungarian newspaper *Vilagossag* reproduced the story, followed by other press outlets. Survivors began sending their testimonies about Mengele's atrocities to Vienna. In a matter of months, victims in Romania, the Netherlands, the United States, and Austria itself had reported what they had witnessed or experienced at Mengele's hands. The Jewish Telegraphic Agency went one step further and published an article stating that the Polish government had asked the US authorities in Germany to extradite Mengele to Poland. Quickly, a group of victims volunteered to serve as witnesses in court. The news also reached the refugee camps in Europe, and several survivors in those camps came forward to testify against Mengele. The news of Mengele's extradition request, although also false, set in motion a trail to record real, yet unimaginable, suffering.

Gisella Perl, the gynecologist who worked as Mengele's assistant, had moved to the United States. She read in a New York newspaper about the arrest of her former boss and the request for witnesses to send in their accounts. Dr. Perl decided to contact the US Army. She wrote a letter offering herself as a witness against "the most vicious mass murderer of the 20th century." She wrote:

> For a long year, I was a prisoner in Auschwitz and was forced to act as a doctor under his command. In this capacity, I had every opportunity to observe Dr. Mengele at his most bestial acts.

Gisella's offer landed on the desk of General Telford Taylor, the American prosecutor who conducted the Doctors' Trial at the Nuremberg Tribunal. He replied that "our records show that Mengele died in October 1946."[196]

---

196 Ibid., pp. 83–85.

"Death" suited Mengele, as there could be no better hiding place than the afterlife, and his own family began to endorse the story. When Mengele's father was arrested, he stated that his son was missing. But Karl Mengele knew what had happened to his firstborn and lied to the denazification authorities to protect him. Irene also went about her life acting like a widow: she only wore black and asked the Günzburg bureaucrats to declare that her husband had died in the war.[197] But her request didn't have the desired outcome, and Mengele's ghost hung over the courts in Europe. He was a conspicuous absence from the Auschwitz trials conducted by the Polish government beginning in March 1947. He was perhaps the only camp doctor to disappear without a trace.[198]

The first defendant in these trials was Rudolf Höss, the commandant of Auschwitz, extradited to Poland by the British authorities. He was convicted in Warsaw and executed near his former office. In a second, much larger trial in Krakow, the Poles tried forty former Auschwitz employees, including several doctors. Of those convicted, twenty-three received the death penalty and six were sentenced to life imprisonment. Only one doctor was cleared, Dr. Hans Münch, a colleague of Mengele's who had refused to take part in the selections. If Mengele had really been arrested and extradited to Poland, he would have been among those convicted. But the Poles never requested the American authorities in Germany to extradite Mengele, perhaps because they believed him to be dead.

Contradictory information and the chaotic postwar conditions provided the perfect opportunity for anyone who wanted to join the flow of immigrants leaving Europe. Furthermore, it was easy to obtain false identity documents or prisoner-of-war discharge papers in the black market. Many Nazis had not yet been identified and could blend in with the refugees. Smugglers got rich offering an escape route from Germany, through Italian ports, to South America. Those who wanted to use the famous "ratlines" to escape Europe needed money to secure a

---

197 Ibid., p. 110.
198 Ibid., p. 114.

142 = HIDING MENGELE

guide, clandestine accommodation, and false documents at each stop. Mengele embarked on one of those lines, with all the financial support a wealthy family could provide. He left Bavaria, went as far south as Austria, crossed the border through the town of Brenner, entered Italy, and traveled all the way to Genoa, where he found a ship headed to Argentina. He was carrying a Red Cross passport bearing the false name of Helmut Gregor issued by the Swiss consulate. He didn't have to explain a whole lot at the consulate, as the official seemed to have heard the same story a few times before:

> You want a Red Cross passport to emigrate to South America because, as a South Tyrolean, you don't have a defined nationality and you can't get a German or Italian passport. Your identity card, issued in the town of Bressanone, serves as the basis for your application, which will be accepted because, according to the statute, the Red Cross will help all people in need, without carrying out an extensive investigation.[199]

On May 26, 1949, Mengele boarded the *North King* for his new life in South America. Juan Domingo Perón had already been in power in Argentina for three years. Sympathetic to Nazism, he welcomed fugitives from the Third Reich with open arms. Among them, the one who seemed to have left the deepest impression on Argentinians was not Mengele, but Adolf Eichmann, the SS lieutenant colonel who organized the logistics of transporting Jews to the concentration camps.

---

199 Ibid., pp. 121–23.

11

NAZIS IN BUENOS AIRES

The mysterious organization known as Odessa, a vast and powerful underground network that supposedly helped former SS members, was just a fantasy in the imagination of Nazi hunters and those who felt nostalgic for Hitler's regime. In the prison camps of postwar Europe, "Odessa" was a password used by former SS members to identify each other; over time, it became a mythical entity fed by books and movies. In recent years, the disclosure of secret documents in the United States and Europe has confirmed that it really never existed as some imagined it. What did exist was an escape route to South America supported by various institutions, among them the Vatican.[200]

It is also true that Nazis—and Germans in general—formed communities in different parts of the Americas. It was just natural, then, that former German officers helped each other in the new places where they lived. But relationships were fluid, and varied according to each one's personal contacts. There was no prearranged network set up by the SS leadership to help its members in case of need. Rather,

---

200 Bettina Stangneth, op. cit., p. 89, 159.

they relied on the goodwill of local sympathizers of the late Third Reich. Foremost among these was the president of Argentina himself, Juan Domingo Perón. The Argentinean president was a longtime admirer of Benito Mussolini, had read extensively about Nazism, and devoured books about the Führer, including *Mein Kampf.* Because of his admiration, Perón considered the Nuremberg Tribunal an infamy and created a scheme to facilitate the escape of Nazis to his distant country.[201] As soon as he came to power in 1946, Perón named a priest from the Catholic Church to be in charge of the Argentine immigration delegation in Europe, which was based in Rome. Father José Clemente Silva was instructed to organize the transfer of four million Europeans to Argentina and given a special recommendation: to carry out the clandestine transportation of undocumented people. This is how a large contingent of Nazis arrived in Buenos Aires after World War II.[202]

The Argentine capital proudly considered itself the Paris of South America, largely because of its architecture and cultural refinement, as attested by its numerous theaters, bookstores, and widely circulated newspapers. Buenos Aires could be seen as a lonely outpost of European civilization, as President Domingo Sarmiento had described it at the end of the nineteenth century. All of Buenos Aires's splendor was born during its golden age, when the country was a major exporter of leather, meat, and agricultural products, and lived up to the promise of being a powerhouse on the American continent. The port on the River Plate estuary integrated the country into the international market and, in 1880, the Argentinian Congress chose the city to be the capital of the Argentine Republic. Perón's Buenos Aires kept the legacy of the nation's glorious past, adding to it the effervescence of the workers' movement and unions under the state's tutelage.

With his charisma and easy appeal to the crowds, Perón attracted thousands of people to the speeches he gave from the balcony of the

---

201 Uki Goñi, *The Real Odessa: How Perón Brought the Nazi War Criminals to Argentina.* London: Granta, 2003, pp. 17, 396.

202 Ibid., pp. 392–93.

Casa Rosada, the presidential palace, alongside his second wife, Evita, who soon became a national icon. However, while Perón wanted to go down in history as the leader who galvanized the masses, he preferred to hide another aspect of his identity from official records: his personal relationship with Nazis.[203] One of them was Hans-Ulrich Rudel, the most decorated pilot in the Luftwaffe, the German Air Force, who had lived in Buenos Aires since 1948. Rudel helped modernize the Argentine Air Force and, in return, won government contracts and licenses. He was sympathetic to comrades newly arrived from Germany and partnered with Konstantin von Neurath, son of the German foreign minister in the early years of the Nazi regime, to set up an emergency fund to assist them. The two men's effort included sending packages, money transfers, and legal representation. Rudel's friendship with Perón greatly facilitated this work, which helped many friends, including Mengele.[204]

Hans-Ulrich Rudel.
Yad Vashem Photo Archive, Jerusalem.

---

203 A lot of documentation was destroyed in the last days of the Perón government, in 1955, in an attempt to erase the traces of the link with the Nazis, as Uki Goñi showed in *The Real Odessa*.

204 Bettina Stangneth, op. cit., p. 110.

The Nazi escapees easily blended in with the population of Buenos Aires, given its considerable number of European immigrants. Furthermore, a large German community had settled in the city and its surroundings since before the war, and thus it wasn't unusual to hear the German language in the streets. The question that remained was what to do with so many idle former Nazi officers, but Perón found a solution for that problem. The government hired Capri, a newly created company run by Argentines and Germans, to build a hydroelectric dam in the city of Tucumán, in northern Argentina. In reality, it was a place of employment for technocrats of the Third Reich; former SS Lieutenant Colonel Adolf Eichmann, for example, was among its employees. Argentinians joked that the company's name, Compañía Argentina para Proyectos y Realizaciones Industriales—CAPRI (literally, Argentinean Company for Industrial Projects and Realizations, i.e., Enterprises)—should be changed to Compañía Alemana para Recién-Inmigrados (German Company for New Immigrants).[205] Perón's connections with the Nazis were extensive, and Mengele himself may have had close ties with the Argentinian leader. Toward the end of his life, Perón told a journalist that a genetics expert used to visit the Olivos presidential residence and entertained him with tales of his amazing achievements. The president said also that, if he remembered correctly, Gregor was the name of the proud Bavarian.[206]

Helmut Gregor, again, was precisely the name on Mengele's Red Cross passport and the name he went by during his early years in Buenos Aires. When he arrived in the city in September 1949, he had some trouble with a customs agent who wanted to inspect one of his suitcases, precisely the one containing his research notes. Mengele argued that they were just "biology notes." Not understanding a word, the official shrugged his shoulders and released him. In his new country, Mengele preferred to hide his status as a doctor,

---

205 Ibid., p. 106.
206 Uki Goñi, op. cit., pp. 162, 411–12.

and the first job he got was as a carpenter in the municipality of Vicente López, in the northern part of Greater Buenos Aires, an area traditionally associated with the upper class. The advantage was that the job entitled him to a bedroom, which he shared with an engineer. His roommate suspected that he was a doctor because he saw some medical equipment in his luggage. Mengele tried to deny it, but finally revealed that he was indeed a doctor when the engineer's daughter fell ill and needed care. Mengele wrote about these details in his diary before he took a long pause, only resuming writing some ten years later.[207]

After the first few grim weeks, Mengele moved to a better place: a colonial-style house in the Florida neighborhood, also in Vicente López. The owner was Gerard Malbranc, a Nazi sympathizer who opened his doors to a circle of Argentinians and Germans who admired the Third Reich. One new friend led to another until Mengele had a fairly wide network of protectors. One of the first people he met was the Dutch journalist Willem Sassen, who had also belonged to the SS. Sassen had become famous among Nazi Germans for writing articles for the extreme right-wing magazine *Der Weg*, which was published in Buenos Aires and distributed illegally in West Germany. Sassen introduced Mengele to Adolf Eichmann and Hans-Ulrich Rudel. Mengele's relationship with Eichmann did not flourish, but his friendship with Rudel did. The latter even accompanied Mengele on his first trips to Paraguay in search of customers for the agricultural machinery of Mengele's father's company in Germany. Rudel, Hitler's most prized pilot, was very well connected, not only with Perón, but also with the Paraguayan dictator Alfredo Stroessner, who was the son of a Bavarian immigrant.

After five years living under the name Helmut Gregor, a simple bureaucratic procedure led Mengele to feel more at ease and less concerned with maintaining his disguise. In 1954, Irene filed for divorce in Germany, and he had to sign a power of attorney at the embassy

---

207 Gerald Posner and John Ware, op. cit., pp. 94–96.

under his real name.[208] The marriage couldn't stand the distance, let alone the clandestine life, and Irene wanted to marry another man. Mengele agreed. Afterwards, he rented half of a house in Olivos, an area in Greater Buenos Aires where many Germans lived, and began to receive visitors from Europe: his father, Karl; company employee Hans Sedlmeier; brother Alois; and sister-in-law Ruth. With family money, Mengele invested in a small carpentry workshop. The business began to thrive and eventually employed half a dozen people.[209] Everything seemed to be going well until, in September 1955, a coup d'état forced Perón to flee Argentina and go into exile. It was a shock for the Buenos Aires Nazi community, who feared what might happen now that they had lost their protector. Their fear, however, soon proved to be unfounded. The newly installed military dictatorship in Argentina closed the National Congress and deposed the members of the Supreme Court, but maintained the Nazis' status quo.

The year after the coup, Mengele embarked on a trip to Switzerland where he met with his son, Rolf; his nephew Karl-Heinz; and his brother Karl's widow, Martha. It was the first and apparently last time that Mengele returned to Europe after the war. It appears that he traveled as Helmut Gregor, the name he had used in Argentina. However, he introduced himself to the children as "Uncle Fritz." Martha obviously knew his real identity (he had been her brother-in-law), and soon they became close and were practically a couple. A few months after the trip, Mengele felt safe enough to live openly under his real name in Buenos Aires. Determined to bury Helmut Gregor, he applied for an Argentine identity card and, to do this, needed a document from the German embassy to prove that he really was Josef Mengele. Everything worked out, and he was issued his new document without any problem. This episode makes it clear that the German authorities knew exactly of Mengele's whereabouts then.

---

208 *In the Matter of Josef Mengele: A Report to the Attorney General of the United States*, op. cit., p. 127.

209 Gerald Posner and John Ware, op. cit., pp. 107–8.

With his new identity card, Mengele was able to get a mortgage to buy a house in Olivos, near the Argentine presidential residence. Martha and Karl-Heinz moved to Buenos Aires so they could all live together. Mengele's father offered him money to become a partner in a pharmaceutical company called Fadro Farm, and later he had the opportunity to work in medical research again, conducting studies for the treatment of tuberculosis—but this time not on human beings, as he had done in Auschwitz.[210] Mengele's new life was beginning to take shape. In July 1958, he traveled with Martha to Uruguay, where they were officially married in Nueva Helvecia, a Swiss settlement eighty miles from Montevideo. The couple spent eight days there and then returned to Buenos Aires.[211] Newly married, a partner in a company, a homeowner, and with a stepson at his side, Mengele seemed to have put down roots. His comfortable and quiet lifestyle, however, would eventually come to an end, thanks to some people who were determined not to let his heinous crimes committed in Auschwitz be forgotten.

WHILE MENGELE WAS SETTLING DOWN in Argentina, justice in West Germany was in its infancy when it came to taking the first steps against Nazi war criminals. In August 1958, a month after his wedding in Uruguay, ten members of an Einsatzkommando were tried in Ulm, a town less than twenty-five miles from Günzburg, where Mengele was born. The Einsatzkommandos were mobile extermination units responsible for some of the most gruesome scenes of World War II. These death squads would advance alongside German troops and shoot the Jews, initially only the men, and then the entire Jewish

210 Ibid., pp. 112 and 115.

211 Andrés Lópes Reilly, "Josef Mengele: Los ocho días que el 'ángel de la muerte' vivió en Uruguay." *La Nación*, April 2, 2021. Available at: <www.lanacion.com.ar/el-mundo/josef-mengele-los-ocho-dias-que-el-angel-de-la-muerte-vivio-en-uruguay-nid02042021/>. Accessed on: July 13, 2023.

community of small towns all over Eastern Europe.[212] It is estimated that 1.5 million people died in this way.[213]

The trial in Ulm happened by chance. The main defendant, Bernhard Fischer-Schweder, had lost his job as commandant of a refugee camp in that city and filed a lawsuit to get his job back in the civil service. However, his lawsuit backfired: not only was he denied his job back, but his nefarious past as an SS officer and police chief came to light. Schweder had commanded the Tilsit Einsatzkommando, which was responsible for the deaths of 5,502 civilians in Lithuania in 1941. He and nine other comrades were sentenced to between three and fifteen years in prison,[214] punishments that seem small in relation to the extent of the crimes committed. The reason for the light sentences was that the German criminal code considered those who pulled the trigger to be only accomplices or accessories to the murders, while the Nazi leaders were found to be the real culprits.[215] Nevertheless, what really matters in this case is that it was the first major trial of mass extermination crimes in a German court.[216] This may have been enough to worry Mengele, since it showed that at least part of German society was beginning to see the Nazi war crimes with different eyes. If most Germans had previously kept absolute silence for fear of having to bear the collective guilt for the Holocaust, now they supported the punishment of war criminals. In this sense, the Ulm trial was a

---

212 "Introduction to the Holocaust." United States Holocaust Memorial Museum. Available at: <encyclopedia.ushmm.org/content/pt-br/article/introduction-to-the -holocaust>. Accessed on: July 13, 2023.

213 Hannah Arendt, op. cit., p. 123.

214 "Der Ulmer Prozess." Stadt Ulm. Available at: <www.ulm.de/tourismus/stad tgeschichte/schicksalstage-und-orte/der-ulmer-prozess>. Accessed on: July 13, 2023.

215 David G. Marwell, *Mengele: Unmasking the "Angel of Death."* New York: W. W. Norton & Company, 2020, p. 173.

216 Interview given by Dieter Pohl to Sonia Phalnikar. "Interview." Deutsche Welle, May 20 2008. Available at: <www.dw.com/en/landmark-trial-pushed -germany-to-tackle-nazi-past/a-3349537>. Accessed on: July 13, 2023.

watershed in West Germany, as the country began to come to terms with its Nazi past.

The first practical consequences of this change ensued very quickly. In December 1958, the Central Office for the Investigation of Nazi Crimes, based in Ludwigsburg, was created by initiative of ministers of justice and senators of German states. The discovery of criminals living free in German society would no longer be left to chance. Rather, the work of identifying and bringing to justice those responsible for war crimes would now be systematized. First, prosecutors would evaluate complaints from all over the world, identify who should be prosecuted, conduct preliminary investigations, and then distribute the cases to the competent jurisdictions, according to the defendant's address.[217] Erwin Schüle, the public prosecutor at the trial in Ulm, became the first head of the Office, which still operates today and has as its main objective to find all perpetrators and accomplices of murders committed during the Third Reich, regardless of the accused's age.[218] For this reason, we still see in the news Germans—now almost all centenarians, since the Third Reich ended seventy-nine years ago—who worked in concentration camps being brought before a court. As the current head of the Central Office put it, when there is an accusation of murder in Germany, it is not a matter of choice whether or not to prosecute: it is a legal obligation.[219]

Among the many letters sent to the Central Office, there was one written by Ernst Schnabel, author of a successful book about the famous Jewish teenager Anne Frank. Schnabel had received a complaint against Mengele from an anonymous young reader and decided to take it to court because he believed that Mengele had been one of the cruelest people in Auschwitz. Erwin Schüle took the matter

---

217 "Task/Preliminary Investigations." Zentrale Stelle der Ländesjustizverwaltungen zur Auflarung nationalsozialistischer Verbrechen. Available at: <zentrale -stelle-ludwigsburg.justiz-bw.de/pb/,Len/Start-page/Arbeitsweise-Translate /Task+_+Preliminary+Investigations>. Accessed on: July 13, 2023.

218 "Der Ulmer Prozess", op. cit.

219 Interview with Thomas Will, conducted on October 18, 2021.

very seriously and sent the complaint to the competent authority, in this case the public prosecutor's office in Memmingen, a town near Günzburg. The head of the Central Office told the local prosecutor that he had received information that Mengele's father had had a car shipped to his son in Argentina, and therefore the customs authorities should know where he lived. He advised, however, that the investigation should be carried out without alerting the family. The police in Günzburg complied with the request and sent to the public prosecutor's office in Memmingen a dossier on Mengele, which included the address registered at the time of his divorce: 1875 Calle Sarmiento, Olivos.[220]

At the same time that the Central Office received the first accusation against Mengele, another accusation reached the Freiburg prosecutor's desk, thanks to the tireless efforts of one man: Hermann Langbein. In addition to being a Holocaust survivor and secretary-general of the International Auschwitz Committee, Langbein had acted as secretary to Dr. Eduard Wirths, the camp's chief doctor. Because of his position, Langbein was able to see Mengele's work up close and wrote a letter listing nine criminal charges against him. As he didn't know Mengele's current whereabouts, Langbein turned to the Freiburg prosecutor, since Mengele had lived there with Irene before going to war. With Langbein's help, the prosecutor took six months to prepare the case and, on February 25, 1959, obtained an arrest warrant for Mengele.[221]

At the same time, in early 1959, Fritz Bauer, who later achieved worldwide fame as the Frankfurt attorney general, also received documents about Auschwitz, including a list of the SS members who had worked in the camp. Bauer had a keen interest in the subject, as he himself was Jewish and had only survived the Holocaust because he managed to flee Nazi Germany. Determined to oversee the case, the attorney general appealed to the Federal Court of Justice, which agreed to transfer all investigations of the concentration camp to the

---

220 David G. Marwell, op. cit., p. 175.

221 Ibid., p. 176.

Frankfurt Public Prosecutor's Office.[222] Finally, German justice was interested in finding out what had happened in the largest Nazi extermination camp.

The preparation for the great Auschwitz trial was long. In the first year alone, more than 350 witnesses were heard in Germany and abroad. The more survivors spoke, the more Mengele's name came up. On the basis of new allegations, on June 5, 1959, the court in Freiburg issued the second arrest warrant against him.[223] The order circulated through German police stations and reached the Foreign Ministry. Two days later, the authorities in Bonn contacted the embassy in Buenos Aires. It seemed that the request for Mengele's extradition would be a swift process, but it stalled right from the start. The German ambassador at the time was Werner Junkers, a former Nazi who had been the Reich Foreign Minister's plenipotentiary in Yugoslavia. He claimed that he didn't remember anything to do with Mengele. On top of that, the embassy only had outdated addresses for Mengele. Due to this lack of interest in the case, the German authorities' request took more than a year to actually reach Buenos Aires.[224] Since the Argentine authorities didn't know where Mengele was, West Germany offered a reward of 20,000 Deutschmarks to anyone who provided information leading to his capture. It was the first time that the German government offered money to catch a Nazi criminal.[225]

At this point, the German and international press finally became interested in Mengele's case. The story attracted considerable attention: an SS doctor, accused of horrific crimes at Auschwitz, had survived the war, but had disappeared in South America with the support of his bourgeois family and local governments.

However, a month before the second arrest order, Mengele was no longer in Argentina. He left Martha and Karl-Heinz behind

---

222 Sven Keller, op. cit., p. 123.
223 Ibid., p. 125.
224 Gerald Posner and John Ware, op. cit., pp. 150–51.
225 Ibid., p. 155.

and moved alone to Hohenau, a small town in Paraguay founded by immigrants of German origin who had left the Brazilian state of Rio Grande do Sul at the beginning of the twentieth century. For more than a year, he was given shelter on the farm of a card-carrying Nazi, Alban Krug, who was introduced to him by his well-connected friend Hans-Ulrich Rudel. In that distant corner of the world, having entered the country on a ninety-day visa, Mengele toured the farms trying to sell his father's agricultural machinery. However, with an arrest warrant against him in Germany and a request for extradition, it no longer seemed feasible to live in Buenos Aires. Mengele considered that it was too dangerous to continue living in the Argentine capital and applied for Paraguayan citizenship. There was no extradition agreement between West Germany and Paraguay, and dictator Alfredo Stroessner, despite his German ties, would not extradite one of his citizens.[226] Mengele would be safe and able to avoid prison. But there was one caveat: in order to obtain Paraguayan citizenship, he had to have lived in the country for at least five years. This impasse was quickly resolved with the help of two friends: Werner Jung, a German Nazi sympathizer who had immigrated to Paraguay before the war, and Alejandro von Eckstein, a former captain in the Paraguayan Army and friend of the dictator Stroessner. They both attested that Mengele had been living near Asunción for almost six years.[227] It was a lie, but it had its desired effect: in November 1959, the request was granted, and the fugitive from German justice became the Paraguayan citizen "José Mengele."

IN BUENOS AIRES, THE NAZI community was no longer the same as in Perón's heyday. Reich supporters began to shun Eichmann, for which Klaus, Eichmann's eldest son, blamed Mengele. According to Klaus, Mengele had told his acquaintances that it was too risky to be close

226 Ibid., pp. 119 and 125–26.
227 Ibid., pp. 105 and 126. op. cit., pp. 331–32.

to Eichmann.[228] The atmosphere had also changed substantially in Germany after the Ulm trial. There was now much greater interest in prosecuting Nazi criminals. For this reason, Mengele distanced himself from Eichmann and all his other former associates from Buenos Aires. In his diary, he recorded that his friends thought he was overreacting by fleeing Argentina to live in Paraguay. The truth is that Mengele's caution kept him safe, while Eichmann's shoddy disguise, under the false name of Ricardo Klement, led him to be found, arrested, put on trial, and hanged.

---

[228] Bettina Stangneth, op. cit.

12

OPERATION EICHMANN

With the determination of someone who had founded a country and won a war, David Ben-Gurion decided that the time had come to deal with an unresolved issue from the past. The Israeli prime minister summoned the head of the new nation's intelligence agency and made a special request: to capture one of the most wanted Nazis so that he could be tried in an Israeli court. Ben-Gurion didn't say who should be caught, preferring not to single out any particular individual. He only emphasized that the criminal had to arrive in the country alive. He knew that the trial of a former Third Reich officer in Jerusalem would have an enormous historical impact.[229] The year was 1957, and, at that time, there was much speculation that prominent Nazis had managed to escape from Europe and were leading free lives, especially in Latin America. The list of bigwigs thought to be still at large included Martin Bormann, Hitler's private secretary; Heinrich Müller, head of

---

229 Interview with Rafi Eitan, Mossad operations commander, conducted on March 29, 2017.

the Gestapo; Adolf Eichmann, responsible for the logistics of deporting Jews to concentration camps; and, of course, Josef Mengele.[230]

The first order that Isser Harel, the Mossad commander, gave to his team was to gather all the information they had on the fugitives. This was a secret mission as, in fact, was the very existence of the Mossad. Other intelligence services, such as the CIA, knew and admired the Israeli agency, especially after the remarkable feat it had accomplished a year earlier: obtaining a copy of Nikita Khrushchev's speech that revealed the horrors Joseph Stalin had carried out in the Soviet Union.[231] Despite the Mossad's great merit, Ben-Gurion forbade anyone to speak publicly about the agency responsible for spying and collecting information abroad for his government. The operations were kept under wraps, without any disclosure or parliamentary approval, because the Israeli leader firmly believed that the security of the young state, surrounded by enemy Arab countries, depended on absolute discretion. That level of secrecy was kept until the Mossad executed the spectacular kidnapping of Eichmann in Buenos Aires. After that episode, the Mossad and its efficiency became famous all over the world.[232]

Among all the notable Nazis on the run, Eichmann was Mossad's first target for the simple reason that the agency discovered his address before others'.[233] It all started with a coincidence—or, more precisely, a youthful infatuation. Klaus, Eichmann's eldest son, attended the same school as Sylvia, the daughter of Lothar Hermann, a German Jew who had moved to Argentina before World War II. The teenagers were close, and the young man often visited the Hermann family home in the suburb of Olivos. On several occasions, he made anti-Semitic

---

230 Decades later, it was proven that Bormann and Müller had been dead since 1945.

231 Rafi Eitan, *Capturing Eichmann: The Memoirs of a Mossad Spymaster.* Newbury: Greenhill, 2002, p. 181.

232 Ronen Bergman, *Rise and Kill First: The Secret History of Israel's Targeted Assassinations.* New York: Random House, 2018, pp. 31–32.

233 Interview with Rafi Eitan.

comments, lamenting that the Nazis hadn't wiped out the Jews once and for all, and one day he mentioned that his father had held an important position in the Third Reich. That was the most he ever revealed about his family, and he never invited Sylvia into his home.[234] Hermann, who had lost his parents and siblings in the Holocaust, began to do his own detective work to find out who that boy was. He had already read in the Argentinian press that Eichmann lived in Buenos Aires and, after a little digging, found out that Klaus was the Nazi official's son. Hermann decided to denounce Eichmann and secretly wrote letters warning of Eichmann's whereabouts to authorities in Germany and Israel, but was ignored by both countries.

It's unclear how one of these letters landed in the hands of Fritz Bauer, the attorney general in Frankfurt. The fact is that Bauer took the matter seriously and began to correspond with Hermann. In June 1957, the prosecutor took the first concrete step to verify the information he had and questioned Eichmann's mother-in-law, who confirmed that her daughter had moved to America. The pieces seemed to fit together. Bauer then approached the Central Office for the Investigation of Nazi Crimes to request that the Interpol conduct an international search. The Central Office's response hit like a bucket of cold water. Given that the institution itself housed former Nazis and thus had no enthusiasm for pursuing them, the Office informed Bauer that it could not comply with his request. The reason offered was that Eichmann was accused of "crimes of a political and racial nature," which lay beyond the scope of Interpol's activities.[235] From then on, Bauer understood that he could not trust the German authorities to carry out this investigation, so he made a bold decision: to collaborate with the Israelis. The prosecutor had the support of the prime minister of the German state of Hesse, Georg August Zinn. The problem was that passing on information about Eichmann to a

234 Uki Goñi, op. cit., p. 387; Gerald Posner and John Ware, op. cit., p. 137.
235 Bettina Stangneth, op. cit., pp. 315–17.

foreign intelligence service, without alarming his own countrymen, was not a simple task.

The Holocaust survivor and Nazi hunter Simon Wiesenthal had already informed the Mossad that Eichmann was in the Argentine capital, but he didn't have his address.[236] A partnership with Bauer could solve this issue, so a Mossad official agreed to travel to Frankfurt in November 1957 to meet with the prosecutor. The meeting took place in a secret location and was the beginning of a fruitful partnership, despite the obstacles the operation faced when it first started.

On their first mission, in January 1958, one of the agents realized that the address provided by Bauer was incorrect. On their second attempt, they found out that Hermann was blind as a result of the beatings he had suffered from the Gestapo in the Dachau concentration camp.[237] This realization took away a lot of his credibility—after all, how could he have identified Eichmann if he couldn't see?[238] Harel was reluctant to continue the investigation in such a distant place and at such a high cost to the agency, which had a limited budget. But Bauer decided to lobby hard for Israel to take action before the Nazi escaped again. In December 1959, he traveled to Jerusalem and complained directly to Israel's attorney general, Chaim Cohen. Bauer said that he had confirmed with a former SS informant that Eichmann was indeed living in Buenos Aires, under the false name of Ricardo Klement. The attorney general asked Harel to reopen the case.[239] He eventually gave in and sent the head of Mossad investigations, Zvi Aharoni, to Argentina. In addition to hidden cameras and communications equipment, Aharoni had the support of a local team: historian Ephraim Ilani, military attaché Yitzhak Elron, and young members of the Argentine Zionist movement who were about to immigrate to

---

236 Interview with Rafi Eitan.

237 Uki Goñi, op. cit., p. 387.

238 Ronen Steinke, Fritz Bauer, *The Jewish Prosecutor Who Brought Eichmann and Auschwitz to Trial*. Bloomington: Indiana University Press, 2020, pp. 4–5.

239 Gerald Posner and John Ware, op. cit., p. 138.

Israel and knew Buenos Aires and the customs of the country well.[240] Aharoni stayed in the city between February and April 1960 and was key to finding Eichmann, for he discovered that the Nazi had moved and was now living at 6061 Garibaldi Street in San Fernando, on the outskirts of the city. With a plan devised down to its smallest detail, a Mossad team landed in the Argentine capital to kidnap the man they called by the codename Dybbuk—in Hebrew, an evil spirit that takes possession of a person.

On the evening of May 11, 1960, Eichmann got off the bus on his way home from work at the Mercedes-Benz factory, as he did every day with clockwork precision. It just so happened that he was running a little late on this occasion, as it was past eight o'clock in the evening. He was walking home with one hand in his pocket when Zvi Malchin, one of the agents, approached him, saying, "Momentito, señor" ("One moment, sir").[241] He then grabbed Eichmann's hands, pushed him into a ditch, and jumped on top of him. The head of the operation, Rafi Eitan, was right behind him. Eichmann screamed, but there was no one around to hear him. He was thrown into a car, where another agent was already waiting. It was Aharoni, who warned him in German not to cause any trouble or he would be executed on the spot.[242] It was a bluff, as their mission was to take him alive to Israel. Eichmann only replied: "I accept my fate."[243]

The way to get him to the other side of the world without raising suspicions had been planned in detail beforehand. There were two options: by sea, using a ship that transported meat from Argentina to Israel; or by air, on an airplane belonging to the Israeli company El

---

240 Rafi Eitan, op. cit., p. 132.

241 Ibid., p. 154.

242 Ronen Bergman, op. cit., pp. 58–59.

243 Aron Heller, "Mossad Opens Archives on Eichmann Capture." *Times of Israel*, February 8, 2012. Available at: <www.timesofisrael.com/mossad-opens-archives -on-eichmann-capture>. Accessed on: October 24, 2022; Gerald Posner and John Ware, op. cit., p. 140.

Al, which had the disadvantage of not having regular flights between the two countries.[244] The Mossad commander opted for the second choice and found a perfect pretext for a chartered flight: fly a delegation of Israeli dignitaries to Argentina for the celebrations of the 150th anniversary of the country's independence. No diplomat could have imagined that the aircraft would then be used for an international hijacking. There was still a small problem: the plane would only return on the 20th.

During the nine-day wait, Eichmann was held captive in a rented house and interrogated by Aharoni, who had been the chief interrogator for the Shin Bet, Israel's internal security service. The Mossad hoped to gather more information about Mengele. Bauer had found out that he was in Argentina, but the agents didn't have his address. Lying shamelessly, Eichmann said he had no idea who Mengele was. Harel didn't much care for Eichmann's claim, for he was obsessed with capturing not only one Nazi, but two: he wanted to take Mengele on the same plane as Eichmann. Rafi was completely against it, as he believed that a second kidnapping could jeopardize an operation that was, so far, successful.

Harel was obstinate and made up an excuse to call the Buenos Aires police and ask for information about Mengele. To his surprise, they provided Mengele's address and said that, until recently, the doctor had lived in the city under his real name. The commander decided to put Aharoni in charge of finding out Mengele's whereabouts, and Rafi unwillingly gave up his chief interrogator for this new mission. One of Mengele's neighbors informed Aharoni that he was on vacation and should be back in a few days. At the time, Mengele was actually living in Paraguay but often came back to visit his wife, Martha, and stepson, Karl-Heinz, so there was a chance that the Mossad might get their hands on him.

The decision was made then to take Eichmann to Israel right away and then return to get Mengele. Rafi and two other men stood by

---

[244] Interview with Rafi Eitan.

in Buenos Aires in case he showed up.[245] On the departure day, the agents drugged Eichmann and took him to Ezeiza International Airport. They issued a fake Israeli passport for Eichmann and had him wear an airline pilot's uniform. He boarded the El Al charter flight to Israel in first class, giving the impression that he was just an unwell crew member.[246]

Initially, the Mossad was not planning to disclose the arrest to the press until Mengele had also been captured, to prevent him from being tipped off and escaping. When Ben-Gurion was informed of the plan, he asked how many people already knew that Eichmann was in Israel. About sixty, was the answer. He reasoned that these many people, plus their wives and children, amounted to a hundred. Too many people, he thought: it was time to spread the news to the world.[247]

On May 23, 1960, Ben-Gurion addressed the Knesset, the Israeli parliament, and announced the capture of Adolf Eichmann. It was sensational news. Eichmann had been the secretary of the Wannsee Conference, held in January 1942, when Third Reich authorities coordinated efforts to implement the "final solution" to the "Jewish question"—euphemisms for the mass extermination of Jews. Soon after the conference, Eichmann became an expert in the forced removal of civilians. From country to country in Nazi-occupied Europe, the Jews were registered, rounded up, and deported to the extermination centers in the East. Before leaving their home countries, they were declared stateless, which prevented any government from interfering and, at the same time, allowed the country in which they lived to confiscate their property.[248] Twenty years later, this same man was in Israel, a country founded by the people he had tried to exterminate. But instead of revenge, the Israelis prepared all the legal formalities for a trial, including the right to a defense.

---

245 Rafi Eitan, op. cit., p. 163.

246 Aron Heller, op. cit.

247 Interview with Rafi Eitan.

248 Hannah Arendt, op. cit., pp. 130–31.

In a meeting with his cabinet, less than a week after the announcement to the Knesset, Ben-Gurion explained the principles that guided him:

> The main point is not punishment, because I don't see an appropriate punishment for these acts. So what if they hang a man who killed millions of children, women, and old people? I think the trial itself is important . . . we must reveal everything that was done to the Jews by the Nazis. All of this must be fully described during the trial. This is necessary for us. There is a new generation that has heard something about it, but has not seen it. It is necessary for us and for the whole world.

He also advocated for the trial to be conducted in accordance with all regular procedures,[249] and his order was carried out to the letter. The police interrogated Eichmann and prepared an investigation, which was submitted to the Public Prosecutor's Office. The government decided that Gideon Hausner, the chief prosecutor, would lead the prosecution.[250] When all this came to light, Mengele disappeared from Argentina for good, and the Mossad agents who had stayed in Buenos Aires never saw him.

THE NEWS OF EICHMANN'S KIDNAPPING hurt international law and Argentina's national pride. As a result, the government took what is considered to be a drastic action in the world of diplomacy: it summoned its ambassador in Tel Aviv, took the matter to the United Nations Security Council, and asked for Eichmann to be returned. The latter demand may seem unimaginable, but the fact is that nothing

---

249 "Special Publication: Behind the Scenes at the Eichmann Trial." Israel State Archives. Available at: <catalog.archives.gov.il/en/chapter/behind-scenes-eichmann-trial/>. Accessed on: July 17, 2023.

250 Ibid.

could be more embarrassing for a country than to suffer such a flagrant violation of its sovereignty. Ben-Gurion knew that the Mossad's mission carried with it the risk of creating animosity between the two nations. To calm the waters, the Israeli government sent Argentina a letter of apology but lied, saying that Argentine Jewish volunteers had captured Eichmann on their own. The story wasn't convincing, though. The Israelis then decided to change their strategy, and pressured the government in Buenos Aires, using the information about Mengele's continued presence in Argentina as proof that the country would not have collaborated had Tel Aviv asked for Eichmann's extradition. As a matter of fact, Germany did request Argentina to extradite Mengele in 1959, but nothing happened. The UN Security Council sided with the Argentines and condemned Israel, asking for appropriate reparation. That UN resolution was enough to begin mending the rift between the two countries and, in August 1960, they issued a joint note announcing that the crisis was over.[251]

The tension in international diplomacy was easing, but it was increasing more than ever in Mengele's life. He knew that the Israelis were after him, so he finally decided to disappear not only from Argentina but also from Paraguay. Mengele calculated that it was only a matter of time before the Mossad arrived at Alban Krug's farm in Hohenau, and his friend, no matter how loyal, would not be able to protect him. "For you the war isn't over yet. Be careful," Krug warned him as they said goodbye. Another friend, the pilot Rudel, was also present at the hasty farewell and provided the contact information for Wolfgang Gerhard, who would later prove to be instrumental in Mengele's escape. Meanwhile, Martha and Karl-Heinz couldn't bear to live as fugitives and decided to return to Europe.[252] It was Mengele's second separation. Once again alone, at the end of October 1960, he crossed the border into Brazil, where he would spend the next eighteen years.

---

251 UN Security Council Resolution 138, June 23, 1960. Ibid.
252 Gerald Posner and John Ware, op. cit. pp. 158–59.

After Eichmann was taken to Israel, Rafi concluded that Mengele would no longer show his face in Argentina but would escape to a nearby country. Instead of betting on Brazil, which would have been an obvious choice, Rafi and his two companions took a train to Chile. They figured it was a beautiful country, more developed than Paraguay and Bolivia, and they had a contact there who could help. However, they couldn't find any clues in Santiago or Valparaíso, so only then did they set off for Rio de Janeiro. After traveling for ten days with no leads, they returned to Israel.[253] Nevertheless, Mengele would never lose his fear of being found by the Jews, even though he lived in remote places, on farms and in the outskirts of urban centers.[254] Eichmann's fate had left a deep impression on him.

IN JERUSALEM, THE TRIAL BEGAN in April 1961 with enormous interest from the world press. Inside a glass booth and wearing a suit and tie, Eichmann heard the fifteen charges against him, which included[255] "crimes against the Jewish people," "crimes against humanity," "war crimes," and "membership in a hostile organization."[256] More than a hundred witnesses gave testimonies, and the prosecutors provided as evidence around 1,600 documents, many of them bearing Eichmann's own signature. Relying on a wealth of detail, the prosecutors presented the judges and the public with the various stages of the Holocaust: the anti-Semitic laws, the incitement to hostility against Jews, the confiscation of property, the imprisonment in ghettos and concentration camps, and, finally, the mass murders. The prosecution demonstrated how Eichmann had been involved in every step of the process

---

253 Rafi Eitan, op. cit., p. 158.

254 Wolfram and Liselotte Bossert's statements to the Federal Police.

255 Eichmann Trial – Session No. 1. Eichmann Trial En. Available at: <www.youtube.com/watch?v=Fv6xbeVozhU>. Accessed on: October 27, 2022.

256 "About the Eichmann Trial." Yad Vashem. Available at: <www.yadva- shem.org/holocaust/eichmann-trial/about.html>. Accessed on: October 27, 2022.

to implement the "final solution." The defense lawyer, the German Robert Servatius, who had defended several Nazis in the Nuremberg trials, did not question the facts or the authenticity of the documents. The line he took was to try to depict Eichmann as a small cog in a great extermination machine. Servatius also tried to defend the idea that Eichmann had had no choice but to obey his superiors' orders. The court rejected these arguments on the grounds that the evidence made it clear that Eichmann fully identified with his duties and had a real obsession with the total annihilation of the Jews. This became especially evident when he took charge of the deportation of hundreds of thousands of Jews from Hungary to Auschwitz in 1944.[257] The court found Eichmann guilty of all charges and sentenced him to death. The defense appealed the decision, but it was in vain. The Court of Appeals, the highest court of justice in Israel, accepted the Jerusalem District Court's arguments, with one addition: the accused had not received any superior orders because he was in fact his own superior and gave all the orders impacting the Jewish populations, prior to and

Adolf Eichmann stands in the glass box and reads his statement before the judges. Also seen in the photo are Eichmann's defense attorney, Dr. Robert Servatius, as well as the chief prosecutor, Dr. Gideon Hausner.

David Rubinger, The Pritzker Family National Photography Collection, The National Library of Israel.

---

257 Ibid.

during the war.[258] The classic argument of "obeying superior orders" to avoid responsibility for war crimes, crimes against humanity, or genocide had already been put forward at Nuremberg. However, this line of defense is not recognized in international law and only serves, in some cases, to soften the sentence.[259] The justification for such a stance is the gravity of these acts, which hurt not only the victims, but also society as a whole. Eichmann also sought clemency from President Itzhak Ben-Zvi, who did not grant it. At midnight on May 31, 1962, Eichmann was hanged, cremated, and his ashes scattered in the Mediterranean Sea.

IN THE SAME YEAR THAT Eichmann was hanged in Israel, Mossad agents returned to South America, determined to catch Mengele. His worst nightmare had come true: the Jews were right on his trail, and this time they had some hot leads. A team left Israel to search the Hohenau district in Paraguay. Their rationale was that Mengele was now a Paraguayan citizen, and that was a likely hideout for him, given the large German colony in that area. It was a valid premise, but the agents got there too late, as Mengele hadn't been in the area for a year and a half. Another Mossad team traveled to Brazil following two leads: one took them to Foz do Iguaçu, and another to the state of São Paulo. The first lead soon proved to be false, but the second was absolutely correct—to no one's surprise, as the information was obtained only after intensive efforts by the Mossad.[260] The agency's first major

---

258 Hannah Arendt, op. cit.

259 Amnesty International, "Eichmann Supreme Court Judgment: 50 Years On, Its Significance Today." London: Amnesty International Publications, 2012. Available at: <www.amnesty.org/en/wp-content/uploads/2021/06/ior530132012en.pdf>. Accessed on: July 17, 2023. Regarding the line of defense, the exception is the countries that are signatories to the Rome Statute, which can accept that "obeying superior orders" is a line of defense in the case of war crimes tried at the International Criminal Court. The same does not apply to crimes against humanity or genocide.

260 Interview with Rafi Eitan.

success resulted from their contact with journalist Willem Sassen, a member of the circle of Nazi expatriates in Buenos Aires. Sassen had recorded hours of Eichmann's confessions about his work during World War II, intending initially to use the recordings for a book. However, he eventually sold them to *Life* magazine in the United States and *Stern* in Germany. The agents reasoned that if Sassen had been close to Eichmann in Buenos Aires, he might very well know where Mengele was. He didn't have that information, but he did know the only person in Europe who was in direct contact with Mengele: Mr. X. The head of the Mossad then assigned Aharoni to persuade Sassen to collaborate with the Israelis. In addition to using his skills as an experienced interrogator, Aharoni offered the journalist a monthly payment of $5,000 if he helped. Thus the agent was able to get Sassen to reveal the mysterious Mr. X's identity: he was none other than the pilot Hans-Ulrich Rudel.[261] About ten agents began to follow Rudel and discovered that he served as an emissary, traveling from Germany to Brazil every six months to bring money.[262]

At the end of June 1962, Sassen sent a telegram informing the Mossad that Rudel would be arriving in São Paulo. The journalist also gave the name and telephone number of a pharmacist named Robert Schwedes, in whose house the former pilot usually stayed. As soon as Rudel landed in the city, the agents began watching and saw when he got in a white convertible car. The key issue was to find out who the vehicle's owner was. The license plate led them to a Wolfgang Gerhard. It was the first time that the agents had heard the name of Mengele's main protector in Brazil, but at that point they were still unaware of how close the two men were.

The next day, when Rudel left for Asunción, the agents began to follow Gerhard. Aharoni discovered that he lived in a house located in

---

261 Gerald Posner and John Ware, op. cit., p. 182; David G. Marwell, op. cit., pp. 184–86; Ronen Bergmann, "Mengeles Glück." *Zeit*, September 17, 2017. Available at: <https://www.zeit.de/2017/37/josef-mengele-auschwitz-arzt-mossad-akten>. Accessed on: August 6, 2023.

262 Interview with Rafi Eitan.

a rural area twelve miles from the city center. They also found out that Gerhard often visited a farm on the outskirts of São Paulo, on a dirt road off the Régis Bittencourt Highway, a major artery connecting São Paulo with the country's southern region.[263]

Planning for the operation had begun at least four years earlier, right after Ben-Gurion gave the order to hunt down Nazis. As soon as the Mossad received information that most of the fugitives were living in Panama, Guatemala, Argentina, or Brazil,[264] Rafi, who commanded the operations division, realized the need to recruit local agents in those countries who spoke the native language fluently. With that in mind, around 1958, long before Mengele crossed the Brazilian border, Rafi tried to identify someone in Israel who might have a contact in Brazil. He eventually met Samario Haychuk, a medical doctor and, through him, his brother Yigal. The thirty-two-year-old Yigal had been born in Presidente Venceslau, in the interior of São Paulo, and Portuguese was his mother tongue. He had been living in Israel for some time, in the southern kibbutz of Bror Hayil with other Brazilian immigrants.[265] Yigal seemed the perfect candidate for a mission in the state of São Paulo, with the added advantage of having that regional accent. When he was contacted about the mission, he immediately agreed, and thus Mossad enlisted its first Brazilian agent.[266]

Rafi embarked for Brazil as head of the operation to kidnap Mengele and take him to Israel, similarly to what had happened to Eichmann two years earlier. Despite the conflict with Argentina that that mission had caused, the Israelis ruled out the possibility of contacting the Brazilian authorities for their assistance in Mengele's arrest. According to Mossad's assessment, Mengele was protected

---

263 Yossi Chen, *Looking for a Needle in a Haystack: In Search of the Auschwitz "Doctor of Death."* Jerusalem: Yad Vashem, 2007, pp. 101–3.

264 Rafi Eitan, op. cit., p. 130.

265 Ibid., p. 135.

266 Telephone interview with Yigal Haychuk, August 25, 2017.

by loyal Europeans, and any communication with Brazilian authorities would only serve to make him run away and disappear once
again. Even at the risk of creating a new diplomatic crisis, this time
with Brazil, the Mossad preferred to conduct the operation on its
own and without informing the Brazilian government. In addition
to Rafi, the team included Zvi Aharoni and Brazilian newcomer
Yigal Haychuk.

The agents drove around the dirt roads of the São Paulo suburbs,
posing as property buyers while they tried to find any information.[267]
Yigal was in charge of speaking to people in Portuguese. Even though
he had no previous experience in espionage, his role was crucial; oth-
erwise the gringo-looking Israeli agents would have had to go around
asking questions in English to Brazilians. Such an alternative would
not only be fruitless but also highly suspicious, and possibly alert the
fugitive. Unbeknownst to the Mossad at the time, Mengele was living
then in Serra Negra with the Stammer family. That didn't keep him
from visiting Gerhard's farm, though, as he so often did.

The Mossad team spent some ten days driving around until they
suddenly found Mengele in a car, in the company of other people and
without security guards. Rafi thought they could have killed him right
then and there if they had wanted to. But they preferred just to photograph him to have physical proof of having found the right person.
Finding Mengele did not mean that he would be captured immediately. Once they had located their target, the Mossad followed their
usual modus operandi, which had a very precise step-by-step approach.
The first stage of the operation was to collect all kinds of information
about the person in question. The second was to put together a plan
based on the newly collected data. Such a plan also included the exact
positioning of each field agent and devised a clear way to transport
their target to Israel. The third stage was to make preparations for exe-
cuting the various parts of the plan. Finally, the last stage was to carry

---

267 Yossi Chen, op. cit., p. 106.

OPERATION EICHMANN • 171

out the mission; in other words, to capture the targeted individual. Rafi was convinced that they could catch Mengele, since they were so close now. All they needed was time.[268]

Time was exactly what they would no longer have. When the agents were in the first stage of the operation, they were ordered to return immediately to Israel. On July 22, 1962, newspapers in Egypt, Israel's greatest enemy at the time, published a bombshell: the country had successfully tested four missiles capable of hitting any point south of Beirut. In other words, the whole territory of Israel was in danger. A few weeks later, it came to light that German scientists had helped develop those missiles, reviving painful memories and fears among Jews. The project was led by two former Nazis who had worked on the creation of the V-1 and V-2 bombs, the forerunners of long-range missiles. All this had happened under the nose of the Mossad, which was taken by complete surprise. Harel put all his agents on alert and used every strategy he could think of in order to stop Egypt's missile project: assassination, letter bombs, intimidation. One other tactic was the final straw: Harel leaked to the press false information that the Germans were building an atomic bomb. The news sent the population into panic and resulted in a huge political cost for the country. Harel clashed with Ben-Gurion and was forced to resign. The prime

---

268 Interview with Rafi Eitan. It is important to note that in the Mossad's report there is a slightly different version of this story. In this report, Zvi Aharoni allegedly saw a person who appeared to be Mengele near the Itapecerica da Serra farm. However, when Rafi Eitan and the Brazilian agent came to Brazil to take part in the operation, they didn't find anyone resembling the Nazi doctor. I decided to adopt the version told to me personally by Rafi Eitan, that he and the agents got very close to Mengele, photographed him, and could even have killed him if they had wanted to, as Rafi said in other interviews. In the Mossad's report, there is apparent dismay when the agents discover that the farm was not in the name of Wolfgang Gerhard, but of a man called Mario Fischer. What they didn't know, and what becomes clear in the letters, is that Wolfgang had spent years trying to resolve a land issue with his neighbor Mario Fischer.

minister himself, founder of the state of Israel, lost support within his party and also left office.[269] The new government decided that the intelligence services would have other priorities than just hunting down Nazis. The understanding among the authorities was that they should not look for revenge, because there was not enough punishment for those who kill small children. Eichmann's trial had been enough. The new Mossad commander, Meir Amit, who had been head of military intelligence, ordered the agents, "Leave Mengele alone; I have another job for you."[270] That was the end of the Mossad's hunt for Mengele, at least for the time being.

---

269 Ronen Bergman, op. cit., pp. 61–74.
270 Interview with Rafi Eitan.

13

THE LOYALTY OF NAZI FRIENDS

As the mission to capture Mengele unfolded, the few weeks Rafi and Yigal spent together in Brazil led to a lifelong friendship. At eighty-five, Guiga, as Rafi affectionally called him, retired after a long career as a trader of frozen meat and fish. On the other hand, Rafi, although slightly older than his friend, was still very active at age ninety when I met him in March of 2017 in his Tel Aviv office and he told me his stories about the Mossad. The former agent said that he had left the world of espionage in 1985 and turned to entrepreneurship, but still kept an adventurous streak. He opened an agricultural improvement and management company that won a contract with Fidel Castro's government to manage a large citrus farm in Cuba.[271] In 2006, Rafi took a new turn in his career and became the leader of an unprecedented political party in Israel, the Pensioners' Party, and eventually became a minister to deal with issues concerning that social segment. The former Nazi hunter was surprised to discover that there were fifty-three organizations of Holocaust survivors in the country;

---

271 Personal interview with Rafi Eitan and telephone interview with Yigal Haychuk.

he decided to centralize assistance to all of them and even obtained a special budget for that purpose.[272] And when it seemed he had settled into a boring life, he appeared as a character in the 2018 Hollywood thriller *Operation Finale*. The movie recounts the mission to kidnap Eichmann and has American actor Nick Kroll playing the young Rafi Eitan.

Rafi Eitan, Mossad commander in the operations to kidnap Eichmann and Mengele. At the age of ninety, in his office in Tel Aviv, March 2017.
Betina Anton.

The smiling old Rafi kept in his sharp mind many details of those distant events. He just couldn't remember one important piece of information: the location of the farm where Mengele was hiding in 1962, when the Mossad carried out its mission on the outskirts of

---

272 Rafi Eitan, op. cit., p. 377.

São Paulo. According to Aharoni, the operation's head of investigations, the farm's location was about twenty-five miles from the capital, São Paulo, on a dirt road off the Régis Bittencourt highway, in the direction of Curitiba.[273] Based on this information and on statements given to the police afterward, it is most likely that the town was Itapecerica da Serra. It was there that Wolfgang Gerhard, the man who received Mengele in Brazil, had a farm that the fugitive visited for almost two decades. At the time of the failed Mossad mission, Mengele had already been living in the country for almost two years. But how did he end up in Brazil? To answer this question, one must retrace Mengele's actions in Paraguay, where the Nazi doctor planned the next steps of his escape with the support of friends. Rudel, Hitler's Air Force ace, had a wide network of relationships among Third Reich sympathizers in Argentina, Paraguay, and Brazil, and gave Mengele the contact information for Wolfgang Gerhard. Gerhard, in turn, was the representative in São Paulo of the Kameradenwerk, a service Rudel had set up in Buenos Aires to help Nazis who recently arrived in Latin America.[274]

Wolfgang Gerhard worshipped Hitler and his ideology to the point of decorating the top of the family Christmas tree with a swastika.[275] Perhaps the greatest demonstration of his love for the Führer was naming his firstborn son Adolf. Gerhard, born in 1925 in the city of Leibnitz, joined the Hitler Youth at the age of twelve, even before Austria joined the Reich. As soon as he turned eighteen, he became a member of the Nazi party; and when the regime collapsed, he could no longer bear to live in his country, now occupied by the Allied forces. In 1949, Gerhard immigrated to Brazil with his mother

---

273 Gerald Posner and John Ware, op. cit., p. 184.

274 Ulrich Völklein, op. cit., p. 263.

275 James M. Markham, "Mengele 'Double' Called Fervid Nazi." *New York Times*, June 13, 1985. Available at: <www.nytimes.com/1985/06/13/world/mengele-double-called-fervid-nazi.html>. Accessed on: July 20, 2023.

and his Brazilian wife, Ruth,[276] arriving in São Paulo at the age of twenty-three. Ruth apparently felt the same appreciation for nationalism as her husband. An acquaintance said that Ruth had gifted her two bars of "Jewish soap," in their original war-era wrapper. The soap had that name because it was said to be made from the bodies of Holocaust victims.[277] In addition to Adolf, the couple had three other children: Erwin, Karoline, and Sieglinde.[278]

In the early 1960s, the family lived in a house on Campo Limpo Road, an area on the outskirts of São Paulo's South Zone, beyond the end of the bus line where land was very cheap. Despite not being well off, Gerhard wrote a letter to Rudel saying that welcoming "Dr. Mengele" into his home was more than a sign of trust; it was a personal reward. The guest was also totally satisfied with his host, and the two men quickly became friends. Mengele even wrote in his diary that he had always wanted to find a conversational partner who understood astronomy and astrophysics more than the basic compendium; Gerhard was that person. Obviously, Gerhard couldn't go around introducing Mengele under his real name, so Rudel had arranged for a Brazilian identity card registered under the name Peter Hochbichler.[279] This was the name Mengele would call himself by in his new life in Brazil. Around that time, Ruth's sister Thea visited the home and later remembered meeting a man who spoke fluent Spanish with a German accent. Thea said that he lived there for a few months. She never saw him again.[280]

Although willing to help his fellow Nazis, Gerhard had very few financial resources. He had no higher education and found work as an industrial technician, welder, or entrepreneur.[281] Even when he

276 Federal Police, "Information from the Austrian Consulate General." Police inquiry n. 1-0097/86, book 6, p. 81; Wolfgang Gerhard's work and social security card.

277 James M. Markham, op. cit.

278 Statement by Thea Maria Kleyer, Mengele dossier from the São Paulo police, file no. 9, July 1, 1985, Mato Grosso Regional Superintendence.

279 Ulrich Völklein, op. cit., pp. 262–63.

280 Statement by Thea Maria Kleyer, op. cit.

281 Ibid., p. 263.

owned a textile printing company in Campo Limpo, he had very obsolete and precarious machinery. This translated into a modest life, and, in the eyes of acquaintances, it seemed that the Gerhards faced financial hardship.[282] However, he was well connected and socialized with expatriate Europeans, who knew him as "Lange," or "long" in German. At six feet three inches tall, he was an impressive presence not only because of his stature but also because of his strong opinions. In conversation, he didn't hide the fact that he was a Nazi and openly called for the return of the regime, sometimes pushing his fervor to border mental instability.[283] In Brazil, he distributed the *Reichsruf,* the Socialist Reich Party newspaper. The party was created in postwar Germany to bring together former Nazis, including Rudel, and was later banned by the German Constitutional Court.[284] In São Paulo, Gerhard used to attend parties organized by the Austrian and Hungarian communities, and it was on one of these occasions, in 1957, that he met the Stammers, the family that would shelter Mengele for more than a decade.[285] Geza and Gitta Stammer were not Nazis, but they wanted to escape communism. After World War II, they left Hungary for political reasons and moved to Austria. The two nations, which had once been part of the same state during the Austro-Hungarian Empire, took completely different paths during the Cold War. While Hungary remained behind the Iron Curtain and became a communist country, Austria managed to escape that fate and remained neutral.

In 1948, the couple came to Brazil to live in São Paulo. Geza, who had an engineering degree from the University of Budapest, soon found a job with large companies such as Volkswagen and Aço Villares. Their two sons, Robert Peter and Miklos Geza, were born shortly after they arrived. Although far away from their roots, the Stammers met other immigrant families who supported each other.

---

282 Ernesto Glawe's statement to the Federal Police, p. 62.

283 Id., p. 61.

284 Ulrich Völklein, op. cit., p. 163.

285 Gitta Stammer's statement to the Federal Police, p. 29.

Everything seemed to be going well, except for the rainy climate in the polluted capital city, São Paulo.[286] Gitta couldn't adapt and wanted to move to the countryside. She visited several small properties but didn't like any of them. One day, an Austrian woman named Martha, who was a tenant of the Stammer family in the Santo Amaro neighborhood, mentioned that her uncle had returned to Austria and had left a property in the countryside for her father to sell. Gitta was interested and decided to visit the place. That's how the Stammer family decided to move to Nova Europa in 1959.[287] The town, founded at the beginning of the twentieth century and named in honor of European immigrants, is located almost two hundred miles from the capital, in the Araraquara region. It was hot almost all year round and was practically unbearable in the summer.[288] Geza bought the small farm,

Geza Stammer.

Criminal Museum of the Teaching Directorate of the National Police Academy / Museu Criminal da Diretoria de Ensino da Academia Nacional de Policia.

---

286 Id., pp. 29–32.

287 Statement by Martha Barbist Novak to the Federal Police, p. 33.

288 "History." Nova Europa City Hall. Available at: <novaeuropa.sp.gov.br/?pag=T1RjPU9EZz1PVFU9T0dVPU9HST1PVEE9T0dFPU9HRT0=&idmenu=214>. Accessed on: December 8, 2022.

where he grew fruit, coffee, and rice, and raised a few head of cattle. However, he couldn't stay there during the week because he worked in São Paulo as a surveyor and only came home on weekends. Gitta had to be in charge of everything.[289]

A few months after arriving in Brazil, Mengele began to complain about life. He had taken up a job at Gerhard's printing company and recorded in his diary, in January 1961, that the work was not very pleasant. What really bothered him, however, was living in a place that caused him feelings of monotony, primitivism, and restlessness, and offered no guarantee of security whatsoever.[290] Around that time, Gerhard paid a few visits to the Stammers in Nova Europa. Whether the visits had ulterior motives cannot be ascertained; however, on one such occasion, he proposed that a Swiss acquaintance of his, Peter Hochbichler, could work for them as an administrator.[291] Geza thought about it and concluded that it would be a win-win situation: he would help a friend and, in return, he would have someone to run the farm. Geza agreed, and around August or September 1961, "Peter" was introduced to the family; later that same year, he moved to the farm.[292]

Hochbichler started working at the Stammers' property but didn't accept any payment. To the contrary, he made a point of paying for his own food and laundry, which Gitta found strange.[293] The arrival of the new farm manager was particularly memorable for one of the employees, Francisco Assis de Souza, who did everything from milking the cows to looking after the crops. He described Hochbichler as an authoritarian person with a nervous temper who argued a lot. He also spoke garbled Portuguese with a strong Spanish accent and said he had lived in Uruguay for a long time.

---

289 Gitta Stammer's statement to the Federal Police, p. 29.
290 Ulrich Völklein, op. cit., p. 268.
291 Gitta Stammer's statement to the Federal Police, p. 29.
292 Geza Stammer's statement to the Federal Police, pp. 85–86.
293 Id., pp. 25–32.

Souza noticed that Hochbichler never left the farm, but sometimes walked around the property. But what impressed Francisco the most was seeing Hochbichler operating on a calf that had a hernia. The surgery was quick and the animal cured,[294] but his actions were quite unusual. Any ordinary manager would have called in a veterinarian and not operated by himself, especially an operation that demanded such a high skill level. Gitta also found the unknown "Swiss" man's behavior strange and was concerned. She thought Hochbichler was discreet and quiet, and noticed that he avoided being photographed. Whenever strangers came to visit, he always asked who they were as soon as they had left. Gitta found this odd and suspected he was not who he said he was. However, whenever she asked him, he always changed the subject.[295]

Life in Nova Europa didn't last long. The region felt like an oven, and the Stammer family decided to move to a place with a more pleasant climate: Serra Negra. Souza didn't want to go along, but Hochbichler did. Although Mengele feared change, it soon proved to be advantageous. After almost four weeks in the new place, he wrote in his diary: "As fierce as my inner resistance to moving here was, I now feel at home in this place, which I rejected so vehemently. But it also has everything it takes to give a home and a place to stay to a person without peace."[296] Even though he felt comfortable in his new environment, Hochbichler continued to behave strangely, until the reason for his behavior was revealed by chance.

A man who bought fruit from the Stammers' farm left them a newspaper, something hard to come by where they lived. One article in the paper talked about Nazi executioners and featured a photo of a young man in his thirties. The face looked familiar to Gitta: it had an unmistakable gaping smile, and she decided to confront Hochbichler:

---

294 Francisco Assis de Souza's statement to the Federal Police, p. 35.

295 Gitta Stammer's statement to the Federal Police, pp. 25–32.

296 Ulrich Völklein, op. cit., p. 271.

"You're so mysterious. You live with us, so please be honest and tell us if it's you or not."

Hochbichler didn't say anything right away. Only after dinner did he speak up to say that Gitta was right. "I live with you, so you have the right to know that, unfortunately, that's me," Mengele said.[297]

After the Stammers learned that Peter Hochbichler and Josef Mengele were the same person, Geza went to Gerhard and demanded an explanation. The Austrian man's reaction was not warm. He made it clear that they should not go to the authorities and threateningly warned Geza that, should they report their discovery to the police, Mengele's friends could harm the Stammer family. The friends' identities weren't made clear, but Geza got the message and just asked Gerhard to get Mengele away from his family as quickly as possible.

The problem was not so easy to solve. Hans Sedlmeier, the Mengele family business representative, had to travel from Germany to Brazil to calm things down and find a new place where the Nazi doctor could live. As Geza recalled it, Sedlmeier went to Brazil at least three times.[298] On the first occasion, he took with him $2,000, which Geza exchanged for cruzeiros, the Brazilian currency at the time. The money apparently helped to pacify the situation. Mengele also wrote in his diary that he contributed $25,000 to the purchase of the farm in Serra Negra and thus became a partner in the property.[299] Mengele stayed with the Stammers until 1974.

The Stammers never mentioned to the police that they had received any money from Mengele but always claimed that the only reason they had harbored the criminal for so many years was that they were afraid of threats. The police, for their part, never investigated the question of the money involved in the Mengele case, because the focus of their investigation was something else: whether the "Angel of Death" from

297 Gerald Posner and John Ware, op. cit., p. 175.
298 Statement by Geza Stammer, pp. 85–86.
299 Ulrich Völklein, op. cit.

Auschwitz had really lived and died in Brazil.[300] People close to the case, as well as his diaries, show that the financial support provided by the Mengele family did play an important role in the success of his clandestine life during the almost three decades he lived in South America. Rolf, Mengele's only son, said that he didn't know exactly how much his father received, but estimated the monthly stipend to have been around three to five hundred German marks.[301]

---

[300] Interview with the chief investigator in the Mengele case, Marco Antonio Veronezzi, conducted on December 12, 2022.

[301] Inge Byham, op. cit., p. 32.

14

NO REST IN SERRA NEGRA

SERRA NEGRA, 1961 TO 1968

If there was ever anyone most deserving of some peace and quiet, that would be Cecília Gewertz, for she had had a very tough life. "No one will ever understand what we've suffered," she always thought. Only now, already in her forties, did she finally have a chance to rest. Every six months or so, she would take a break from her job in São Paulo and travel with her husband and son to her friend Anézia's farm in Serra Negra. There they liked to go to the swimming pool of a nearby hotel, where they could swim to their hearts' content. During those relaxing days, Cecília was able to forget the past for a little while; maybe even forget her own real name, Cyrla.

After passing through several concentration camps and being rescued by the Red Cross in Ravensbrück when the war ended, Cyrla was twenty-three years old and skin and bones. She left Germany on the fourth bus of a convoy of five, although the Germans bombed the fifth vehicle in an attempt to prevent the prisoners from escaping. It was a miracle that she had survived, considering all the adversities she had faced. Once safe, she couldn't eat anything but soup and oatmeal.

Some of her camp fellows gorged on food when they finally had the chance, but died because their bodies were no longer able to digest. The Swedish government warmly received war refugees like a mother would, and Cyrla was one of them. She was "rebaptized" in Sweden with the name Cecília, and given a house, food, and clothes, and even attended nursing school for free. However, nothing assuaged the loneliness of someone who had lost her entire family in Treblinka. Only one brother survived, hiding in the forests, joining the partisans, and finally moving to the United States.

Cecília moved to Brazil at the insistence of her husband, Simon, who soon changed his name to its Portuguese equivalent, Simão. The two survivors had married in Sweden, and part of his family had immigrated to Brazil. Their disappointment upon arriving in São Paulo was tremendous: their relatives asked how much money they

Cyrla Gewertz, one of the survivors of Josef Mengele's experiments in Auschwitz.

Betina Anton & Jose Martin Gewertz.

were carrying, and Cecília replied that fifty-nine US dollars was all they had. Feeling despised, the couple found an apartment in the Bom Retiro neighborhood and lived their lives the best way they could, as they no longer had a visa to return to Sweden. Neither did they want to go to Poland, where Cecília had been born and had the worst possible experiences. Until the end of her life, she was unable to sleep well through the night. She had to stop taking sleep medication on doctor's orders, and keeping her eyes closed was hard for her, as the darkness brought back all the painful scenes from her past.

In one of those memories, the then-named Cyrla was once more standing in the morning Zählappell, the endless counting of prisoners at Auschwitz. Mengele chose her along with three other girls: a Greek, a French, and a Hungarian. None of them knew each other. They were taken to the special barracks where Mengele conducted his experiments; there they saw some bathtubs already filled with water. Naked and with her hair shaved off, Cyrla entered the first tub.

"Oh, it's burning!" she shouted in German, a language she had learned during the Nazi occupation.

"Put your head under the water, or I'll kill you," said Mengele.

Cyrla spent fifteen minutes in the scalding water, as the doctor timed it on his watch. She thought the ordeal was over then, but that was only the beginning. From the boiling water tub, she was forced into another one containing freezing water. The experience was repeated from one bathtub to the next throughout the day. Cyrla thought she was going to die. The Greek girl, tiny and very thin, didn't survive, and her body was carried away on a stretcher. Night fell, and the barrack was now empty. Cyrla heard noise outside and screamed for help. Other inmates soon came to her aid. They ripped off a board from the wall of the experiment block and managed to get her out through the hole. But she couldn't walk, for her legs were swollen and red from burns. She spent two days lying on top of a bunk bed, but even then she had to take part in Zählappell every morning. The other prisoners showed her great solidarity, carrying her to the morning count. They also found a scarf to cover her head, perhaps so that

Mengele wouldn't recognize her. Years and decades passed, and still Mengele's face always came back to haunt her in her worst nightmares.

Breathing the fresh air of Serra Negra was, therefore, an immense relief for Cecília. Surrounded by green hills, this little town on the water circuit sits almost a hundred miles from the hustle and bustle of São Paulo. Cecília's friend's ranch was an even quieter place, as it was located in a remote neighborhood, perfect for relaxing. On one of the pool days at the nearby hotel, a local resident came running to tell her some news.

"Do you know who's living in Serra Negra?" he asked. Nobody had any idea. "Mengele!" he replied, excited.

It's a mystery how that resident found out about Mengele, since only the Stammer family knew Peter's true identity; but upon hearing the name, Cecília shuddered and felt ill. What were the odds of being so close again to that man, more than twenty years later and at that end of the world? She didn't think of reporting him to the authorities, but only of running away. "What if he's here to kill Jews?" thought Cecília, without realizing that it was a rather absurd possibility in the new environment where she lived. Frightened, she packed her things and never went back to Serra Negra.[302] It was another stroke of luck for Mengele. With a simple phone call to the local police, to the German or Israeli embassy, or even to a Nazi hunter like Simon Wiesenthal, Cecília could have brought that criminal to justice. But her trauma and wounds were still too fresh in her mind, and she chose to keep quiet. Her only consolation was that she never had to face her tormentor in Brazil.

Mengele lived with the Stammers on the Santa Luzia farm, a property near the hotel where Cecília's family enjoyed swimming. The doctor had become a rural administrator and had to manage the farm's employees, who called him "Seu Pedro," the Portuguese equivalent to Mr. Peter. He hired the workers himself and paid their salaries. But he didn't have the slightest social skills and could be very rude, which led

302 Interview with Cyrla Gewertz conducted on July 14, 2017.

to horrible arguments with the staff. Gitta would intervene in those situations. She wanted to avoid any problems, terrified that any disagreement might draw attention to Mengele's presence in her house.

Now that Mengele's identity was no longer a secret to Gitta, she tried to find out more about what he had done during the war. Mengele confirmed that he had been in Auschwitz, but said that he had contracted typhus and had been removed for treatment elsewhere. At no point did he confirm that he had experimented on human beings, as the newspapers reported. Whenever the subject of "war" came up, Mengele immediately turned away. Gitta was able to extract little from him about the period when he lived on the run after the conflict. He told her only that he had fled from Germany to Italy and then crossed the Atlantic Ocean on a small French ship to Buenos Aires. He said he'd lived in the Argentine capital for a few years before moving to Paraguay, and confessed that he hadn't lived in Uruguay, the justification he had given earlier for his Spanish accent, but only spent a short time in that country. In Geza's absence, conversations with Mengele dragged on into the night. Gitta considered him cultured and intelligent. He read books on philosophy and history and liked classical music, especially Mozart. She believed that Mengele hardly left the estate, at most going downtown or, sometimes, to Lindoia, a neighboring town known for its hot springs.[303] The neighbors viewed it differently.

Across from the Stammers' property on the main road was the farm of the Silottos, a family of Italian origin like many of the settlers in Serra Negra. To this day, the family's oldest members remember Mengele as the "Hungarês"—probably because he lived with the Stammers, who were Hungarian. As a teenager, Alfeo Silotto used to hang out with the Stammer brothers and believed that Mengele was Gitta's lover. The rumor circulated widely, because the two of them were always together and her husband, Geza, would only show up on weekends, sometimes staying away for as long as fifteen days.

---

303 Gitta Stammer's statement to the Federal Police, p. 223.

Alfeo says that every Sunday, Mengele would go to an Italian bar at lunchtime but would leave early, before it got too crowded. Although he only met the locals occasionally, some anecdotes became well known. For example, it is said that Mengele once saved a drunk man who had fallen into a stream that was rising rapidly because of heavy rain. He crossed a bridge, dragging along the intoxicated man, and delivered him to his girlfriend's house. On another occasion, he treated a cousin of Alfeo's, José Osmar Silotto, who was suffering from a disease caused by worms and popularly known as "Amarelão." After using a home remedy prescribed by Mengele, he was cured.[304] At the age of twelve, José Osmar helped with the coffee plantations on the Santa Luzia estate and was impressed by his boss's ability as a taxidermist, which he used to perfectly preserve dead little birds.[305]

Mengele was living peacefully in Serra Negra when his colleague Adolf Eichmann was hanged in Israel at the end of May 1962. Afterward, he was greatly afraid of being kidnapped by the Mossad and suffering the same fate, so he decided to build a thirty-foot-tall observation tower. A bricklayer helped with the work, and Mengele himself used his woodworking skills to make the floor, door, windows, and roof. The Santa Luzia farm was the last property on top of a hill and there was only one way to reach it. From the windows of the white tower, a person had a panoramic view and could see anyone approaching on the dirt road. As long as he was on sentry duty, often using binoculars, it was practically impossible to take him by surprise. Whenever he left his safe haven, though, Mengele liked to be accompanied by his fifteen mongrel dogs,[306] as he usually did any time he walked Gitta to the stop where she took the bus into town. However, Mengele was never in real danger from the Mossad in Serra Negra.

---

304 Interview with Alfeo Silotto on November 21, 2020.

305 Noedir Pedro Carvalho Burini, O anjo da morte em Serra Negra. [S.l.: s.n., 19--], p. 10.

306 "Casa em Serra Negra, agora atração turística." O Estado de S. Paulo, June 14, 1985.

Mengele's observation tower in Serra Negra.
Betina Anton.

At that time, Rafi Eitan's team came close to Wolfgang Gerhard's estate in Itapecerica da Serra, which Mengele visited very often, but no Israeli agent ever considered going to Serra Negra. The fact is that the fugitive was well-hidden and didn't know it.

Mengele was constantly worried about his safety, especially if news emerged of Nazi criminals being caught by the authorities. On February 28, 1967, shortly after six thirty in the afternoon, the Austrian Franz Stangl returned to his home in the South Zone of São Paulo. Before he even had a chance to reach the front door, DOPS (Department of Political and Social Order) agents arrested him. Stangl didn't react, but was relieved to hear them speak Portuguese, for his greatest fear was being kidnapped by the

Mossad.[307] The next day, the state governor, Abreu Sodré, personally went to the Department of Public Security to congratulate the police and announce the arrest to the press. He must have known that the arrested Nazi was no small fish, despite leading an unremarkable life in Brazil. Stangl never bothered to hide his real name, had been working at the Volkswagen plant in ABC Paulista for eight years, and lived in a house in the Brooklin neighborhood with his wife, three daughters, and a grandson. But this apparently average citizen had a dark past: he had commanded the extermination camps of Treblinka and Sobibor during World War II.[308] It is almost impossible to hear the survivors' stories, for the simple reason that very few people came out alive from those two places.[309]

From 1942, when the Holocaust extermination campaign began to accelerate, hundreds of thousands of Jews were transported to Treblinka, Sobibor, and Belzec, a third extermination camp. All three were built for Operation Reinhard, the codename for a plan to liquidate all the Jews in Nazi-occupied Poland. Unlike Auschwitz, which also functioned as a forced labor camp, these sites were created with a single objective: the immediate murder of prisoners in the gas chambers. The employees of the three camps were recruited from the T4 euthanasia program secretly conducted in Germany. And that's where Stangl stepped in. He was an SS Obersturmführer, a rank equivalent to lieutenant colonel, and had taken part in the operation to secretly kill "undesirable" Germans. Because of his position and experience in mass extermination, he was selected to command Sobibor. Later, he was summoned to head Treblinka, which was in disarray due to the excessive number of dead bodies scattered everywhere. The chaos was such that trains bringing prisoners to Treblinka had to be suspended for a week until the SS put the place in order. Once

---

307 "A prisão do nazista." *Jornal da Tarde*, March 3, 1967.

308 "Polícia prende chefe nazista." *O Estado de S. Paulo*, March 2, 1967; "A Áustria quer nazista de volta." *O Estado de S. Paulo*, March 3, 1967.

309 Nikolaus Wachsmann, op. cit.

the transports resumed, the first victims arrived from the Warsaw ghetto.[310] Together, the three Operation Reinhard camps took the lives of 1.5 million Jews.[311]

When Wolfgang Gerhard heard that Stangl had been arrested in São Paulo, he decided he needed to take action. He thought of a radical solution: rescue Stangl in his VW Kombi, which he normally used to drive his children everywhere. Gerhard only needed to modify the front of the vehicle and install a false bottom near the engine. It would be a tight fit, but he thought his friend could lie on the floorboard. He shared his crazy plan with Mengele, who rejected it outright. Mengele believed that if Gerhard tried to carry out his plan, he would attract the authorities' attention to the many Germans living in Brazil, and even to the Austrians. This would only lead to more problems, especially for him, Josef Mengele, the most famous and wanted fugitive Nazi. Gerhard didn't like the reaction and called him selfish, saying he was shying away from helping a comrade. It was true, Mengele lacked the same camaraderie with his fellow Nazis that Gerhard felt in abundance. In any case, the rescue was never attempted, because modifying the Kombi was a time-consuming job and time quickly ran out.[312] Stangl was soon transferred to the capital, Brasilia, and from there extradited to Germany. The Treblinka and Sobibor commander finally went on trial; but before his sentence was declared final he died of a heart attack in prison, in June 1971.[313]

310 Laurence Rees, op. cit., pp. 345–48.

311 "Operation Reinhard (Einsatz Reinhard)." United States Museum of Holocaust. Available at: <encyclopedia.ushmm.org/content/en/article/operation -reinhard-einsatz-reinhard>. Accessed on: February 20, 2023.

312 Wolfram Bossert's statement to the Federal Police, p. 19.

313 "Um comandante nazista na Volkswagen do Brasil." Deutsche Welle, July 20, 2017. Available at: <www.dw.com/pt-br/um-comandante-nazista-na-volkswagen-do -brasil/a-39853635>. Accessed on: February 20, 2023.

Mengele was right in his assumption that Stangl's arrest would cause problems for him. At the time, the newspaper *O Estado de S. Paulo* published the following:

> The presence in Brazil of other Nazi war criminals and the existence of clandestine entities designed to facilitate the entry into the country of former collaborators of Hitler's regime are some of the main points of the interrogations to which the Austrian (Franz) Paul Stangl is facing now in Brasília, where he is being held. . . . On the other hand, the Federal Police have indications that the Nazi doctor Mengele was in Brazil, but had already fled.[314]

The information was somewhat correct. Mengele was still living in Serra Negra, but he and the Stammers would soon be moving to another town. According to some neighbors, the reason was the construction of a large hotel near the Santa Luzia farm. There was also another, more personal reason: after living with Mengele for some time, Gitta realized that he was a very authoritarian person, which constantly caused friction in her family. Moving to a farm in Caieiras, just twenty miles from São Paulo, would relieve the tension at the Stammers' home and allow her husband, Geza, to not have to be away from home for so long.

CAIEIRAS, 1968 TO 1974

The Stammer family and their guest moved to the estate in Caieiras in 1968. A chauffeur who worked for Geza later recalled two things he found odd. Firstly, that Seu Pedro stayed indoors most of the time. Secondly, his boss stopped by the post office every day to check the mailbox he had rented. However, if Geza was too busy, the driver

---

314 "Nazista teria proteção." *O Estado de S. Paulo*, March 7, 1967, p. 36. Available at: <acervo.estadao.com.br/pagina/#!/19670307-28187-nac-0036-999-36-not/busca /Stangl>. Accessed on: February 18, 2023.

himself would pick up the mail, which was most often sent from Germany addressed to Peter.[315] Mengele loved to write and receive letters, and he maintained an intense epistolary exchange with various people: his son Rolf, his stepson Karl-Heinz, his family in Günzburg, and, later, some of his friends in Germany and Austria. His most regular correspondent was Wolfgang Gerhard, who returned to Austria in 1971.

In a letter written in April 1969 and addressed "to everyone" in the Mengele family, the Nazi fugitive summarized his routine in Brazil and his state of mind:

Everyone,

Since you really know very little about me and the course of my life here, I thought it might be very useful to tell you what I do, what I think, and how my life here is going. So I'd like to start with a description of my routine on an average day:

We usually start the day between seven and eight; often the owner of the house has already left for work with his eldest son. Then we have breakfast and then, of course, there's lots to do—around the house, in the yard, and in the garden. The renovation of the dilapidated house, which has now become a very imposing country house, requires considerable manual labor and, as you can imagine, the garden also requires a lot of work. The walkways have to be maintained, the grass cut, new planting done, as well as lots of little jobs. The last big job was roofing the front house, which was completed last year. In the meantime, there has been a pause in the work due to a lack of materials. However, there are always possibilities and needs for improvements and repairs, and so the handiwork is still needed.

---

[315] "A Vida na Sombra: Mengele teve a proteção de uma rede de amigos em seus dezenove anos de Brasil." *Veja*, June 19, 1985.

Most of the time, I do this work by taking a short walk in the surrounding area, accompanied by my faithful dogs. In the afternoon, I have more time to myself. This has been especially true in recent months, when I've put some things in writing and I've also been able to read more. As far as my writing is concerned, I decided to record the history of my time in a longer account, based on my own life story and, at the same time, weave in the family history. It is supposed to be a representation of the rise of a family that has its roots in agriculture and then rises to the upper class.

My own life, as representative of a national destiny, must shine. Of course, I don't know how successful I will be. What I wrote seven years ago still meets my standards today, so I now have the courage to continue writing about it. Occasionally I write down a small incident or anecdote. I also keep a little diary, and sometimes my mood is right to write a little poem. In the second part of this description, I'd like to give you some examples.

And when the day comes to an end, we sit together in the evening, usually just Gitta and the kids, and tell each other what we want to get off our chest, discuss our problems, listen to good music on the record player or play some—albeit worse—ourselves. And so the day finally comes to an end: even if you haven't done much, you've spent the day, as the saying goes. In the past, about a year ago, the days were even busier, mostly with lots of work. Cows had to be milked as early as six in the morning, and many other tasks and duties occupied the time of the farmer and peasant. You also had to look after the animals and everything else that crawls and flies on a large farm. Even today, of course, there is still a bit of difficulty from time to time, especially in relation to the employees, who, however, are now just an inept maid who has been fired and a lazy farm worker.

If you had to work harder in the past, or if it's much easier and more enjoyable today, you might get the impression and the question might arise as to whether such an existence still makes much sense. I ask myself that question too but am inclined to answer it in the affirmative. It's not so essential what you do, but much more essential what you get out of it for a lasting benefit. All work, almost all professions, eventually becomes routine and therefore uninteresting.

But I have formed a different idea of the meaning of my existence. I want to prove with my existence that only those who give themselves up are lost, as a good comrade once wrote in one of his books, or as Hemingway made his old man say: You can be destroyed, but you can't give up.

As for my reading, I have daily newspapers, magazines, and the like at my disposal. I'm also always reading a book, currently McLuhan. Music is provided by our friend Musikus. He is an enthusiastic fan of the music of Händel, Bach, Mozart, and Haydn, and during our weekly visits we always enjoy such wonderful classical music, which can offer so much pleasure. Lately, we've also become a bit daring, going to the small cinema on the outskirts and watching mostly old films that are now outdated. I like the Old West productions best, because in those movies you can see such beautiful horses and brilliant riders and, at the end of the day, the hero always escapes unscathed, even though a lot of ammunition is fired at him.

In addition to shorter excursions by car, mainly on Sundays, in the vicinity of our location, we have also gone on some longer excursions. Last year, I spent nine weeks at Farm 1, where I introduced the harvest. In the meantime, we made another visit to make some arrangements with the new tenant. Now I've just gotten back, also from a longer excursion, i.e. further into the jungle. I went there with Musikus, who is an avid speleologist and photographer. Although we didn't manage to finish our planned trip, because we lost a camera and the flash had suffered from the humidity, this excursion resulted in several hundred photographs of parasites, trees, waterfalls, plants, streams, and, finally,

196 · HIDING MENGELE

cave entrances and their surroundings. As you can see, my life is not
as monotonous as it may seem. But the principle also applies here that
life is only as interesting as you make it, and that's a personal matter.

. . . Real life is just experience . . .

I also have good people to talk to in Gitta, Musikus, and Lange, and
during our get-togethers we have lively conversations and discussions
on a wide variety of topics. In particular, about modern society, astronomy, the theory of relativity, scientific problems.[316]

Mengele didn't usually sign his letters with his name. At most, a
"Dein . . ."—"Your . . ." As a fugitive from justice, he knew that if this
material fell into the wrong hands, he would betray himself and give
the police clues to where he was hiding. He also avoided mentioning the names of towns, using codes such as "Farm 1" to refer to the
Santa Luzia estate in Serra Negra. He normally referred to relatives
and friends using one syllable, especially in later letters. In this one,
Mengele even writes "Lange," Wolfgang Gerhard's nickname. Later
on, he just calls him "La." Musikus was the codename of Wolfram
Bossert, a friend who will inaugurate a new era in Mengele's life in
Brazil and establish his tropical Bavaria once and for all.

---

[316] "Letter from Mengele to his family." National Museum of the Federal Police,
file no. 67, Brasília.

15

TROPICAL BAVARIA

CAIEIRAS, 1968 TO 1974

It was a summer evening in February 1968, and Wolfram and Liselotte Bossert were at the home of their good friend Wolfgang Gerhard and his wife, Ruth, whom they visited every week. As usual, the Bosserts brought Austrian cold cuts and German sausages for the adults and chocolates for the children, a habit rooted in their common origins. The two families' children had fun together while the adults chatted, always in German. At some point in the evening, the two men would lock themselves in a room to work on a book about cave exploration that they were co-writing.[317] But that night something was different: another guest was present. He was a widower who said his name was Pedro. Gerhard explained to the Bosserts that his friend was very lonely, had problems, and needed as many people as possible by his side. Wolfram Bossert tried to be helpful. He talked to Pedro at length and gave him his address, inviting the newcomer to spend a

---

[317] "Filho de Gerhard acusa os Bossert." *O Estado de S. Paulo*, June 12, 1985; Federal Police, police inquiry n. 1-0097/86, book 6, p. 125.

day with him at his house whenever he wanted. A coincidence made their friendship easier: Bossert worked for the Melhoramentos company in Caieiras, which was less than three miles away from where Pedro lived.[318]

Josef Mengele (center) enjoys the company of Wolfgang Gerhard (left) and Wolfram Bossert (right).

Stern Magazine.

Such convenient proximity meant that the two soon got into a routine together. Every week, Bossert would leave work, pick Pedro up, and take him home for dinner. The two enjoyed listening to German records, drinking wine, and chatting until the early hours. Among the supposed widower's favorite subjects were medicine and domesticating animals. The next morning, Bossert would give him a lift back to the farm. Their affinity only grew with each encounter. Liselotte and the children, Andreas and Sabine, also grew fond of Pedro, and eventually the whole family began to call him "uncle." Almost a year after they became friends, Peter confessed: he was Josef Mengele, the man being sought all over the world; however, he insisted that what was said about him was untrue.[319] The revelation of his real identity would certainly have been a tremendous shock for anyone—but not for the Bosserts. It didn't affect their relationship at all, and life went on as normal.

---

318 Gitta Stammer's statement to Federal Police, p. 30.

319 "Assustado, agressivo, vivia com medo." *O Estado de S. Paulo,* June 7, 1985.

Josef Mengele with Liselotte Bossert and her children.

Stern Magazine.

Josef Mengele in a canoe with Sabine and Andreas Bossert in Caieiras, São Paulo.

Stern Magazine.

Josef Mengele showing Sabine and Andreas Bossert his workshop in Caieiras.

Stern Magazine.

Josef Mengele, Liselotte, and their children in Bertioga.

Stern Magazine.

THE MOSSAD'S DORMANT HUNT FOR Mengele gained a new and unexpected impetus in early 1968. A thirty-five-year-old woman approached the Israeli consul in São Paulo and claimed that her brother-in-law was harboring Mengele in Brazil. The complainant was Thea Maria Kleyer, Ruth Gerhard's sister. She said that Gerhard had threatened to kill both women, and thus she decided to contact the consulate. Amidst the many reports about Mengele that the Israeli authorities received, Kleyer's caught their attention for one reason: she commented that the fugitive's hiding place was a farm in Itapecerica da Serra, information that raised a red flag for the Mossad. The agency's local representatives decided to talk directly to her, sidestepping the consular formalities. Kleyer began by telling them her personal story. She had been married twice, had a child with each husband, and was twice divorced. In a second meeting, Kleyer told one of the agents that she was afraid of Gerhard. She also confessed that her main reason for going to the consulate was a dispute with her second ex-husband, who had taken her youngest son, aged eight, away from her. She offered to help the Israelis find Mengele in exchange for assistance in getting her youngest back. They agreed, and she told them everything she knew.

Kleyer said that Mengele spent Christmas at Gerhard's house in 1962 and then moved in with "a very simple woman of Hungarian origin"—referring to Gitta. She also told the Mossad that Mengele had bought a farm in the state of São Paulo and that his wife, Martha, was living in Europe, something the agency already knew since they kept a close watch on her. Other information that Kleyer shared with the Mossad included Gerhard's illegal textile-printing factory at home, and that every six or eight weeks her brother-in-law would drive his Kombi to meet Mengele and deliver the checks he had received from Germany in his post office box.

To make her testimony more credible, Kleyer offered the names of a few people in her brother-in-law's inner circle: Hans Rudel, the former German Air Force pilot who helped Mengele get to Brazil; and Erich Lessmann, a businessman and close friend of Gerhard. Both Lessmann and Gerhard had traveled together to visit Mengele. Furthermore, it appeared that, at some point, Lessmann employed Gerhard as a technician in his welding shop. Such a job was indeed noted on Gerhard's work permit, which he would later pass on to Mengele. One more name came up in Kleyer's testimony: Wolfram Bossert. She said that he lived in Caieiras and visited Gerhard every week. Some of those names, such as Rudel's, were already well known to the Mossad; yet the leads received from Kleyer were certainly hot.

Preparations to capture Mengele began immediately on three continents: Asia, Europe, and South America. The agency assigned an agent codenamed Mirambo to coordinate the mission to identify the Nazi criminal. In February 1968, the same month that Mengele met the Bosserts, Mirambo arrived in São Paulo with a series of instructions. He was not to act against any local laws; not to do anything that might alert the fugitive; and finally, he should not kidnap Mengele in the same manner that had been done to Eichmann. This time, the order was to only identify the fugitive, help local authorities arrest him, and extradite him to Germany, where there had been a warrant for his arrest since 1959. Two days after his arrival, Mirambo conducted an in-locus analysis of the situation and established a relatively simple plan. The agent would follow Gerhard as soon as he received the money to hand over to Mengele. However, some questions remained unresolved: When would the next remittance arrive? When would Gerhard travel? Could surveillance be organized without alerting anyone?

While the Israelis prepared for the operation, they continued to meet with Kleyer to get more information. Looking back, it's really impressive how much correct data she provided. The only problem was that all the information she had was outdated, as Mirambo soon realized. Everything she had related corresponded to 1962 and 1963, when Kleyer had lived with her sister and brother-in-law. But the informant didn't know, for example, that Mengele was now living in Caieiras, or where the Stammer family estate was located. Mirambo didn't see any way forward and made a daring suggestion: seize Gerhard and take the information from him by force. Mirambo's method was violent, and Mossad chief Meir Amit's position remained unequivocal: the mission to localize Mengele should be discreet. Against his will, Mirambo returned to Israel. He regretted this because he believed that they had never been so close to catching Mengele. The Mossad sent another agent to take Mirambo's place in Brazil.[320] The new agent,

---

[320] Yossi Chen, op. cit., pp. 135–40.

codenamed Zohar, was briefed on Gerhard's, Kleyer's, and Mirambo's activities but found nothing despite several efforts, and the Mossad ended their contact with Thea.

In September 1968, the Mossad command changed again. The new chief, Zvi Zamir, informed Prime Minister Levi Eshkol about the search for Nazi criminals. The commander said that the agency was inundated with reports, mainly about the whereabouts of Mengele and Bormann, Hitler's private secretary. Many of these reports were sincere; others were just attempts to obtain money. Zamir said he would need more resources to examine each report, so Eshkol determined that they were to only collect information about Nazis, which would then be passed on to the Israeli Foreign Ministry to share with concerned governments. The Mossad would no longer be directly involved in any mission, with the exception of Mengele's and Bormann's cases. "It is appropriate and proper that your team be instructed that they are allowed to do something about this," said Prime Minister Eshkol to the head of the Mossad.[321] In regard to Mengele, the problem was that they had lost track of him at that point.

Famous Nazi hunters, such as Tuviah Friedman and Simon Wiesenthal, indicated from time to time that Mengele was in Paraguay. In response to a letter from Friedman, German president Gustav Heinemann asked his counterpart in Asunción to extradite Mengele in November 1970. The Paraguayan government replied that it had no way of arresting Mengele, let alone extraditing him, given that the criminal was not in the country. As we know today, that was correct, but nobody believed it at the time. To satisfy the Germans, the Paraguayan authorities issued an arrest warrant for Mengele, but made it clear that they would only act if he actually turned up. Wiesenthal soon announced to the world that the German government was offering ten million marks in exchange for Mengele's extradition.[322]

---

321 Ibid., p. 151.

322 Ibid., pp. 152–53.

Initially, the Israeli ambassador in Paraguay received only one lead about Mengele per month. After Wiesenthal's announcement, however, an average of two people a day showed up at the embassy with information about Mengele.[323]

Meanwhile, in Brazil, the possibility of following Gerhard to reach Mengele was gone for good in 1971. That year, the Nazi doctor's chief protector decided to return to Austria. His wife and his eldest son, Adolf, had cancer, and the family thought that treatment in Europe would be better for them. From then on, Wolfram and Liselotte Bossert became responsible for Mengele's well-being in the country, while Gerhard maintained constant contact with his friend.

Some characteristics of Mengele's writing stand out in the letters he exchanged with Gerhard. His meandering and supposedly poetic style and the codenames he used to describe friends and places made for difficult reading at times. For example, Wolfram Bossert became Musikus, then shortened to "Mu." Mrs. "Mu" referred to Liselotte. The "uncle" was himself, Mengele. Finally, it's interesting to note that he used Portuguese words in his letters, such as "sítio" (small farm), "foice" (sickle), and "João de Barro" (a typical Brazilian bird). Mengele was mixing the new language with his mother tongue, employing a form of speech that was typical of expatriates from the Germanic community.

In one of his first letters, Mengele described the farm in Itapecerica da Serra, the same site the Mossad mission had come very close to almost a decade earlier. Mengele returned to the place, now with the Bossert family, on the Proclamation of the Brazilian Republic holiday. There he experienced happy moments of peace and quiet, instead of persecution from intelligence agents.

In December 1971, Mengele wrote to Gerhard: "For so many years I had heard about the farm and yet it remained unknown to me. Now, however, my curiosity was out of control: not even bad

---

[323] Ibid., p. 153.

weather would make us give up; we would make the trip no matter what."[324] On the way to the farm, with Wolfram Bossert at the
wheel, they were indeed caught in bad weather, but Mengele was
happy. "What's the harm? We'll tell some more silly jokes, laugh,
and sing a little louder," he later wrote. As they approached the property, some memories started rushing back to him, suggesting that it
had been a long time since he had visited the place: "My memory,
which initially recalled the small church on the road, only begins to
really function again when we arrive in front of the Fischers' house.
Perhaps there is nothing for me 'to remember' anyway, since everything has changed so much."

Mengele continues the letter, seemingly ecstatic as he writes about
the flora and fauna and comments on every detail of the lush Atlantic
Forest:

> We had to go back to the car to get the rest of the luggage. So we
> walked in another direction along the friendly green of the forest path,
> discovered the tranquil and rare splendor of a blue-violet flowering
> bromeliad, and finally worked up a big appetite for the roast chicken
> we brought with us, which we then devoured at the terrace table.
> Over our light meal, I thought about what the seating arrangements
> must have been like for his large family—especially with visitors and
> guests—and remembered an observation my mother made once, that,
> according to Viennese etiquette, you can also use your fingers when
> eating chicken thighs.

Although Mengele had plenty to worry about, he enjoyed some
happy moments with friends, amidst nature, and with fond memories
of the past. Some of the passages he wrote to Gerard are reminiscent
of some old, bucolic TV commercial. Nothing in the letter supports
the other scholars' theories that Mengele had become a depressed

---

324 "Letter from Mengele to Wolfgang Gerhard," December 1971. Museum of the
National Police Academy, archive 38, Brasília.

old man leading a miserable life in Brazil; quite the opposite, as this excerpt shows:

> Before the children go to sleep, there is a lot of laughter. . . . The cozy living room keeps us there until late at night, and I tell them what I know about the farm's beginnings, which is to say, part of the story of our friendship and of an illustrious and unusual time.

Mengele reports that the next day,

> the children bring the peaceful Sunday morning to life and chase away the older ones who sleep late. . . . The housewife prepares a hearty breakfast. . . . Mu is already waiting for his children and their uncle so we can all go for a walk in the woods.

After describing their walk exploring the property, the Old Nazi paints another portrait of the family dynamic of which he, the beloved uncle, is part.

> Mu stretches out on the corner seat and reads Plüschow's adventures; Mrs. Mu makes some noise as she prepares lunch; the children play barber with their uncle; and the weather is improving.

It's worth noting that Gunther Plüschow was a German aviator who fought in World War I and became famous for being the first pilot to film the archipelago Tierra del Fuego and the Argentine Patagonia from the air. This is one example of how the family stayed connected with its own culture and history. Not surprisingly, some of the books the police later found with the Bosserts had been bought in a traditional German bookstore in São Paulo's Brooklin neighborhood.

Mengele's long letter continues, narrating the end of another day with the Bossert family:

At nightfall, a small fire glows on the lawn in front of the terrace, delivering a happy Sunday spent in the forest to the night and its stars. After a few more songs from our youth, we retired to the secretive air of the house by candlelight and ended the day eating, reading, and chatting.

At the end of his extensive account of the visit to the farm, Mengele expresses his hope that his friend didn't feel too nostalgic. "Hopefully some things will trigger memories in you without your heart feeling too heavy."

His final reflection draws parallels with his own life on the run:

It's probably the fate of the times to have to leave "something" behind. A house in B.A. [Buenos Aires], a jungle in Br. [Brazil], or a suitcase in Berlin. But what matters here is what the item meant to you.[325]

In April 1972, Gerhard replied to the letter and thanked Mengele for the report he had sent about his place. Gerhard took the opportunity to tell him about a visit he had made to Günzburg, his friend's hometown. As always, Gerhard began his letter with "Dear old man":

You know better than anyone how nice it is to receive news from home. Coincidentally, I was also able to take a look at "your home." Albeit with the eyes of a "foreigner," but with my heart and soul so close to you, trying to see and experience it with your eyes, that for a while I thought we were walking together through alleys and squares. It's not easy, in one short afternoon, to take away something long-lasting from this small city so rich in culture, to go through a thousand strange and unknown experiences, and still feel as close to it as your heart dictates.[326]

325 Id.

326 "Letter from Wolfgang Gerhard to Mengele," April 15, 1972. Museum of the National Police Academy, archive 3, Brasília.

In his usual sentimental and philosophical style, Mengele sent his reply in August 1972:

> I would like to thank you very much for your occasional postcards and even more for your dear and well-lived "small-town experience" that so delighted (and hurt) my heart. Now you know another part of me. You used to listen to me well and attentively; how else would you have been able to describe it so vividly and accurately? It made me think and realize that I was just a humble traveler in my beloved old city. Yes, it is tough and only gives back love and loyalty to those who stay. So it was with various generations who grew up in it, but then left again just as they had once arrived. The average citizen barely knows their names. . . . It probably has something to do with the history of our world, which according to O. Spengler is "the history of wars," in the past and probably also in the future, despite all the talk of international understanding and humanity![327]

Mengele's routine seemed to be going well, even with Gerhard on the other side of the Atlantic. In October 1972, however, a sudden disruption happened. Bossert, who worked and lived in Caieiras, was fired by Melhoramentos during a company restructuring, which threatened to halt his weekly dinners at home with Mengele and his visits to the doctor at the Stammer family estate. In November, Wolfram Bossert wrote to their mutual friend Gerhard to tell him the news and said that he was considering his options for the future:

> The idea of returning to Europe has come up again. But what do we know about Europe today, apart from the fact that Willy Brandt has

---

[327] Letter from Mengele to Wolfgang Gerhard, August 1972. Oswald Spengler is a German historian and philosopher, best known for his work *The Decline of the West*. He tried to deny the political and philosophical principles of the Enlightenment and had a great influence on other historians and thinkers of the twentieth century.

been re-elected?[328] We know nothing about work, income, living conditions, or the important human relationships on which our well-being largely depends. . . . I don't even want to talk about politics, which was the main reason I left at the time and in which probably nothing has changed in the meantime. . . . There's probably nowhere else in the world that's as comfortable and jovial as here in Brazil.[329]

Returning to Austria wasn't easy and didn't seem to be an option for Bossert. Gerhard's family, who had returned the previous year, faced major financial difficulties, exacerbated by Ruth's illness and that of Burli, the eldest son's nickname. Gerhard decided to ask the Mengele family directly for help. In his view, the wealthy Bavarian industrialists owed him a debt of gratitude, since he had welcomed their criminal brother to Brazil with open arms and lent him money in times of need. Now it was his turn to receive some compensation. However, this idea provoked a serious disagreement with Mengele, who recorded his displeasure with Gerhard in a typewritten, nine-page-long letter, the addressee of which is unclear:

The view of friendship, according to which friends should support each other even in material hardship, is obviously shared, with the only restriction that this hardship must be through no fault of one's own.

---

328 Willy Brandt was a Social Democrat politician who was prime minister of West Germany between 1969 and 1974. He won the Nobel Peace Prize in 1971 for his policy of rapprochement with the countries of Eastern Europe, known as Ostpolitik, one of the movements that helped end the Cold War.

329 Letter from Wolfram Bossert to Wolfgang Gerhard, November 22, 1972. Museum of the National Police Academy, archive 48, Brasília. Excerpts from this letter were published by the newspaper *Folha de S. Paulo* on November 24, 2004, by Ana Flor and Andrea Michael, "Mengele trabalhou dez anos no Brasil." Available at: <www1.folha.uol.com.br/folha/brasil/ult96u65893.shtml>. Accessed on: July 20, 2023. In the article, the letter was wrongly attributed to Mengele, which resulted in the claim that the doctor had worked for Melhoramentos. In a statement, the company categorically denied that Mengele had ever been one of its employees.

Reasonably enough, "support" cannot be a permanent arrangement for a healthy man. We are all struggling to survive, we have to provide for our own relatives, or have no means of earning our own money, for well-known reasons.[330]

Mengele wrote the above thinking that Gerhard was using his son's health as an excuse to explain his poor economic situation in Europe. In the old Nazi's view, his friend should have saved money for unforeseen circumstances and should have found a job that offered a steady— even if low—income. Instead, he had gone into the watch business, an uncertain venture that required him to travel often.

Beyond the quarrel between the two, the letter reveals an important point worth highlighting: Gerhard lent Mengele money to buy the Serra Negra estate in the early 1960s. At the time, Mengele was short the equivalent of $1,666 to buy the property, and the Austrian had that amount in a Brazilian bank. He agreed to advance the money until Mengele was able to make a transfer, a transaction that was very complicated and difficult, given his status as a fugitive from justice. Mengele believed that there was no risk for Gerhard in the whole operation, as everything had been settled in US dollars, a strong currency. For Mengele, Gerhard's assistance was just a "friendly courtesy not unlike lending a friend a book you don't need at the moment." The record of Mengele's payment for his share in the purchase of the Serra Negra estate proves once again that he was a partner of the Stammers, not just a "Swiss" who appeared in their lives and was later revealed to be a war criminal.

Mengele continued to express his anger in his letter and accused Gerhard of only thinking about money. He also came to the defense of his family in Günzburg, especially his younger brother Alois, who had succeeded his father as head of the business: "For an entrepreneur of my brother's caliber, money is only a means to an end, to creative

---

330 Mengele's account probably to Wolfram Bossert. Federal Police Museum, archive 43, Brasília.

fulfillment." Nevertheless, Mengele later revealed that he always shared the little money he received from Germany with Gerhard.

> How should I evaluate his "services out of altruistic friendship" for which he now demands payment from my relatives? I sent him my last savings to protect him during his family's worst needs without thinking about my future and, in a situation of personal crisis, I asked my brother for a loan to prove what he said in his letter . . . about "thanks and friendship." If he asks me to make this sacrifice, it's a concept of friendship that can perhaps still be discussed.

But even though he cursed and criticized Gerhard harshly, Mengele still recognized the other man's merit:

> To conclude these statements, I would like to expressly mention and emphasize my gratitude for your camaraderie in my difficult situation. I never made a secret of the means at my disposal and always managed them in such a way that all the "participants" were always protected from the worst possible hardships. Personally, I only used a ridiculous fraction of this support money from my relatives. This in itself is uninteresting, and relevant only insofar as the restriction imposed on me freed up the funds for other uses.

Mengele's arrival in Brazil was intrinsically linked to Gerhard, about whom he complains so much. Much more than his first contact in the country, Gerhard was the man who promised to always look after a comrade in trouble, and introduced Mengele to all his future friends. No one could have imagined, however, how their contact—initially of a purely utilitarian nature—would turn into a deep relationship. In the excerpt below, Mengele offers a glimpse into his intimate self that allows us to understand how his friendship with Gerhard blossomed:

212 = HIDING MENGELE

I would like to refer again to the relationship that existed between La [Gerhard] and me. It has always been rightly emphasized that it was sustained by the spiritual efforts of two seekers. This is how a helpful welcome in a political emergency led to a spiritual encounter and a friendship. I met a man who was almost exclusively guided mentally by Kolbenheyer's ideas and considered him to be the second greatest German "mental acrobat" after Goethe.[331] At that time, I was still mainly involved with my interests in natural sciences, but I soon found pleasure in the idea of considering the results of natural science in a broader context. . . . I liked his originality of thought, but at the time I didn't think I could get along with him, at least not in the long term. . . . After I moved to S. N. [Serra Negra], his visits became more frequent and I was also very happy to have a good comrade and intellectual exchange partner in him. . . . No one demanded anything from the other, no one talked about obligations, everyone believed that the other was doing the right thing. Later on, he [Gerhard] didn't tell me about his growing impoverishment and I still thought of him as an ambitious businessman until my eyes were opened.

Mengele also highlighted the beginning of his relationship with Wolfram Bossert:

A new phase in our friendship began when I moved in and met Mu at the same time. . . . I had hoped that a larger circle of friends might develop, but certain reasons only allowed it to flourish in a more restricted way. In any case, it was a fruitful period of mutual encouragement. My isolation was relieved and his burden spread a little.

Finally, Mengele acknowledged his family's financial support throughout his time on the run. He concluded that the "people there"

---

331 Erwin Guido Kolbenheyer (1878–1962), a German-language writer who wrote novels defending Nazi ideas.

had had to endure "a heavy fate" since the end of the war, and had provided "an enormous amount of money."[332]

There was a strong friendship triangle between Mengele, Gerhard, and Bossert. The latter wanted the other two to get along, as he made clear in some letters to Gerhard:

I'm once again in the awkward situation of being in the middle of two parties who don't understand each other, having to understand both men's opinions and motivations, although I don't fully approve and am only trying to clarify [some issues] in order to help avoid future mistakes. I must ask for your forgiveness in advance and for your understanding that I will be forced to tell you many unpleasant things, but what's a real friendship good for, if not helping others through the truth?[333]

In another letter, Wolfram once again got straight to the point:

The people there [the Mengele family] have nothing to do with you, me, or anyone else, so they have no obligations to repay debts of gratitude, obligations of friendship or camaraderie, or whatever. Your only connection is with the "old man," whom you should have contacted and who would have mediated. He would probably have gotten more than just a thousand German marks, despite the strained relations between him and his family (whom you, like me, know and who make it clear that they are not happy when his friends go there for money). You probably wouldn't have thought that your relationship would have improved in any way as a result of your action.[334]

332 Mengele's account, probably to Wolfram Bossert. Museum of the National Police Academy, archive 43, Brasília.

333 Letter from Wolfram Bossert to Wolfgang Gerhard, November 22, 1972. Museum of the National Police Academy, archive 49, Brasília.

334 Letter from Wolfram Bossert to Wolfgang Gerhard, November 29, 1972. Museum of the National Police Academy, archive 47, Brasília.

The thousand marks Bossert refers to is an amount Gerhard apparently received from the Mengele family when he sought them out in Bavaria, although he had hoped to obtain much more. Despite this major disagreement over money, Mengele and Gerhard later resumed their friendship.

WHILE THE RIFT BETWEEN THE two friends was eventually mended, the same could not be said for the relationship between Mengele and the Stammers. The situation with them only went from bad to worse. Gitta said that Mengele liked to constantly interfere in the running of the family's daily affairs. She finally decided that she no longer wanted the old Nazi in her home, even though she didn't know what to do with him.[335]

Mengele was often so nervous—fearful of the Mossad, a fight with a friend, lack of money—that he caused himself a serious and, to say the least, bizarre health problem: he swallowed an excessive amount of hair from his moustache and accumulated a Ping-Pong ball–sized clump of hair that caused a blockage in his intestines. At first, the doctors couldn't figure out the problem, but an X-ray revealed it. Mengele underwent surgery at the Santa Elisa Hospital in Jundiaí to remove what they classified as a trichobezoar in the rectum. It was a very rare case in humans and caused quite a stir in medical circles. Dr. Eduardo Fredini Júnior, who treated him, never forgot the incident; however, he had no idea that the man who spoke Portuguese with a thick accent was a war criminal wanted by the justice system. Years later, he saw Mengele's photos and recognized him by his large moustache and hat, without which he never left the house.[336]

---

[335] Statement by Gitta Stammer to the Federal Police, p. 30.

[336] Statement by Fredini Júnior to the Federal Police, p. 69.

An older Josef Mengele with bushy moustache and signature fedora.

Criminal Museum of the Teaching Directorate of the National Police Academy / Museu Criminal da Diretoria de Ensino da Academia Nacional de Policia.

AS FATE WOULD HAVE IT, the eldest Mengele brother, who spent more than half his life on the run, outlived his two siblings. In February 1974, Alois, the youngest, who ran the family's company and whom Mengele admired, died at the age of sixty. The news quickly reached the Mossad, which sent photographers to infiltrate the funeral in Günzburg. It was an opportunity to find out if Mengele was still alive. He might appear at the funeral, which was scheduled to be held five days after the death to allow time for guests from abroad to arrive. On the day of the funeral, snow was falling; the attendees were wrapped in their winter coats and many carried umbrellas. As a result, the photographers were unable to identify anyone at the site. And no photos published in the next day's newspaper showed any face resembling Mengele's.[337]

---

337 Yossi Chen, op. cit., p. 156.

It was a difficult year and, at that point, Mengele had become a hot potato: no one wanted to have him in their household. Not knowing what else to do to get rid of the nuisance, Geza asked Bossert to take him into his home. Although they were very close, the Austrian declined. Instead, he advised Geza to rent a property and find a maid for Mengele; that way, they all would have an easier life. Bossert, however, despite having moved to the capital after losing his job in Caieiras, pledged to continue seeing his friend every week for dinner.[338]

Once again, the Mengeles' loyal employee, Hans Sedlmeier, had to come from Germany to resolve the impasse with the Stammers. In December 1974, Geza, Gitta, and their children moved into a house in the Água Fria neighborhood, in the North Zone of São Paulo, but this time Mengele didn't accompany them. He lived alone on the farm in Caieiras until February 1975, when he moved to his last address, in the Eldorado neighborhood. It was here, on the outskirts of São Paulo's South Zone, that Mengele would spend the last four years of his life. The money for the purchase of the two houses—both Mengele's and the Stammers'—came from the sale of the farm in Caieiras. They would still maintain some connection but, for the most part, the partners were breaking up the business, which had lasted more than a decade.

---

338 "Assustado, agressivo, vivia com medo." *O Estado de S. Paulo*, June 7, 1985.

16

LIFE ON THE EDGE

SÃO PAULO, 1975 TO 1979

Mengele was about to turn sixty-four when he had to start a new phase in his life. The only option he had now was to live alone in the small house in Eldorado, on the edge of the Billings reservoir. At this point, the weight of age was already showing. He suffered from rheumatism and had an unusual, very noticeable swelling in his left leg. Liselotte observed that his leg had swollen so much that it was almost twice the size of the other one. In addition, he had frequent cramps and some difficulty walking. He told Gitta it was a consequence of a disease he had contracted in Paraguay or Uruguay. Mengele also suffered from unbearable migraines, which appeared in his teens and never went away. He was in poor physical health, and it would get even worse the following year. Mengele, however, always adhered to the philosophy that he shouldn't surrender in any way, for he strongly believed that whoever surrenders is dead.

This new phase in his life brought great concern to Mengele's inner circle. A letter, probably written by his son, Rolf, discusses his physical and mental state:

It is my firm conviction that P. can no longer live alone. Humanly speaking, he couldn't cope and, besides, he moves around so clumsily that constant injuries, sunstroke, heart attack, or something similar are possible. Even the help of a maid wouldn't be enough, because he wouldn't have the conversation, the intellectual exchange of ideas, to which he had become accustomed over the years with Gitta.

The letter refers to Mengele as "P.," which could mean Papa, an affectionate way of referring to his father in German. In any case, the fact is that whoever wrote it was also concerned about Mengele's safety, as he was a fugitive from justice:

We all know that every change, even in favorable conditions, always involves risks. Everything has been quiet for more than ten years. No one worries about family connections or the behavior of relatives anymore, because "that's the way it's always been" and they've gotten used to it. Even in a very favorable place, there are always moments of risk—disquiet, changes, curiosity from neighbors, relatives, and acquaintances.

This excerpt makes clear the concerns Mengele's small support network had: changing homes could be dangerous and raise suspicion.[339]

WHEN A STRANGER APPEARED AT his gate on the Alvarenga Road, Mengele trembled with fear. He didn't dare open it. If his gardener, Luís, was at home, the old man would ask him to see who it was first. In the meantime, he would wait, hiding inside. Usually it was just people asking for directions.[340] Nevertheless, his fear seemed to dissipate as he walked around his new neighborhood, always wearing a hat, as if

---

339 Letter from an unknown sender, September 4, 1974. National Police Academy Museum, archive 41, Brasília.

340 Testimony given by Luís Rodrigues to the Federal Police, p. 51.

he felt safer under the felt protection. He thought he lived in a beautiful place, which was true in a way. The bromeliads on the trees, the pine trees, and the dam were beautiful. On his wanderings, he made friends with Jaime, a retired metalworker who now had a job as a caretaker on a small farm. Jaime said that the foreigner with the strong accent was known as "Seu Pedro" and was a well-liked person in the neighborhood, as he treated everyone with respect and cordiality. The ex-metallurgist's wife washed Seu Pedro's clothes for a few years, until she died in 1978. The caretaker also recalled that when the gringo fell ill, Dr. Roberto, a doctor from the Eldorado and Diadema area, took care of him.[341]

In his solitary daily routine, Mengele always ate salads to "stay fit." When night fell, he would turn on the television to watch the evening's first soap opera, followed by another one at seven, and the third soap opera at eight o'clock at night. He only broke that habit on Wednesdays, the day set aside to receive Wolfram Bossert. Sometimes Liselotte and her children would also come for dinner with their uncle. Mengele loved to chat in German and philosophize about the current times. On Sundays, he was visited by his gardener, Luís, who had still been a teenager when he began working for him. The young man would bring his younger sister, and the three of them would watch television together. On those occasions, the host maintained the German custom of serving afternoon coffee with bread and jam.[342]

Without ever revealing who he was, "Seu Pedro" sometimes commented that he had been in the Second World War and had then been forced to flee and sleep alone in the bush. In his long conversations with Luís, he said that he didn't like Black people and advised the gardener not to interact with them. Seu Pedro would point at Blacks passing by on the Alvarenga Road and comment: "Look how ugly they

---

341 Testimony given by Jaime Martins dos Santos, caretaker of a farm on the Alvarenga Road, to the Federal Police, p. 50.

342 Letter from Mengele to Martha, February 1976, National Police Academy Museum, archive 75, Brasília.

are." He openly expressed his hateful racism, for example criticizing the soap opera *Escrava Isaura* (*The Slave Isaura*), one of the biggest hits on Brazilian television then, saying he didn't like it because there were too many Black actors on the series. But he watched it anyway, for the pleasure of seeing enslaved people mistreated. Mengele used to say that "Black people really deserved to be beaten," without disguising his disgusting sadism and intolerance.[343]

After the soap operas, Mengele used to spend hours on end writing and reading. He devoured the biography of Joseph Freiherr von Eichendorff, a great author of German romanticism. He also read Georg Büchner, the forerunner of Expressionist theater with his play *Woyzeck*. Coincidentally, the protagonist Woyzeck is a Jewish soldier who agrees to take part in a doctor's outrageous experiments, in which he is only fed peas. The "scientist" is thrilled to see the degradation of Woyzeck's body. In the meantime, the doctor's wife cheats on him, and his superior in the Army accuses him of being immoral for not having married in the church. As if that had been the immorality! Mengele also read E. T. A. Hoffmann, one of the greatest names in fantasy literature, whose stories inspired the ballet *The Nutcracker*, the opera *The Tales of Hoffmann*, and Sigmund Freud's psychoanalytic theory on "Das Unheimliche," or The Uncanny, which describes something familiar that appears strange or even frightful. By studying the three German authors—Eichendorff, Büchner, and Hoffmann—Mengele said that he wanted to better understand the historical context of the French Revolution.[344] He also enjoyed researching other historical subjects, such as German immigration to Brazil. When he watched movies, they were usually old ones with actresses such as Sophia Loren or Natalie Wood, going to bed late, well after midnight.

---

343 Luís Rodrigues's statement to the Federal Police, p. 53.

344 Letter from Mengele to Wolfgang, March 10, 1976, National Police Academy Museum, archive 55, Brasília. Eichendorff wrote the novel *Das Schloss Dürande* (1837), which depicts class differences in pre-revolutionary France. Büchner wrote the play *Danton's Death* (1835; premiere, 1902), set during the French Revolution, and Hoffmann was a contemporary of the French Revolution.

In the morning, he prepared his own coffee. He used to say that he was "his own housewife," even though he had a maid. On Wednesdays, when Luís came to take care of the garden, Mengele would wake up early to get the gardener's coffee ready too. Then the two of them would start working together. The young man would weed the lawn and the flower beds, and his employer would rake the leaves that had fallen from the trees, especially the rubber trees. Mengele also trimmed the vines and any other overgrown plant. He picked the raspberries, which then became part of his dessert. If there was nothing else to do in the garden, there was always something to fix in the house—a light bulb or switch or a dripping tap.

From time to time, Mengele would go out shopping: beverages, milk, fruit, meat, and whatever else he needed. When he returned with his heavy grocery bags, his "boys," the dogs Zigan and Buxi, were already waiting for him for a walk on a neighboring property, where they would sniff around the woods and sometimes get lost. During his walks in the forest, Mengele picked more raspberries, which grew everywhere. Once or twice a week, the Nazi doctor went into the "city." By this, he meant the more urbanized districts of the South Zone of São Paulo, where he ran all sorts of errands: he mailed letters, paid the electricity bill, bought something at the German bookshop and a piece of strudel from the German patisserie. These were his little pleasures, as he explained in a letter to Martha, his ex-wife.

Mengele's life was so prosaic that he bore no resemblance to the malignant person who had sent thousands of innocent people to the gas chambers in Auschwitz. Although he always felt anxious and fearful of being caught at any moment, especially by the Mossad, he had enough freedom to do whatever he pleased. In a letter, he wrote of indulging in another simple pleasure: he had bought new furniture for his house—a sofa, two armchairs, and a Provençal-style table for the TV. "My cage is becoming more and more habitable, but I wonder: why so many places to sit? Seldom does any of the few people I know come to visit!" he wrote to Martha, keeping up his strong personality trait of complaining.

In the letter, Mengele revealed that he had had a pleasant exchange of ideas with Martha's son Karl-Heinz, who was both his stepson and nephew. The subject of their conversation had been two books by Peter Bamm, a German doctor who had been at the front during World War II and became a bestselling author. Mengele had lived with Karl-Heinz in Buenos Aires and had a closer relationship with him than with his own son, Rolf. He asked his ex-wife:

> I had always hoped for this spiritual connection. Karl-Heinz described his new house to me, and I wished him a good domestic life and a wife. He hasn't yet discovered how much better it is to live as a couple. Or do you have a different opinion?[345]

At the turn of the year 1975, Mengele received a visit from his good friend Gerhard, who had traveled to Brazil because he was having difficulties with his property in Itapecerica da Serra. His daughter Karoline had joined him because he had given her the trip as a Christmas present. She later told the police that he had to resolve land-registration or lawyer issues.[346] The two of them spent New Year's Eve in Rio, then visited the Bossert family and the estate. Gerhard took the opportunity to leave Mengele updated versions of his own Brazilian documents: his foreign identity card, his work permit, and his driver's license. Mengele simply replaced Gerhard's original photos with his own and, just like that, became a legal foreigner. The only potential problem was the fourteen-year age difference between the two men, but that never turned out to be an issue.

Always eager to increase Mengele's support network, Gerhard decided to contact an acquaintance who might have some affinity

---

345 Letter from Mengele to Martha, February 1976. Museum of the National Police Academy, archive 75, Brasília. In the letter, Mengele refers to Karl-Heinz only as "Kh." For clarity, the full name has been used.

346 Bundeskriminalamt, *Mengele Dossier.* Wiesbaden, June 28, 1985, p. 7, archive.

Josef Mengele's national driving license.

Criminal Museum of the Teaching Directorate of the National Police Academy / Museu Criminal da Diretoria de Ensino da Academia Nacional de Policia.

with the old man: Ernesto Glawe, a textile engineer who lived in the South Zone of São Paulo. Glawe had been born in Buenos Aires to a German father and an Argentinian mother, and spoke German fluently. Gerhard approached Glawe, told him he was returning to Austria, and asked if he would be willing to provide assistance to an elderly friend of Austrian origin. The assistance Gerhard was suggesting required Glawe to visit and chat with the old man, and to help him with anything he might need. Glawe was surprised, since they weren't really close enough for Gerhard to make such a request. However, he agreed to meet the "Austrian" gentleman because, Glawe said, he liked helping others.

Gerhard took Glawe to the house on Alvarenga Road, where he introduced him to Mengele under the name Peter Gerhard, another of his aliases. After that first meeting, the engineer started visiting "Peter" every month. He would always arrive with a small gift—like cookies or chocolates—and the two of them would chat for a while.

"Peter" was very polite and courteous. Sometimes Ernesto's family would come along, especially his son Norberto, who soon began to call him by his Brazilian name, Pedro. On one of these visits, Ernesto met the Bossert couple, whom he had known for years because Liselotte had been his children's teacher. But only on this occasion did he find out that they were also friends with "Peter." Glawe's family and the Bosserts had a lot in common—they all spoke German and enjoyed spending time in nature—and thus they began to frequent each other's homes.[347] Furthermore, both the Glawes and the Bosserts belonged to a community wherein everyone knew each other, if not personally, then most likely through a mutual acquaintance. After that, Gerhard felt there was a good chance that the old man's social circle would expand. He returned to Europe, but his leaving was hard on Mengele, who wrote to Gerhard in March 1976:[348]

> The first week after his departure brought my days back to my consciousness. Understandably, I found loneliness to be even more painful. In addition, I had no money until Wolfram finally came for a routine visit and I borrowed some. In the meantime, Ernesto was also present, with whom I had a good conversation throughout the evening.

The lonely criminal also told his friend that he had visited Geza and Gitta to find out about the sale of the apartment he had in São Paulo. This property was obviously not in his name, nor was any other estate he had bought in partnership with the Stammers. Mengele told Gerhard that the Hungarian couple had been very friendly and helpful, and continued: "At the same time, I could clearly see that my great

347 Ernesto Glawe's statement to the Federal Police, p. 61.
348 Letter from Mengele to Wolfgang, March 10, 1976. Museum of the National Police Academy, archive 55, Brasília. In this letter, Mengele refers to Wolfram Bossert as "Mu," but his real name has been used here to facilitate the reader's understanding.

adversary is Pe, who apparently keeps them from visiting me." "Pe" was the codename for Robert Peter, the elder Stammer son.

Gerhard had recommended that Mengele buy a sailboat to relax, as there was a dam right in front of his house, and the Germans who lived nearby loved sailing. He replied that he considered it sometimes, but argued that it wasn't that easy without help. In conclusion, Mengele said that he was preparing himself mentally and morally for his birthday on March 16, when he would turn sixty-five. "I don't know whether to consider it as a symbol of a conclusion or a new beginning. In any case, I decided that I would be calmer after it, as befits my age."[349]

In mid-May 1976, Ernesto's son Norberto was visiting "Pedro" with his fiancée. As they were saying goodbye, around nine in the evening, the old man began to feel unwell. Suddenly, he had trouble speaking and moving. Norberto went to a clinic near the Billings dam to ask for help. After describing his condition, a doctor advised him to take "Pedro" to a better-equipped hospital. From the symptoms, it was probably a stroke.

Norberto returned home to ask his father for help, but the older Glawe had hepatitis, and so the young man had to sort it out himself. He called Bossert and asked him to come to "Pedro's" house. After Bossert got there, Norberto took his father's car and, with Bossert's help, transported Mengele to the Santa Marta Hospital, located behind the Santa Casa de Santo Amaro Hospital. Mengele had to be hospitalized, and Norberto took care of it, presenting Pedro's documents. These were the same ones that actually belonged to Wolfgang but had been tampered with and now showed Mengele's photo. Norberto also had to leave a deposit, paid for with a $100 bill that "Pedro" had given him.[350]

---

[349] Id.

[350] Statement by Norberto Manfredo Glawe to the Federal Police, pp. 58–59. 14 Ibid., p. 59. 15 Ibid., p. 60.

When he was discharged, Mengele couldn't be alone and, therefore, stayed in Ernesto's home for almost two weeks. Meanwhile, Norberto took care of Mengele's house in Eldorado so that it wouldn't be left deserted.[351] As he always did with anyone who belonged to his circle, Mengele created a codename for Ernesto Glawe: he was "Santiago," because he had a house on a beach with that name, located between Bertioga and São Sebastião.[352] In a letter to his family in Germany, Mengele described his stroke and recovery:

On May 16, I suffered a kind of stroke, which temporarily paralyzed the left side of my body. With the exception of my left hand, which I can now use 50% of the time, all the after-effects disappeared quickly. From time to time, I'm still plagued by headaches and urgent complaints about my intestines, which I now want to have thoroughly examined in a laboratory. Next week, I'll get my new teeth and the junk will look more or less decent again. I'm still living with Santiago, where I'm in good hands in every respect. As he himself is ill with hepatitis, his wife is more of a nurse than a housewife.

However, I will soon be returning to my little house, where Santiago's son is currently holding down the fort, albeit with some difficulties on Luís's part. The two young people got engaged at the same time and plan to get married around February. It hasn't yet been decided whether we'll live together after the small garden cottage is renovated, or in a new house in another area. . . . In time, everything will "be all right again," which is the dearest offspring of human hope.[353]

351 Ibid., p. 59.

352 Ibid., p. 60.

353 Letter from Mengele to his family, June 25, 1976. Museum of the National Police Academy, archive 76, Brasília.

Barbecue organized by Norberto Glawe at the house on Alvarenga Road, São Paulo.

Criminal Museum of the Teaching Directorate of the National Police Academy / Museu Criminal da Diretoria de Ensino da Academia Nacional de Policia.

When Pedro returned home, Norberto continued to live with him for another month,[354] as the old man was very isolated and needed company. As he mentioned in his letter, he even suggested that Norberto move in with his future wife for good. That, however, never happened because she didn't like the idea.[355] To celebrate "Pedro's" improvement, Norberto organized a barbecue and invited his fiancée, her sister with her boyfriend, and a couple of other friends.[356] The famous photo of the event appeared years later in the Federal Police dossier and in the press: the Nazi fugitive surrounded by young people enjoying a Sunday afternoon. Norberto later told the authorities that "Pedro" was generally very attentive to the girls who came to his house

---

354 Statement by Norberto Manfredo Glawe to the Federal Police, p. 59.

355 Statement by Ernesto Glawe to the Federal Police, p. 66.

356 Statement by Norberto Manfredo Glawe to the Federal Police, p. 59.

and showed an interest in young people. "Pedro" once told Norberto that he had been on the battlefront in World War II, but did not reveal that he was Josef Mengele. In 1985, Norberto told the police that he only found out that the criminal had lived in Brazil when the news hit the papers and the whole world was abuzz. Norberto also said that he had distanced himself from "Pedro" after realizing that he was very authoritarian, and he never saw the old man again.

Mengele had a different version of how his and Norberto's relationship unfolded; he wrote:

> At first things went very well, but it became increasingly clear that the boy, obviously much loved by his mother, was not willing to support our domestic community, but regarded me more or less as his maid. Since he almost only came home to bed (usually after eleven o'clock), I was always on my own, even more than before, for Luís had quit because he didn't get along with the young man.[357]

A little over a month after his stroke, Mengele wrote about his recovery, which was progressing as expected, albeit slowly: "The only abnormal things in my existence are stress, the depressing sadness of feeling abandoned and, at times, the tormenting disappointment with my own life," he reported in a dramatic tone. Mengele also wrote that, during vacation, Ernesto wanted to travel with his wife to some land he owned in the coastal mountains and invited him along. Mengele accepted the invitation, and the trip seems to have done him a lot of good: "The beautiful air and scenery of the mountains gladdened my heart, as did the new and attractive road along the coast," he wrote.[358]

According to Mengele, the final straw in his relationship with Norberto was after his little house on Alvarenga Road was broken into. According to Mengele, one Saturday morning, Bossert picked

---

357 Museum of the National Police Academy, archive 52, Brasília.
358 Letter from Mengele to Wolfgang, July 2, 1976. National Police Academy Museum, archive 53, Brasília.

him up to take pictures of him, something unusual, as Mengele hated being photographed, afraid that any photo could be used to identify him. That same morning, Norberto also decided to go out to see his parents and fiancée. When Mengele returned home in the afternoon, he found that his house had been burglarized. The robbers had taken objects that were easy to carry, such as watches, razors, calculators, umbrellas, and Geza's gun—nothing of much importance, except for the weapon. The theft brought him a new element of uncertainty and worry, particularly because the pistol could fall into the hands of people investigating the Nazi fugitive's whereabouts. Although it was registered in Geza's name, the Hungarian didn't want to report the theft because that would have required everyone involved to go to the police station. From then on, the old Nazi didn't think he could trust Norberto any longer. The young man went out too often and came back home only late at night, which frustrated the old Nazi. After all, the main reason for Norberto being there was to keep him company. Mengele concluded: "The former experiment with Santiago Jr. went badly, but it was stopped at the right time, at least before the house was transferred to his name, which I was repeatedly urged to do."[359]

In another letter to Gerhard, Mengele wrote:

We probably made a mistake with Santiago, and as soon as I can get my money that I had given him to keep, and put it somewhere else (safe), I want to distance myself from him . . . By the way, he bought an expensive car (a Maverik) and an apartment for his son, although he didn't give Wolfram a penny back. Suspicious?! You can't talk to these people about anything other than everyday things, which I found out recently when they visited me again, many weeks later.[360]

---

[359] Letter from Mengele to Wolfgang Gerhard, November 10, 1976. National Police Academy, archive 50, Brasília.

[360] Id. In this letter, Mengele referred to Wolfram Bossert as "Mu," but I kept his real name to make it easier to read.

Life went on without the "Santiagos." Mengele told Wolfgang that he now had a driver and could take care of his own affairs, the most important of which were the regular visits to Geza and Gitta to discuss business. The Hungarian had finally found a buyer for the apartment that, as mentioned before, belonged to Mengele but was not registered in his name. In a letter, he explained how the scheme worked: "All previous purchases of the property were made without a bill of sale. . . . Geza, who has always owned the deed, has never said a word about it."[361]

IN THE MIDST OF SUCH practical problems, there was always time for a breather outside the city. Five months after his trip with Ernesto, Mengele paid another visit to the Itapecerica da Serra farm with the Bossert family. It was a wonderful opportunity to spend a few days with Wolfram, Liselotte, and the children, away from the confinement and monotony of his own home. The adventure began with Mengele sleeping at the Bosserts' house on Friday so that they could leave early the next morning. On the way to the farm, they stopped by the cemetery in Embu das Artes. It was a sunny day, and yellow marigolds shone on Wolfgang's mother's grave. Mengele took a tour of the cemetery with the family, talked about the dead, and mentioned that this could be his last resting place. Two years and four months later, he would be correct. On the day of their visit, however, he commented, "But there's still a bit of time [for me]"; and before continuing on their journey, they stopped at a steakhouse, where they ate heartily.

It was November 1976, and spring was in full swing. When they arrived at the farm, they marveled at the beauty of the flowers they had planted on previous visits: yellow lilies, pale blue hydrangeas, and white daisies. There were also red-billed lilies, and radiant *manacá* bushes with purplish-white flowers. The hearty barbecue meal had

---

[361] Letter from Mengele to Wolfgang Gerhard, September 6, 1976. Museum of the National Police Academy, archive 52, Brasília.

depleted everyone's energy, and they needed a short rest before Bossert took them to the orchidarium below the house. Later, the children and Uncle Peter left their parents and went for a walk, picking up flowers to make a bouquet for Liselotte.

During those days, they went into the woods and visited a waterfall. Mengele also mentioned a neighbor named Mario Fischer, who appears frequently in Bossert's letters to Wolfgang, the estate's owner. Apparently, the situation of the property was not regularized, and the two always spoke of the need to go to the National Institute for Colonization and Agrarian Reform (INCRA), the body responsible for maintaining the national rural property records.[362] Perhaps for this reason, in the 1960s, the Mossad believed that the property was not Wolfgang's, a discouraging factor in the search for Mengele. According to reports, the paperwork really wasn't up to date, but Wolfgang was indeed the owner.

Another Christmas was approaching in the isolated house on Alvarenga Road, and Mengele wrote to his stepson, Karl-Heinz, in December 1976:

> For the elderly, the date is significant, above all, for the memories it brings back. First of all, of my own childhood, of the presents that fulfilled burning desires, then of the many experiences with loved ones—with the fiancée, the wife, the "son," and perhaps (still) with the grandchildren. In between, there were Christmases in enemy territory with comrades whose names are unknown.

The letter continues with an account of a Christmas episode, when Mengele was just twelve years old, that reveals a great deal about his personality and way of thinking since his early years. On the afternoon of December 24, he agreed to go on a sleigh ride with two friends from school. but his classmates never showed up. Although it was getting

---

362 Letter from Mengele to Wolfgang Gerhard, November 10, 1976. Museum of the National Police Academy, archive 50, Brasília.

dark, Mengele decided to set off alone in the wild, snowy landscape, and got home late on that special night. His mother and father weren't happy, but welcomed him warmly anyway. He further wrote:

> I recovered my well-being in a hot bath and satisfied my voracious appetite with the traditional Christmas ham. Then I spent one of many unforgettable Christmas evenings with my parents, siblings, and cousin Lina. . . . The harmless story seems very characteristic of me and the course of my life. I was always driven to do something special, and that started with becoming acquainted with the surroundings of my home. Once I had set a goal, it was hard to talk myself out of it; I was ready to make a personal commitment and had a lot of patience. Every agreement and every promise was an unquestionable obligation for me.

The excerpt above shows his obstinate side and the belief that he was destined to do something "special."[363]

In 1977, the routine in the Eldorado house changed when Elsa Gulpian, a woman from Rolândia, in the southern Brazilian state of Paraná, started working as a maid for "Seu Pedro." The twenty-five-year-old was responsible for cleaning and cooking, as well as all the shopping. Mengele told Gulpian he was Gitta's cousin, although Elsa had never met her. However, Gitta's husband, Geza, paid Mengele a visit every month, always carrying a briefcase. The two men would talk behind closed doors for about half an hour. "Seu Pedro" would say that his "cousin" had brought him money and, as soon as Geza left, he would pay Elsa and the gardener, Luís, who had returned to work in the house.

The maid considered "Seu Pedro" to be a good person and well-liked in the neighborhood, although he had few friends. When Wolfram Bossert showed up on Wednesday evenings, the young woman had usually already left for the day. Only on three occasions had she stayed

---

363 Letter from Mengele to Karl-Heinz, December 18, 1976. Museum of the National Police Academy, archive 74, Brasília.

longer at Mengele's home and prepared dinner for the two men. On another occasion, when Bossert came during the day, Elsa also met Liselotte and served lunch for everyone. Mengele and the couple talked a lot, but she didn't understand anything because they only spoke German.[364]

The boss called the young woman "Perle." Luís soon noticed that there was something more to their relationship. "Seu Pedro" had a special affection for Elsa and gave her a gold bracelet and other nice gifts. Sometimes he took her to the cinema, and they even went out for dinner. Her sister used to join them on those occasions, and once, at the Santo Antônio restaurant in São Bernardo, someone took a photo of them that became famous years later.

In conversations, "Seu Pedro" made it clear that he didn't like Black people. "Slavery should never have ended," the old Nazi once said to Elsa. Whenever it was time for Elsa to leave his house, the boss himself made a point of escorting her home to protect her. One day, he told Luís that he was in love, but he didn't say with whom. He used to invite the young gardener to listen to music, and "Seu Pedro" would even dance if a waltz was playing.[365] Elsa remembers that he had lots of tapes of classical music and especially liked Beethoven's Symphony No. 5. Elsa also met Rolf, who stayed at the house for a few days and was introduced to her as a nephew of "Seu Pedro" who had arrived from Germany.[366]

Rolf had not seen Mengele in person since he was a teenager. On their first meeting in Switzerland in 1956, Rolf actually thought Mengele was "Uncle Fritz" and not his own father. The two met again in October 1977, in São Paulo; but in previous years, the two had exchanged intense letters. In one of them, from 1969, Mengele discovered that he had become a grandfather:

---

364 Elsa Gulpian de Oliveira's statement to the Federal Police, p. 48.

365 "Antes da morte, a depressão." *O Estado de S. Paulo*, June 11, 1985, p. 17.

366 Elsa Gulpian de Oliveira's statement to the Federal Police, p. 48.

As I am biologically oriented and used to thinking in terms of generations, the happy event appealed to me in a special way. It's one of those fundamental events that have had the same significance in all times and among all peoples, because they connect us so directly with the natural [world], that is, with the principles linked to this Earth, and which we call life. And what possibilities exist within him. But it will be what he makes of it. The environment and education should not be forgotten. But they are also linked to the family. I don't actually know any of the actors involved in this event, but I still feel connected to this leader of a new generation, like someone who belongs to me too. All my best wishes go to him.[367]

Josef Mengele and Rolf Mengele during their visit to Brazil in 1977.

Stern Magazine.

Josef and Rolf Mengele, together with Lisolette Bossert and her children, Sabine and Andreas, during the 1977 meeting of father and son.

Stern Magazine.

---

367 Letter from Mengele to Rolf, April 1969. Museum of the National Police Academy, archive 57, Brasília.

A year later, Mengele was thrilled with another important event in his son's life—his graduation:

I cannot express how happy I was at the successful completion of your studies, but you can believe me when I say that it was very great. Despite the report of your success having reached me late, I never really doubted it.[368]

ROLF'S TRIP TO SÃO PAULO was discussed for a long time before it became a reality, as Mengele was extremely cautious in his every move. He held a "war council" with his small inner circle to consider all factors, the two most important of which, in his opinion, were the need for a visit and the risk involved. He wrote, "In the absence of a truly valid reason, the risk rises to the limit of what is responsible. This time, the behavior of third parties does not oblige one to accept great risk." On the other hand, Mengele considered it necessary for his well-being to receive someone "from over there"—in other words, from Germany—every year.

Rolf traveled to Brazil with the passport of a friend, Wilfred Busse. If he tried to enter the country with his own passport, he would raise suspicions and could be followed. He carried with him $5,000 provided by the Mengele family, which he would hand over to his father in the same way as Hans Sedlmeier and Hans Rudel had done previously.[369] The meeting with Rolf was certainly the one Mengele most eagerly awaited. Later, the old man wrote:

Unfortunately, he was only able to devote himself to me for a week; he spent another three days with a (French-Swiss) university colleague

368 Letter from Mengele to Rolf, April 15, 1970. Museum of the National Police Academy, archive 68, Brasília.
369 Yossi Chen, op. cit., p. 203.

in Rio. We also fulfilled a respectable schedule in which we visited
all our friends and acquaintances; paid a visit to Farm I [Serra Negra]
and II [Caieiras] accompanied by Geza; spent a beautiful day (by bus)
in Santos-Guarujá-Bertioga; and a Sunday at the Itapecerica da Serra
farm with a visit to the waterfall. The reunion went as I'd hoped, so
all in all it was positive. The two of us got on well, even though we
didn't share many similarities. In our political views, however, we are
so far apart that I considered such discussions pointless and avoided
them. He was enthusiastic about the country and the people here (he
expected abysmal conditions) and therefore wants to come back soon
(probably with his second wife) to spend a "dream vacation" with me
on the sidelines. However, I fear that his career as a lawyer, his export
business, and the construction of a large house will postpone his South
American plans, if not frustrate them. Of course, the visit satisfied
many desires for things worth knowing and not usually written about.
His mother was involved in a very serious car accident, which left some
irreparable damage (instant disorders, memory impairment, etc.). This
prompted me to contact her again.[370]

Rolf's mother was Irene, whom Mengele had married when he was
young and who later visited him in Auschwitz.

THE HUNT FOR MENGELE HAD come to a stop since Levi Eshkol had become
Israel's prime minister in the early 1960s, and little or no action had
been taken for almost a decade. However, the 1977 elections shook
up Israel. The new prime minister, Menachem Begin, had a different
vision than his predecessors and, from then on, Mossad was perma-
nently tasked to hunt down Nazi criminals; Mengele was number one
on their list. In the national imagination, Mengele was the symbol of

---

370 Museum of the National Police Academy, archive 51, Brasília. In this excerpt
written by Mengele, he uses only "Ge" for Geza, "Farm I and II," and "La-Sítio."
These are all codes used in the letters, but for clarity of reading, the names and cities
have been written out.

cruelty, a man responsible for personally sending hundreds of thousands of Jews to their deaths, in addition to torturing his victims, killing with his bare hands, and conducting gruesome medical experiments. In short, in the Jewish collective consciousness, he was the incarnation of evil itself.

When the Mossad was given the task of finding Mengele, the agency had to reorganize itself. For various reasons, the reorganization took time and was only finalized in March 1978. That's when the agency created a division called Messer ("knife" in German; codename for Mengele) that would be dedicated to finding the fugitive once and for all. The Mossad's best bet was that he was in Paraguay, because that's where their informants were pointing. In order to resume the search, the agents decided to prepare a list of all of Mengele's former contacts, among them Alban Krug (a farmer who welcomed him in Paraguay) and Hans Rudel.[371] But when the Mossad took the next steps to catch Mengele alive, it was already too late.

THE YEAR 1978 WAS ALREADY drawing to a close. Elsa found a new love and decided to get married. This meant she was no longer going to work at "Seu Pedro's" house. When he found out, he cried but soon found another "Pearl" to take her place, Inês Mehlich. He was always saddened when the workday was over and his employees left, because he felt utterly alone. Thus, he often asked Inês to stay a little longer and watch the soap operas with him.[372]

Meanwhile, in Austria, his good friend Gerhard moved in with his two sons, Adolf and Erwin. His wife, Ruth, had died of cancer and his two daughters were busy with their own lives. On the afternoon of December 11, 1978, Gerhard went out with his eldest son and an acquaintance to a bar. There he began to feel unwell and was taken home. He vomited and decided to go to bed early. The next day, instead of getting better as expected, he felt much worse. They decided

---

371 Yossi Chen, op. cit., p. 163.

372 "Antes da morte, a depressão." *O Estado de S. Paulo,* June 11, 1985, p. 12.

to contact the doctor who had been looking after Ruth and monitoring Adolf's health after his bout with cancer. The doctor called for an ambulance and sent Gerhard straight to a neurological hospital. Three days later, he was dead from a stroke.[373] At two o'clock in the afternoon on December 20, his body was buried in the city of Graz, in a funeral paid for by the government because his children couldn't afford it. After the funeral, Adolf called the Bossert family and broke the news.[374] Precisely at that moment, Mengele was by their side, for he had joined the Bosserts to spend the end of the year at the Itapecerica estate. He wrote to his stepson, Karl-Heinz, in his last letter:

> Christmas was marked for me by the loss of such a unique friend and comrade. He is also irreplaceable as a correspondent, with whom I could discuss my intellectual concerns. It is regrettable that he was unable to make full use of his above-average talent due to a lack of discipline and aspiration.[375]

Mengele's letter continued:

> I would first like to thank you and Dieter for your willingness to help when my friend Wolfgang died suddenly. While one may come up with some not very pleasant things to say about his way of life, it must be pointed out, on the other hand, that he was an exemplary friend and patriot. His readiness to act at any moment, whenever a man was needed, I haven't experienced that again in my life—at least not after the war. Hardly anyone would have run such risks, not even in exchange for much larger amounts of material aid.

---

373 Telex from the Austrian Federal Foreign Office, sent on June 12, 1985, to the Austrian Consulate General in São Paulo (Federal Police, police inquiry n. 1-0097/86, book 6, p. 79).

374 Bundeskriminalamt, Dossier Mengele. Wiesbaden, June 28, 1985, p. 9, file 15.

375 Letter from Mengele to Karl-Heinz, February 1979. Federal Police Museum, archive 56, Brasília.

Karl-Heinz and his cousin Dieter had taken over the family's company after the death of Dieter's father, Alois, Mengele's younger brother. Mengele asked the two cousins to provide financial assistance to Wolfgang's children, who were now orphans, and promised to provide the details for the money remittance. He wrote:

Lately I've been in a very depressed state, perhaps triggered by Wolfgang's illness and sudden death. So I feel alone and abandoned . . . which for me is painful and almost unbearable. Sometimes I have a strange fear of being at the mercy of a cold reality in which there is no trace of human warmth. If a maid cooks and takes good care of you, in the end only the physical body will find its care. What can and should you talk about with a woman like that? About the past, the lost, the unfulfilled, the existential, or the simple, practical issues? Because of my isolation and Wolfram's almost morbid isolationist lifestyle, there's no chance of meeting anyone interesting.

Although I should fix my water pump, which broke down again, I'm going to the beach tomorrow to get out of the circle of everyday life. Wolfram is only there this week on vacation, so I have to hurry. Maybe I can find accommodation for the period after the summer season as well. I hope I get lucky with the weather.

In this state of mind, at the age of sixty-seven, Mengele took the bus to Bertioga to meet the Bosserts. It was February 1979. On that summer trip, Mengele would die in the arms of his friends, after drowning in the sea. Despite the deep fear of ending his existence without love and without affection, he took his last breath surrounded by his faithful protectors. It was the end of life for him, but not the end of his story. That would attract all the world's attention six years later.

17

THE FINAL HUNT

Almost two years had passed since Mengele's death when the Frankfurt Court of Justice issued a new arrest warrant for him. The 1959 warrant was canceled and replaced by a much broader one that contained more evidence. It stated that Mengele was "strongly suspected of having killed, attempted to kill, and of having instigated, aided and abetted the killing of people" in a "malicious and cruel" manner. The exact number of murders was impossible to determine, but from a series of facts and testimonies detailed over thirty-five pages, it probably reached the thousands. One such accusation in the arrest warrant, for example, is the killing of a woman in 1944: she had just arrived in Auschwitz from the Lódz ghetto and didn't want to be separated from her thirteen-year-old daughter. Mengele resolved the impasse by shooting both mother and daughter. Then, "out of rage," he sent everyone on that transport to the gas chamber, even those who had already been selected for work.[376] The records of his atrocities were abundant.

---

[376] Order for the arrest of Josef Mengele, Frankfurt am Main, January 19, 1981.

One of the people who documented Mengele's crimes was West German investigating judge Horst Von Glasenapp, whose role was equivalent to that of a prosecutor. His work began after the great Auschwitz trial of SS members that took place in Frankfurt in the 1960s. Mengele avoided the docket then simply because his whereabouts were unknown. From then on, his case became detached from the Auschwitz trials and was examined separately by Von Glasenapp. The judge traveled to several countries and collected more than three hundred interviews around the world. The witnesses told what they had seen in the extermination camp: Mengele's activities and how he treated his victims. All this Herculean investigative effort, however, had to be shelved in 1974 for a simple reason: there was nothing to be done about the accusations without knowing Mengele's whereabouts.[377] In an interview for a documentary aired on British television in 1978, Judge Von Glasenapp made it clear that he did not believe the criminal would ever be arrested.[378] So the new warrant issued in 1981 renewed hopes of an arrest, although, by then, as it proved, it was too late.

MEANWHILE, THE MOSSAD WAS ALSO trying to reach Mengele. The hunt had resumed at the end of the 1970s, at the request of the Israeli government. In 1982, the agency considered kidnapping the son of former pilot Hans-Ulrich Rudel, with the purpose of using the boy to force his father to reveal where Mengele was. However, Rudel died in December of that year from a stroke, before the Mossad could carry out the operation.[379] Rudel's funeral in Bavaria attracted hundreds of

---

377 David G. Marwell, op. cit., p. 208.

378 "The Hunt for Doctor Mengele." *World in Action*, temp. 15, ep. 5. Production: Michael Beckham and Brian Lapping. Editing: Ray Fitzwalter. Music: Shawm Phillips. United Kingdom: Granada Television, November 20, 1978 (30 min). Available at: <www.youtube. com/watch?v=W2UjdyZLBrs>. Accessed on: June 6, 2023.

379 "Why Did Israel Let Mengele Go?" *New York Times*, September 6, 2017. Available at: <www.nytimes.com/2017/09/06/sunday-review/israel-mengele -auschwitz-holocaust.html>. Accessed on: June 13, 2023.

people, including neo-Nazi leaders, and a flyover by the Luftwaffe jets provoked controversy. According to the Defense Ministry, the planes were on a routine mission for NATO, the North Atlantic military alliance. Witnesses, on the other hand, claim that it was an obvious tribute to Hitler's most decorated pilot. Afterwards, a prosecutor opened an investigation into the people seen performing the Nazi salute during the funeral.[380]

The Mossad then decided to focus on another possible link to Mengele: his own son. Israeli agents bugged Rolf's home, office, and telephone. Rolf was living in Berlin in the early 1980s and had the same birthday, March 16, as his father. The Mossad thus hoped to intercept a phone call between the two on that date. Unbeknownst to them, Mengele was already dead, which made their plan worthless.[381]

In 1984, another attempt was made to close in on Rolf. He had placed an ad on the real estate market, and an undercover Israeli agent, Rafi Meidan, presented himself as a potential interested party. A woman, also a Mossad agent, claimed to be his secretary. During a meeting in a restaurant, Rolf revealed some interesting details about himself. He said he was anti-Nazi and a pacifist. He also played down the importance of the rise of neo-Nazism and said that he was German only because of his roots: that he would not be willing to fight for Germany. He called the Nazi regime a "crazy little group" and never mentioned his father's name. The "secretary," who was very attractive, arranged to meet Rolf alone with the aim of seducing him, but that didn't work either. She reported to her superiors that, in her opinion, the only way to extract meaningful information from Rolf would be through violence, kidnapping, or extortion. The Mossad agreed that "carrying out such a non-routine act is the only way left for us to obtain information about his father," but there are no records of what

---

380 "Controversy over Alleged Tribute to Dead Nazi War Hero." Jewish Telegraphic Agency, December 30, 1982. Available at: <www.jta.org/archive /controversy-over-alleged-tribute-to-dead-nazi-war-hero>. Accessed on: June 13, 2023.

381 "Why Did Israel Let Mengele Go?" op. cit.

happened next.[382] The fact is that only through a joint international effort would it be possible to find Mengele.

AT LAST, THE SYMBOLIC YEAR of 1985 catapulted all efforts toward the same goal. January 1985 was the fortieth anniversary of the liberation of Auschwitz, and Mengele's twin victims, led by Eva Mozes Kor, marched through the site of the concentration camp in Poland to mark the date. In February of that same year, Mengele's symbolic trial took place in Jerusalem, an event that finally exposed his crimes to the whole world. A significant number of his victims were present to offer first-person accounts of their unimaginable suffering at the hands of the Nazi doctor. The televised testimonies seemed to have finally convinced public opinion that such a vile, heinous criminal like Mengele could no longer be allowed to remain at large. The day after the hearings, the US attorney general announced that the State Department would open an investigation to locate Mengele.

The pressure on the authorities was mounting everywhere. At the end of February, the minister-president of the state of Bavaria was visiting Israel when a reporter confronted him. The journalist wanted to know about an alleged Swiss account used by the Mengele family company to send dividends to the fugitive. The politician said he knew nothing, but promised an investigation. For the first time, Mengele's nephews, Karl-Heinz and Dieter, were forced to go public. They declared that they had never sent any money to their uncle, let alone to an account in Switzerland. They also stated that "Mengele was never involved in the firm." They thus chose not to tell the truth, despite the growing commotion to find out Mengele's fate.[383]

---

382 "The Hunt for the Nazi 'Angel of Death': How Israel Tried — and Failed — to Capture Dr. Josef Mengele." *Haaretz*, September 9, 2017. Available at: <www.haaretz .com/israel-news/2017-09-09/ty-article/.premium/how-israel-tried-and-failed-to -capture-dr-josef-mengele/0000017f-db30-df9c-a17f-ff3809da0000>. Accessed on: June 12, 2023.

383 Sven Keller, op. cit., pp. 173–74.

In May of that same year, another episode added to the worldwide search for an answer. The famous German Nazi hunter Beate Klarsfeld left Paris, where she lived, and flew to Paraguay, where she began to demonstrate in front of the Palace of Justice in Asunción. About twenty young Paraguayans joined her, holding placards that read "Stroessner, you lie when you say you don't know where Mengele is"; soon, around a hundred armed police officers arrived to disperse the demonstrators. Beate and her husband, Serge Klarsfeld, had already succeeded in bringing to justice the Nazi Klaus Barbie—known by the nickname of the "Butcher of Lyon" because of his role as head of the Gestapo in that French city—who had been hiding in Bolivia. Now the German activist was convinced that she could do the same with Mengele and believed that he lived in Paraguay. "If you think logically, there is nowhere else he could be. If he's left, the police have to know, it must be in their files," she told journalists.[384] Beate promised to pay $25,000 for information leading to Mengele, who was then the world's most wanted Nazi. The reward she offered was in addition to others totaling $3.4 million.

Public interest in the case was at an all-time high, which led to a major turning point in May 1985. The United States, West Germany, and Israel announced a coordinated effort to find Mengele and bring him to trial for crimes against humanity. It was the most intense international hunt for a Nazi since World War II. Representatives from the three countries met for two days in Frankfurt and agreed to open a direct line of communication among them to share the progress of their investigations.

It is unclear why the case took on such extraordinary proportions just then. According to the *New York Times*, some authorities said it was because of the fortieth anniversary of the defeat of Nazi Germany and also because, after a long delay, the time was ripe to address, head-on,

---

384 "Nazi Hunter, in a Protest in Paraguay, Demands Mengele's Arrest." *New York Times*, May 25, 1985. Available at: <www.nytimes.com/1985/05/25/world /nazi-hunter-in-a-protest-in-paraguay-demands-mengele-s-arrest.html>. Accessed on: June 8, 2023.

issues related to the Holocaust. These were inadequate explanations for such an important historical moment, when all forces converged to try to resolve an issue that had been all but ignored for decades. Now, suddenly, there was an urgency that made it seem a case of life and death. The main bets were that Mengele was alive, aged seventy-four, and living in Paraguay. At the same time, a flood of disinformation and even fake photos emerged, which hindered the investigation.[385]

At the end of that long month of May, the right lead finally came from Germany. A university professor told the police that, while on vacation, he had met a man named Hans Sedlmeier, the Mengele family company's loyal employee. According to the source, after a few drinks, Sedlmeier started bragging about having helped the Nazi doctor by personally taking money to him in South America. The conversation had taken place almost a year earlier, but only now had the professor decided to report it, perhaps hoping to get a reward or simply joining in the effort to arrest the fugitive.[386] Sedlmeier had already answered questions about Mengele four times: in 1964, 1971, 1984, and March 1985. The first time, he confessed to German authorities that he had met Mengele in Argentina at the end of 1957, and in Paraguay at the beginning of 1960. He then lied, claiming that he had cut off all contact with the Nazi doctor after that.[387]

Based on the professor's account, the police made a decision to search Sedlmeier's house, but their request for a search warrant was denied.[388] The investigators did not give up and submitted another piece of evidence to support the need for a search: a letter intercepted in a German prison. Gert Luk, a German living in Paraguay, wrote

385 "3 Nations Joining to Hunt Mengele." *New York Times*, May 11, 1985. Available at: <www.nytimes.com/1985/05/11/world/3-nations-joining-to-hunt-mengele.html>. Accessed on: June 13, 2023.

386 "Mengele Trail: Clues of Paper, Then of People." *New York Times*, June 23, 1985. Available at: <www.nytimes.com/1985/06/23/world/Mengele-trail-clues-of-paper-then-of-people.html>. Accessed on: June 14, 2023.

387 Yossi Chen, op. cit., pp. 201–2.

388 "Mengele Trail: Clues of Paper, Then of People," op. cit.

it to Manfred Röder, the leader of a neo-Nazi movement who was in prison for planning a bomb attack on immigrants. The letter said that the "uncle" had died some time ago "on the beaches of Brazil." The German authorities deduced that the "uncle" was Mengele. With this new argument, a judge authorized officers belonging to the federal investigating agency to enter Sedlmeier's residence in Günzburg, Bavaria, on the morning of May 31.

Sedlmeier and his wife, Renate, were taken by surprise. This time, their informant in the local police was unaware of the raid and unable to alert them as he had on other occasions. Sedlmeier still tried to run for a jacket hanging in a closet, but the investigators got there first and found a notebook in a pocket.[389] It contained several contacts in Brazil, including a post office box for Geza Stammer, Liselotte Bossert's full address, the address of the Alvarenga Road house, and the name Glawe.[390] The German police also found some letters that Sedlmeier's wife had kept in another closet without his knowledge. Renate herself had been a close friend of Mengele's before the war, and the two wrote to each other while he lived in Brazil.

Among the letters found in the Sedlmeier house was the one sent by Wolfram Bossert announcing that Mengele was dead—"with deep regret I announce the death of our mutual friend"—without explicitly mentioning the old man's name.[391] In another, the sender said he had a new telephone number in Brazil. There was also a letter that gave instructions for a visit: "As our little street is almost unknown to taxi drivers, I advise you to call it Rua Guararapes, 650, from where ours begins." This was the exact way to get to the Bossert house in Brooklin, São Paulo.[392] The discovery was a bombshell for Mengele's protectors in Brazil; in a very short time, the police would be reaching them.

---

389 Ibid.

390 Federal Police, police inquiry n. 1-0097/86, book 6, pp. 11–3.

391 Gerald Posner and John Ware, op. cit., p. 315.

392 Federal Police, police inquiry n. 1-0097/86, book 6, pp. 11–3.

That same day, the police put Sedlmeier under house arrest and contacted the German consulate in São Paulo.[393] It was crucial to act quickly, before the information leaked out and alerted Mengele's inner circle. Although it was already Friday afternoon, the time zone worked in their favor. The deputy consul general, Sepp Wölker, contacted the office of Romeu Tuma, the Federal Police regional superintendent, and arranged a meeting for two o'clock in the afternoon. Tuma readily agreed to help the Germans, but Dr. Aparecido Laertes Calandra, Tuma's chief of operations and personal aide, said that it wouldn't be possible to start the investigation over the weekend. Coincidentally, Calandra was a graduate of a training course at the German Federal Investigation Agency (Bundeskriminalamt, BKA), the equivalent to the US FBI, and he proposed a telephone meeting with his German counterparts on Monday to determine the next tactical steps. The Germans agreed, for they would then have more time to decipher the codes used by Mengele. By cross-referencing the phone number written on a letter with the one in Sedlmeier's address book, one of the police officers discovered, for example, that "Mus" was Wolfram Bossert.[394] However, what the German agents perhaps didn't know was that Calandra had been accused of being a torturer for the infamous Information Operations Detachment - Internal Defense Operations Center (DOI-CODI) in São Paulo, during the Brazilian military dictatorship. In his dark past, he was known among political prisoners by the codename Captain Ubirajara. Calandra always denied having inflicted torture on any prisoner.[395] Now, ironically, he was involved in the search for a man who had also denied the crimes he was accused of committing under another dictatorship—that of the Third Reich.

On Monday afternoon, the attorney general of the state of Hesse, Hans-Eberhard Klein, who was in charge of the Mengele case in

---

393 Gerald Posner and John Ware, op. cit., p. 315.

394 David G. Marwell, op. cit., pp. 232–33.

395 "Aparecido Laertes Calandra," in São Paulo's Resistance Memorial. Available at: <memorialdaresistenciasp.org.br/pessoas/aparecido-laertes-calandra/>. Accessed on: June 24, 2023.

Germany, met with German authorities to report on the findings at Sedlmeier's house. Although the country had pledged to maintain a direct line of communication with Israel and the United States to report new leads, it was decided at that meeting that nothing would be revealed until there was more clarity about what was going on. The press was also to be kept in the dark for the time being. Later that day, the German Federal Investigation Agency contacted Calandra again. They agreed that two German federal agents, along with one from the state of Hesse, would travel to São Paulo to monitor the investigations.[396]

On Tuesday, the German consulate sent a telex to Tuma with an urgent request from the German authorities: an interview with Mrs. Liselotte Bossert and Mr. Wolfram Bossert. The message said that "they are involved in aiding and abetting the fugitive Nazi Dr. Josef Mengele, suspected of murder."[397] Tuma called in the head of the DOPS (Division of Political and Social Order), Marco Antônio Veronezzi, and assigned him the task. Veronezzi, however, wouldn't be alone when interrogating the Bosserts. Although one of the letters found in Sedlmeier's house announced the death of their "mutual friend," the police considered the possibility that this could have been a ploy to throw the authorities off the scent. Therefore, it was still unclear whether Mengele was alive or dead.[398] Calandra deployed a team to find out who was living in the Bossert family's home. The order was to investigate whether Mengele was there and to arrest him if necessary. There was a great sense of excitement; after all, it wasn't every day that the São Paulo police dealt with a case of such magnitude. The agents set up a camera and began to observe the movements in and out of the house. A man and a woman entered, left, and returned. After two days, the man left and never returned. The investigators became suspicious. Was this Mengele himself, who

396 David G. Marwell, op. cit., p. 235.
397 Federal Police, police inquiry n. 1-0097/86, book 6, p. 10.
398 Interview with Marco Antônio Veronezzi, December 12, 2022.

had sensed the police presence and fled? The feeling of excitement gave way to frustration. Had they lost the opportunity to put such an important figure behind bars? Their next step was to enter the residence.[399]

To everyone's surprise, there was no resistance. Liselotte was helpful and readily cooperated with Veronezzi, the first authority to hear her version of the whole story. She told the chief officer that Mengele had drowned in Bertioga six years earlier. She also told him about his burial under a false name in the city of Embu das Artes. He then asked her for the documents. She produced an envelope and, as a sign of affection, pressed it against her chest before handing it to the deputy. Inside was a plastic bag containing a foreigner's ID, driver's license, and work permit—all bearing Mengele's photo, but with Wolfgang Gerhard's personal information. In the same envelope there were several photographs of the old Nazi in Brazil. Some included Liselotte's children with their "uncle."[400] Veronezzi took all the material to the Federal Police Superintendence. At the Bossert home, the police seized a typewriter on which Mengele typed most of his letters. They also found two folders: one marked "A-Z Briefe Gerhard," which contained letters from his friend Wolfgang Gerhard and newspaper clippings; and the second, labeled "Weihnachts Briefe," containing Christmas correspondence. Additionally, the police seized an important item that corroborated Liselotte's story: a receipt for the burial tax issued by the Embu town hall. No one was arrested, but Liselotte and her husband had to go to the police that same day, to give the first of many official statements.[401] For Veronezzi, there was no longer any doubt: Mengele was dead. The remaining issue was to confirm whether the body buried in Embu was really that of the criminal—an extremely difficult confirmation to

---

399 *Eldorado: Mengele Alive or Dead?* Directed by Marcelo Felipe Sampaio. São Paulo: Laguna Films, MS Pictures, 2019 (71 min.).

400 Interview with Marco Antônio Veronezzi.

401 Federal Police, police inquiry n. 1-0097/86, ledger 6, pp. 14–15.

obtain under tremendous international pressure, especially at a time when DNA testing was not yet available. On that long day, June 5, 1985, Veronezzi submitted a request to federal judge José Kallás to exhume the remains from tomb 321 in the Rosário Cemetery in Embu. The next day, the judge authorized the exhumation, which became a huge media circus and was publicized all over the world.[402]

Josef Mengele's work permit.

Criminal Museum of the Teaching Directorate of the National Police Academy / Museu Criminal da Diretoria de Ensino da Academia Nacional de Policia.

---

402 Ibid., p. 25.

Josef Mengele's foreign identity card.

Criminal Museum of the Teaching Directorate of the National Police Academy / Museu Criminal da Diretoria de Ensino da Academia Nacional de Policia.

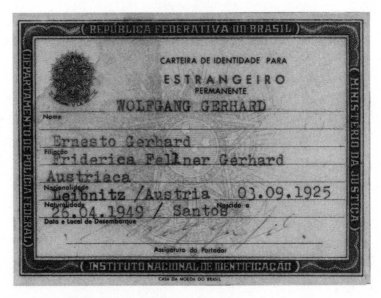

Josef Mengele's foreign identity card.

Criminal Museum of the Teaching Directorate of the National Police Academy / Museu Criminal da Diretoria de Ensino da Academia Nacional de Policia.

REPÚBLICA FEDERATIVA DO BRASIL

ESTADO DE
São Paulo

MUNICÍPIO DE
Santos

COMARCA DE
Santos

DISTRITO DE
Bertioga

CARTÓRIO DO REGISTRO CIVIL

, PU 321

Walter Pereira Prado
Escrivão do Registro Civil das Pessoas Naturais

REGISTRO CIVIL BERTIOGA
DISTRITO DE BERTIOGA
Município e Comarca de Santos
WALTER PEREIRA PRADO
OFICIAL

CERTIDÃO DE ÓBITO

CERTIFICO que sob n.º __56__ às fls. __56__ do livro n.o __C-1__
de Registros de Óbitos, encontra-se o assento de WOLFGANG GERHARD
, falecid o dia __07__ de Fevereiro de 1. 979
às __17:45__ horas em BERTIOGA
do sexo MASCULINO , profissão TECNICO MECANICO
natural de AUTRIA
com __53 anos__ de idade, estado civil VIUVO
filh_o_ de ERNESTO GERHARD
e de FRIDERICA FELINER GARHARD
Foi declarante LISOLOTTE BOSSERT
Atestado de óbito firmado p_or_ Dr. Jaime Edson Andrade Mendonça
que deu como Asfixia por Submerssão n'água
;e o sepultamento foi realizado no
Cemitério de Embú –
O registro foi efetuado no dia __08__ de Fevereiro de 1. 979
Observações:

O referido é verdade e dou fé

Bertioga , 08 de Fevereiro de 19 79

ESCRIVÃO

Ordem 507

Wolfgang Gerhard (Mengele) death certificate.

Criminal Museum of the Teaching Directorate of the National Police Academy / Museu Criminal da Diretoria de Ensino da Academia Nacional de Policia.

18

EXHUMATION

SÃO PAULO. THURSDAY, JUNE 6, 1985

" I've got a really tough nut for us to crack," José Antônio de Mello, deputy director of São Paulo's Forensic Medical Institute, began his phone call to Daniel Muñoz, the young coroner who headed the Institute's Anthropology Department and its only employee. That Thursday, the beginning of the Corpus Christi holiday, promised to be sunny, and Muñoz left his three young children at home to rush to the Institute. He certainly didn't expect to hear the bombshell that Mello was about to drop: a body buried in the Embu das Artes cemetery was suspected of being none other than that of Josef Mengele, the world's most wanted Nazi. According to Mello, the police had asked for the exhumation of the body to take place that same day; therefore, he wanted Muñoz to identify the bones right away. Of course, Dr. Muñoz wouldn't be working alone on such an important mission and was already thinking of names of colleagues he could invite to join him in the effort. At the very least, he would need someone specialized in dental identification and an anatomist to help assemble the skeleton.[403]

At seven o'clock in the morning, the first police officers on the scene were walking around the Rosário Cemetery in Embu das Artes, located fifteen miles from the center of São Paulo, with their walkie-talkies, as they waited for the judge's order before they could start the exhumation. Police superintendent Tuma had arrived in the company of the German deputy consul and the Bossert couple, who had to wait inside the cemetery chapel under heavy security, to avoid press scrutiny.[404] The court order to exhume the body only came in the early afternoon; the sun was shining brightly, even though it was almost winter in the Southern Hemisphere. By then, the news that Mengele's body had been found had spread to all corners of the globe, and dozens of Brazilian and foreign journalists crowded into the small cemetery. Cameramen and photographers fought for space to get the best shot of tomb 321, where the grass had grown so much that it looked completely abandoned. Only after a closer look would anyone notice that the tombstone read Friderieke Gerhard, since Wolfgang's mother was also buried there. Amidst all the commotion, Liselotte and Wolfram Bossert approached the grave as if they were movie stars. In a sense, they were indeed the main attraction in that extraordinary international event.

Armed with hoes and wearing rubber boots and gloves, two gravediggers began the spectacle, digging the soil out of the grave. Once they had dug a little more than seven feet deep, one of them opened the casket, which was already rotting and starting to crumble. From the bottom of the grave he brought out the skull and handed it to Mello. The medical examiner held the skull with one hand and showed it around as if it were a trophy; the journalists surrounding the grave were stunned by the dramatic Shakespearean scene. The gravedigger proceeded to remove bone by bone, handing each one to the doctor who, in turn, deposited them in a box. To the dismay of the

---

403 Interview with Daniel Romero Muñoz, August 2 and 15, 2017.

404 "6 de Junho de 1985." *O Estado de S. Paulo*, June 7, 1985.

The gravedigger passes bones one at a time to Dr. Antonio de Mello.

Criminal Museum of the Teaching Directorate of the National Police Academy / Museu Criminal da Diretoria de Ensino da Academia Nacional de Policia.

Mengele's bones are placed in a box to be transported to the Forensic Medical Institute.

Criminal Museum of the Teaching Directorate of the National Police Academy / Museu Criminal da Diretoria de Ensino da Academia Nacional de Policia.

three German police officers accompanying the exhumation, Mello wore no gloves or shoe coverings, nor was there any sort of protection for the box; in fact, Mello stepped in it as if it were a canoe. Later, the Germans criticized their Brazilian colleagues' lack of professionalism and said that the gravedigger's boots had damaged the skull face.[405] But what the Brazilians lacked in technique, they made up for in humor: in a solemn tone, Tuma declared to the reporters: "I can state categorically that he is absolutely dead."[406]

Liselotte watched everything from the graveside. At some point, she inquired whether the deceased had been buried with his arms alongside his body, as she had asked the funeral service director to do six years earlier, and Mello answered in the affirmative. She recognized pieces of the shirt, pants, belt, and socks in which her friend had been buried. Liselotte signed an affidavit certifying that that was the same coffin in which Mengele's body had been buried;[407] but before it was all over, she claimed that she wasn't feeling well and asked to leave. Nevertheless, she had to face a horde of reporters eager to extract any additional information from her extraordinary story. They had many questions, but she offered few—and false—answers. For example, Liselotte told the press that Mengele had risked his life many times to treat Auschwitz prisoners who had contagious diseases, perhaps in a very twisted allusion to the "Mengele method" to end typhus in the concentration camp; conveniently failing to mention the pointless killing of hundreds of women who ensured his "method" would work.

The old teacher also said that the horrendous experiments Mengele had been accused of were outright lies, and he complained because he had been "painted as the devil himself" all over the world.[408] Her

---

405 Ulrich Völkein, op. cit., p. 310.

406 Alan Riding, "Key Man in Mengele Case: Romeu Tuma." *New York Times*, June 16, 1985.

407 Federal Police, report, police inquiry n. 1-0097/86, book 6, pp. 14–15.

408 "Sepultado em posição de sentido." *O Estado de S. Paulo*, June 7, 1985, p. 26.

statements bear the question: What would she have thought had she talked to Eva Mozes Kor, Ruth Elias, Cyrla Gewertz, or any other of Mengele's victims who had experienced their worst nightmares at his hands? In a complete denial of the truth, Liselotte went on to say that Mengele had been sent against his will to Auschwitz. In fact, she really didn't know about the young Nazi doctor's professional goals and the connection between that death camp and the Kaiser Wilhelm Institute in Berlin.

Wolfram also defended the Nazi fiercely and with conviction. "He was my friend, he died in my arms, he visited my house, he was loved by my children. He was a good man and many times said that because he was a soldier, he had to follow orders, denying everything they attributed to him," he said.[409] The Austrian made use of extremely tenuous arguments to defend his dead friend, first of all because Mengele was not a soldier, but rather an SS officer. Furthermore, his own boss at Auschwitz, Dr. Eduard Wirths, conducted himself very differently, which proves that Mengele was not there just following orders; he had his own plans.

Only around three o'clock in the afternoon were the bones finally transported to the Forensic Medical Institute in São Paulo. Once the bones arrived, Muñoz was ready to begin his task but, as soon as he started, he noticed that some parts were missing. The coroner decided to go back to the Rosário Cemetery, where he had the coffin removed again, and he took sixteen bags of earth from the newly reopened grave back to his lab. Each bag of dirt had to be carefully sifted so Muñoz could find tiny bones, teeth, and even strands of hair that had been left behind. It was meticulous archaeological work, as he put it. The larger bones, such as the femur and tibia, were still in good condition. However, some of the smaller ones were broken and crumbled in his hand. The Embu cemetery is very humid, which had accelerated the skeleton's deterioration.[410]

---

409 "Assustado, agressivo, vivia com medo." *O Estado de S. Paulo*, June 7, 1985, p. 26.
410 Interview with Daniel Romero Muñoz.

Wolfgang Gerhard when he made his first identification in Brazil in 1950 (left). Wolfgang Gerhard, 1976 (right).

Criminal Museum of the Teaching Directorate of the National Police Academy / Museu Criminal da Diretoria de Ensino da Academia Nacional de Polícia.

Seven natural teeth were found in Mengele's jaw—four upper and three lower molars—and there was also a gold crown. Mello, Muñoz's boss, was excited by the discovery and told journalists that the teeth could help identify the body accurately.[411] But the process wasn't so simple, and it would take at least fifteen days to get the result. Tuma declared that there was a 90 percent chance that the body was really Mengele's and made it clear that the Brazilians would lead the forensic analysis.[412] However, he did so in a manner that wouldn't alienate the foreign experts who had traveled to Brazil: "We are in charge, but science has no borders." That was enough for the *New York Times* to declare that Tuma was the most skilled police chief in the country.[413]

---

[411] "Sete dentes, chave da resposta." *O Estado de S. Paulo*, June 7, 1985.

[412] "Descoberto em SP corpo que pode ser de Mengele." *Folha de S. Paulo*, June 7, 1985.

[413] Alan Riding, op. cit.

IN 1985, BRAZIL WAS TAKING its first steps as a democratic nation after the military regime that had ruled the country for twenty-one years. This meant that many of the authorities involved in the Mengele case had participated in the persecution of political dissidents during the dictatorship. This was true in the case of Calandra, who had been accused of torture, and of Mello, who was denounced decades later for issuing fraudulent necroscopic reports as a coroner.

Tuma, on the other hand, had headed the São Paulo branch of Brazil's infamous DOPS, which fought clandestine left-wing political organizations and strike movements in the ABC region of São Paulo. The political landscape began to change in São Paulo in November 1982, when Franco Montoro, who opposed the dictatorship, won the elections for state government. As soon as the election results were in, the sitting governor, José Maria Marin, ordered Tuma to transfer the DOPS archives to the Federal Police Superintendence, thus preventing the opposition from having access to the documents. In 1983, the DOPS was effectively extinct, and Tuma joined the Federal Police.[414] Despite having been the head of a political-repression agency during the dictatorship, Tuma publicly condemned the use of torture for ethical and moral reasons and because he considered it an inefficient way of obtaining information from prisoners: he favored investigating and finding evidence as better methods.[415]

UBATUBA. FRIDAY, JUNE 7, 1985

It was Friday of the extended Corpus Christi holiday, and Wilmes Teixeira, director of the Mogi das Cruzes Forensic Medical Institute, was relaxing at his beach house in Ubatuba when the phone rang. It was his assistant, telling him to turn on the television: the news was reporting the exhumation of the skeleton that allegedly belonged to

---

414 "Tuma, Romeu," CPDOC-FGV. Available at: <www.fgv.br/CPDOC/acervo/ dicionários/verbete-biografico/tuma-romeu>. Accessed on: August 4, 2023.

415 Alan Riding, op. cit.

Mengele. Soon, Teixeira received another phone call, this time from a US forensic expert seeking information about the exhumation. He had obtained Teixeira's number from the American Academy of Forensic Sciences register, which listed him as one of two Brazilians accredited with the organization. Indeed, Teixeira was a forensic medicine enthusiast and had traveled to the United States more than thirty times to attend seminars and training courses on the subject. In Mogi das Cruzes, a town near the capital city of São Paulo, he was often given permission from the mayor to exhume remains, and he set up a collection of forty skeletons on his own.

Because of his keen interest in forensics, he made friends with various American experts in the field. Forensic anthropologist Clyde Snow thought it was quite a coincidence that Teixeira was from São Paulo where the Mengele case was unfolding. Snow asked his Brazilian counterpart if he could accompany what was considered the most important forensic investigation in history. Teixeira explained that he lived in the state of São Paulo, but that his district was Mogi das Cruzes; he had nothing to do with the work being done in the capital. However, the director of the São Paulo Forensic Medical Institute, Rubens Brasil Maluf, eventually agreed to let Teixeira coordinate a team of foreign scientists.[416]

In the end, nine US forensic scientists traveled to Brazil to follow the Mengele case up close: three from the Department of Justice, three from the Simon Wiesenthal Center in Los Angeles, and three experts in documents and handwriting sent by the US government.[417] Germany also sent an expert in this field, as well as an odontologist

---

416 Interview with Wilmes Teixeira conducted on September 9, 2017.

417 *In the Matter of Josef Mengele: A Report to the Attorney General of the United States*, op. cit. Among the experts from the Justice Department were coroner Ali Hameli, anthropologist Ellis Kerley, and dentist Lowell Levine. From the Wiesenthal Center came radiologist John Fitzpatrick, coroner Leslie Lukash, and anthropologist Clyde Snow. The document experts were Gideon Epstein, Antonio Cantu, and David Crown.

and a forensic anthropologist,[418] and Israel dispatched Menachem Russak, head of the police division responsible for investigating Nazis. That Friday, Neal Sher, the head of the Office of Special Investigations (OSI), the US unit responsible for prosecuting Nazis, arrived at Guarulhos International Airport.

Although they were doubtful about the Brazilians' competence, the foreigners could only follow the investigation as observers. During the four-day weekend, Muñoz assembled his team of skilled professionals: Moacyr da Silva, a specialist in forensic odontology from the University of São Paulo (USP); and doctors Ramón Manubens, professor of anatomy at the Marília Medical School, and Marcos de Almeida, from the Paulista School of Medicine. Muñoz also needed records of Mengele's biometrics so that he could compare them with those of the skeleton. To do this, he enlisted the help of the OSI, who had brought Mengele's SS archive to Brazil.[419]

Meanwhile, Veronezzi continued his work at the Federal Police Superintendence. That Friday, Gitta gave her first statement; Geza didn't accompany her because he was traveling. The new details she revealed about Mengele's life in Brazil confirmed the information given by Liselotte and Wolfram. The sheriff also summoned Mengele's former maid Elsa and his neighbor Jaime, who lived on Alvarenga Road, to take part in a photo-recognition test. The police arranged seven photographs of Mengele provided by the Bosserts on a table, mixed with ten others of a person with similar physical characteristics. Both Elsa and Jaime were able to unequivocally identify "Seu Pedro," the name by which they knew the Nazi.[420]

The investigation was going full speed ahead. The director of the forensics service sent the police two photos of Wolfgang Gerhard from

---

418 Rolf Endris, an odontologist from the Johannes Gutenberg University in Mainz, and Richard Helmer, a forensic anthropologist from the University of Kiel.

419 *In the Matter of Josef Mengele: A Report to the Attorney General of the United States,* op. cit. p. 241.

420 Federal Police, police inquiry n. 1-0097/86, ledger 6, p. 49.

1950, when he had obtained his first identification document in Brazil. A quick glance at them revealed clearly that Wolfgang was not the mustachioed old man who appeared on the foreigner's ID bearing his name. That same day, authorities in Argentina also provided the documents of Helmut Gregor and Josef Mengele, who in reality were the same man. The Brazilian police compared the fingerprints sent by the Argentines with Wolfgang's and concluded that they belonged to two different people.[421]

The Bosserts' accounts were beginning to make some sense, but it was still a complex case. Mengele had evaded justice for decades, and many people thought he might have staged the whole story to throw off his persecutors. In New York, Simon Wiesenthal, the world's most famous Nazi hunter, stated that he did not believe that the remains exhumed in Embu were Mengele's. Rather, there was "concrete evidence" that the criminal had passed through the United States in 1984 and had been in Asunción a few years earlier. He said:

> Every day, reporters stand in front of Mengele's second wife's house in Italy in search of information about his whereabouts, and she is forced to protect herself with dogs to avoid being harassed, as well as constantly changing her phone number. I believe that as soon as he dies, his own family will break the news so that they can finally have some peace and quiet.

Perhaps the Nazi hunter didn't want to accept as true the incredible discovery made by the German and Brazilian police authorities because it showed that he had been wrong all along, despite his reputation as the leading authority on the subject. In any case, Wiesenthal cast doubt on the investigations: "Who will be found buried in Mengele's place?"[422]

---

421 Ibid. p. 70.

422 "Wiesenthal, o caçador, contesta." *O Estado de S. Paulo*, June 7, 1985.

Another Nazi hunter, Beate Klarsfeld, who had traveled to Paraguay in May of that same year to protest that country's supposed cover-up, was convinced that "the government of General Alfredo Stroessner would have every interest in informing us that Mengele is dead, if that was true."[423] In a single statement, she reinforced the negative perception that many Europeans and Americans held of the Paraguayan and Brazilian authorities, as if Germany, the United States, or Israel had done enough to capture Mengele during the thirty-four years he had lived in hiding. The former head of the Mossad, Isser Harel, was also skeptical. In an interview with the Brazilian newspaper *O Estado de S. Paulo*, he stated that in the past many people had spread rumors that Mengele was dead in order to disrupt the search for the Nazi doctor. Therefore, his conclusion was that Mengele's body being found was a lie.[424]

Similarly, Holocaust survivor Ben Abraham, who lived in São Paulo, didn't swallow the news: "Mengele is very intelligent, so intelligent that I refuse to believe that he left so many photos, documents, and other signs of his passage here, unless it was for the purpose of deceiving us. I can't believe he drowned in Bertioga. Mengele must be laughing at us right now," he said.[425] With so many people doubting the news, and so many supposed plots to deceive the authorities, the Forensic Medical Institute thought it best to keep the skeleton under permanent surveillance until the mystery was solved.

SATURDAY, JUNE 8, 1985

Adolfo Krause was the principal at the German school where Liselotte had taught kindergarten. He had been named after Adolf Hitler. Thus, one might hastily conclude that Krause was a Nazi; but nothing could

---

423 "A Exumação do Enigma." *Veja*, June 12, 1985.

424 "Wiesenthal, o caçador, contesta ." *O Estado de S. Paulo*, June 7, 1985.

425 "Carrasco empregava cobaias humanas em suas experiências." *Folha de São Paulo*, June 16, 1985.

be further from the truth. The son of German immigrants, he was baptized as Adolfo simply because it was a popular name. His father was a Lutheran pastor who had moved to Brazil to spend six years, at the end of which he would return to Germany. But when that period ended in 1944, Europe was in the middle of the war and the Krause family decided to stay. Herr Krause, as he was respectfully called at the school, had a slight "gaucho" accent and a friendly and caring manner, and never in his life had he supported any Nazi ideas.[426]

That Saturday, he went out for a late lunch with his family, had a coffee, and then went home to watch the evening *Jornal Nacional* newscast. To his surprise, the first image he saw when he turned on the television was that of Liselotte, giving an interview to explain why she had covered up for Mengele in Brazil. That was the first time he had heard of the teacher's deep involvement with Mengele. Before long, she called him at home.

"Did you see the news on the *Jornal Nacional*?" Liselotte asked.

"Yes, ma'am," he answered.

"It's true. And I'm not going to work at the school anymore," she replied.

Even before Herr Krause had enough time to process what had happened, Liselotte was already resigning. However, her decision was not as spontaneous as it seemed, and she didn't reveal her real reason at the time. Many years went by before she admitted that the German government had put pressure on her to resign and warned her that the school would no longer receive a cent in subsidies from Germany if she stayed on as a teacher. For this reason, she thought it best to resign right away, rather than waiting to be fired, which would happen sooner or later.

---

[426] Interview with Adolfo Krause, August 25, 2017. The "gaucho" accent is the distinct regional accent of the southernmost state of Rio Grande do Sul, whose natives are known in Brazil as "gauchos."

SUNDAY, JUNE 9, 1985

On Sunday, a woman named Evelyn was with her family at the Náutico Paulista Club, on the banks of the Guarapiranga reservoir, when she saw the big headline in that week's *Veja* magazine[427]: "The mystery of the Mengele case may be coming to an end." Turning to the article, she read that "Some letters from Mengele himself were seized, two of them sent by an Austrian couple, Wolfram and Liselotte Bossert." Another passage read that "in a crying fit, she [Liselotte] said that she and her husband had covered up for Josef Mengele in São Paulo." It was a terrible shock for Evelyn to find out that her two young children's teacher had protected the man who had left such a lasting, painful mark on her family.

Evelyn's family's connection with Mengele had begun in Auschwitz. Helga, Evelyn's mother, had been sent from the Theresienstadt ghetto to the death camp as a teenager. When she disembarked from the cattle train, Mengele personally separated her from her parents and sent them to queue for the gas chamber. Helga stayed in the camp until its liberation by the Soviets, and there she endured horrifying experiences. For example, she was temporarily blinded by working as a slave in a mine, was given horse bones to eat, and had to share a shriveled blanket with another girl. Trying to stay warm, the two of them breathed together underneath the blanket, and the fact that the other girl had tuberculosis didn't matter at all to Helga. In fact, nothing else mattered to her, an only child who had been orphaned thanks to Mengele. Helga carried those painful memories with her for the rest of her life. Even when she was an old woman living in Brazil, she would still wake up screaming in the middle of the night. She felt very conflicted because she hated the Germans, despite having been born in Germany herself. Nevertheless, her grandchildren attended

---

427 Interview with Evelyn (who preferred not to give her last name) on September 8, 2022.

a German school, even as Evelyn kept thinking to herself, "But they would never set foot in that school again."

Evelyn grew up hearing her mother's stories of persecution, about Auschwitz and so much death. That's why she never told anyone in São Paulo that she was Jewish. She dropped her family's surname, which in her opinion sounded too Jewish, and adopted her husband's. She had her children baptized when they were two months old because she thought it was important to have a document in case they needed to prove they weren't Jewish. She warned them never to tell anyone of their origins, because she was terrified of potential consequences. Yet, despite all her fear, she didn't see anything wrong with the German school community: quite the opposite, she felt comfortable there. The other mothers were friendly, didn't worry too much about clothes or appearance, and the children got along well. At school functions, Evelyn never came across any apologists for Nazism, which would have made it impossible for her to remain a member of the school community. The news in *Veja* magazine, therefore, shook her small world. Evelyn had no idea what she would do with her children, but they wouldn't be staying at that school any longer.

Meanwhile, that Sunday morning, the German consul phoned Herr Krause with a request: "Since you know Liselotte very well, could you go to her house and check if all this story is really true or not?" he asked. The two agreed to meet at the consulate to talk about it. There, Consul Sepp Wölker explained that Germany wanted to clarify the facts. Herr Krause initially agreed to help but then, back in his car, had second thoughts: As the school principal, should he get involved in that kind of situation and, worse, play the role of policeman? If his name appeared anywhere, he would inevitably be branded as an accomplice of Liselotte and her husband. Thus, as soon as he got home, he called the consul and told him he had changed his mind: "There's no way I'm going to play that role; I must preserve the school image."

MONDAY, JUNE 10, 1985

As he did every workday, at seven o'clock in the morning on Monday, Herr Krause was already at the school. About fifteen minutes later, one of the janitors called to him: "There's a TV crew here." It was a US TV crew trying to enter the school to interview him. Once again, Herr Krause had to make a quick decision in a moment of crisis, a situation he had never faced before. "Let everyone in," he ordered. He gave an interview and allowed the TV crew to walk around, filming. After about forty-five minutes, the journalists left.

Shortly afterward, the principal began to receive angry phone calls from parents questioning the fact that a US TV crew had entered the school.

"Our children have been filmed, they're going to be presented as Nazis on US television," said one of the parents. With his usual calm and wisdom, Krause replied: "Can you imagine if I *hadn't* let them in? They would have jumped over the wall and announced in all the news programs: 'Here's the proof, they're neo-Nazis, they didn't let us in!'"

During each exchange he had with a caller, the principal stood firm in his reasoning: it had been a wiser decision to open the doors than to keep them shut to the journalists.

After that stressful morning incident, Herr Krause prepared Liselotte's resignation papers and drove to her house in Brooklin. He parked his car about three blocks away and, when he approached on foot, the journalists pounced on him. He explained to the reporters that he was going to the Bossert residence, but he wouldn't answer any questions at that point. Inside, away from the cameras, Liselotte told him the whole story. She repeated that, at first, she hadn't known that her friend was Mengele. She also said that her children had been very fond of their "uncle." "What was I going to do?" she asked, seeking complicity. Herr Krause listened to her for at least half an hour. The decision, however, had already been made: her contract was to be terminated and she would never set foot in the school again.

When Principal Krause had hired Liselotte at the end of the 1970s, nothing about her raised any red flags: she never expressed any sympathy for Nazism or any other radical ideas, and nothing in her behavior suggested that she might be covering up for the world's most wanted Nazi. Thinking back, he remembered the party when she introduced him to an older German relative at the school gate. It must have been *him*, but how could Krause have guessed? Now, however, it seemed clear: Liselotte had been friends with Mengele even before she'd been hired.

It would be naïve to imagine that São Paulo's German community was totally isolated from Nazis. In the decades after World War II, some of them moved openly in various social circles. That was the case of Franz Stangl, who had been the commander of the Treblinka and Sobibor extermination camps, and overtly worked for Volkswagen in Brazil, using his real name. Similarly, Stangl's successor as head of Sobibor, Gustav Wagner, was the caretaker of an estate in Atibaia, a town not far from the city of São Paulo. According to Herr Krause, the property where Wagner worked belonged to a family whose children attended the German school. Coincidentally, Superintendent Tuma took part in Wagner's arrest in 1978, a case that had international repercussions.

Another Nazi criminal who also lived and worked in São Paulo was the Latvian pilot Herberts Cukurs, who set up an air taxi company at the Guarapiranga reservoir, not far from Billings, where Mengele had lived. During the Nazi occupation of Latvia, Cukurs, who was part of a group that became notorious for murdering thousands of Jews, was nicknamed the "butcher of Riga." In Brazil, he became friends with an Austrian businessman, Anton Kuenzle, who persuaded him to expand his business to Uruguay. In February 1965, the two traveled to Montevideo but, once there, Cukurs discovered that his friend was actually a Mossad agent and was murdered.[428] Kuenzle's real

---

[428] André Bernardo, "Herberts Cukurs: O nazista que viveu 20 anos no Brasil e foi executado no Uruguai por agentes do Mossad." BBC, March 6, 2022. Available at: <www.bbc.com/portuguese/geral-60481793>. Accessed on: July 13, 2023.

name was Yaakov Meidad, a German-born Jew who lost his parents in the Holocaust and, in 1960, took part in the kidnapping of Adolf Eichmann in Argentina.[429]

Nevertheless, stories about Nazis were sporadic among the German community in São Paulo. Many parents at the German school didn't even know who Mengele was until they heard about him through the press. One of the mothers, who frequented her German father-in-law's house in Bertioga, recalled that she was on the beach on the same day that Mengele died. She had clear memories of that afternoon, because her husband was one of those who ran out to help the man who was drowning, and she made a point of walking her little daughter away so that she wouldn't see the scene. When it happened, neither she nor her husband could remotely imagine that the drowned man was Mengele. Only now, hearing the news, had she connected the dots.

The teachers at the German school didn't talk much about what had happened to Liselotte. Normally, they were very close to one another, especially because Herr Krause always invited the whole staff to a get-together at his house every time a new employee was hired. And, according to Krause, no prospective hire would ever have a place at the school if there was any indication that they supported Nazism. Evelyn, along with her mother, Helga, felt relieved knowing this, and she was pleased when she heard that Liselotte was no longer at the school. Yet, they remained apprehensive about Sabine, Liselotte's daughter. At the time, Sabine was a young kindergarten teacher at the German school, and Evelyn's daughter was in her class. Evelyn finally decided that the best course of action was to let it be: "Sabine is such a sweet person—what does she have to do with her mother's actions?" Evelyn concluded that she couldn't blame the younger generation for what the previous one had done: her children would continue at school.

---

429 Robert Philpot, "How the Mossad Hunted the 'Butcher of Riga,' Who Murdered Up to 30,000 Jews." *The Times of Israel*, August 1, 2020. Available at: <www.times ofisrael.com/how-the-mossad-hunted-the-butcher-of-riga-who-murdered -up-to-30000-jews>. Accessed on: August 14, 2023.

MUNICH. TUESDAY, JUNE 11, 1985

On the other side of the world, Rolf felt the weight of the previous generation's actions more than anyone else. Five days after the body was exhumed in São Paulo, a spokesman for Rolf in Munich issued the following statement:

> I have no doubt that the remains exhumed in the Embu cemetery in Brazil on June 6, 1985, are those of my father, Josef Mengele. I am sure that the coroners will confirm this promptly. The family is willing to provide any additional information that may be necessary. I traveled to Brazil in 1979 to confirm the circumstances of his death. I have kept silent until now out of consideration for the people who had been in contact with my father over the last thirty years. Please accept my deepest condolences, and those of my family, to all the victims and their relatives.

In Frankfurt, the Mengele family's lawyer handed over the statement text to Attorney General Hans-Eberhard Klein, who had been in charge of the case against Mengele since 1974. That day in Munich, fifty reporters, photographers, and cameramen waited for a word from Rolf, but he did not appear in public. Sabine Hackenjos, Rolf's sister-in-law, spoke to them: "I hope there will be no more doubts after this," she said. Ever since the Mengele case made headlines around the world, Rolf and his family had been receiving death threats and lived in fear.

The statement didn't convince Menachem Russak, the head of the Israeli police division responsible for investigating Nazi crimes: "It only reinforced the great fraud," he told the press. Isser Harel, the former head of the Mossad, went further: "Until the case goes to an international team of experts, including Germans and Americans, and they decide that it is Mengele, this story has no basis in truth," he said.

At a time when there was no DNA testing, the pressure on the Brazilian forensic experts was enormous. During those very hectic days, Muñoz would go to the Forensic Medical Institute at six in the morning and wouldn't return home until eleven at night. His work method consisted of carrying out a thorough investigation in order to compare all the data harvested from the skeleton with Mengele's records. He worked under the assumption that someone was trying to deceive him and could have buried someone else's body in that grave in Embu. He also knew that two people can be very similar but not the same. Therefore, the coroner systematically looked for any discrepancies.

The first few days of the investigation were dedicated to gluing the skeleton together bone by bone until it was entirely assembled. Ramón Manubens, professor of anatomy at the Marília Medical School, helped with the arduous work. A few pieces of vertebrae and other small bones were left out, but that didn't interfere with the big picture. Once the skeleton was ready, Muñoz began to identify the most important element: the deceased's sex. The pelvis was typically male. The infrapubic angle was around sixty degrees. In a woman, it would be around ninety. The measurement of the head of the femur also corresponded to that of a man. Muñoz then was able to determine the corpse's race based on an examination of the skull, concluding that it was a Caucasoid individual—i.e., white. The skull also helped define the age, which was confirmed by the dental specialist. Dr. Moacyr, from the University of São Paulo, examined the teeth and jaw and concluded that the individual was between sixty-five and seventy years old. When Mengele died, he was sixty-seven. Based on the length of the femur and tibia, Muñoz calculated the height of the skeleton at five feet seven inches, give or take an inch. Mengele was five feet eight inches tall. So far, everything confirmed that the remains matched Mengele's biometrics.

One of Mengele's most striking features when he was alive was his gapped front teeth. The problem was that the skull's dentures made it impossible to see what in dentistry is called "diastema." However, the exhumed skull had a huge hole in it, which experts call the incisal foramen, and that is precisely the main cause of diastema: there is no bone to hold the teeth in the correct position, so they come in a little far apart, causing a gap in the person's smile. In this way, the coroners were able to confirm a rare commonality between the skeleton and Mengele.

But the examination of the remains didn't end there; everything was meticulously analyzed in an effort to uncover any discrepancies.

While analyzing the skull, the Brazilian team found three strands of hair. Almeida, from the Paulista School of Medicine, who had obtained his specialization in England, concluded that they were moustache hairs. The examiners also found a small yellow spot on the face of the skull, which suggested that that part of the bone hadn't formed all at once, but rather little by little, on different occasions. The cause for this condition is a chronic bone infection, or osteomyelitis. After identifying this problem on the skull, Muñoz turned to Mengele's military dossier and found in the Nazi's records that he indeed had osteomyelitis. For many, that discovery in itself would be sufficient to support the conclusion that those were Mengele's remains. The forensic scientists, however, continued their meticulous work.[430]

In the pelvis area, the examiners found a spur, or a bone scar. What could have caused it? According to Muñoz, it most likely happened as the result of a hip dislocation: the head of the femur came out of the acetabulum (the hip socket). Mengele's military dossier said that on June 21, 1943, Mengele was riding an SS motorcycle through the Auschwitz concentration camp when a tractor attempted to overtake a truck and collided with the motorcycle, injuring Mengele. In Muñoz's opinion, that accident could have caused the scar found on the corpse's pelvis.[431]

---

[430] The American scientists who accompanied the investigation found no signs of osteomyelitis in the skeleton, and this was one of the factors that left doubt, as explained in *In the Matter of Josef Mengele: A Report to the Attorney General of the United States*, op. cit., p. 155.

[431] The bone spur in the pelvis area was another point of contention, because the record of the accident at Auschwitz does not say what type of injury Mengele suffered (Ibid., p. 154).

The forensic team asked the sheriff for Mengele's items seized from the Bosserts' home, among them a beige Burberry trench coat. The measurement from the middle of the collar to the sleeve matched the skeleton's measurements perfectly. In other words, the trench coat could very well have belonged to the person whose remains were being examined. The team also checked with the witnesses about Mengele's medical issues. Gitta said that he suffered from dental problems, abscesses that he drained himself by sticking a needle between the gum and the tooth. Tooth abscesses are a very common condition in those who suffer from chronic sinusitis, which, in turn, can cause osteomyelitis, especially if it is not treated with antibiotics. According to Muñoz, this may have happened to Mengele, who had osteomyelitis at the age of fifteen, in 1926, while the use of penicillin only became popular later, at the end of the 1940s.

WEDNESDAY, JUNE 12, 1985

The Brazilian police also asked Austria to verify the death of the real Wolfgang Gerhard and thus confirm the version told by the Bosserts. A telex from the Austrian Foreign Ministry confirmed that he had died of a stroke on December 15, 1978, in the neurological hospital in Graz. Austrian and German investigators also visited Wolfgang's eldest son, Adolf, better known as Burli. Adolf told them that more than a hundred journalists had sought him out since the exhumation of Mengele's body. His siblings Karoline and Erwin were present when the investigators went to his home and initially said they didn't remember Mengele. Two days later, Burli confessed to the police that he and his siblings knew the man in the photos very well: it was "Onkel," their uncle. However, he denied they knew that the man was actually Josef Mengele.[432]

---

[432] Bundeskriminalamt, Dossier Mengele. Wiesbaden, June 28, 1985, p. 10, archive 15.

FRIDAY, JUNE 14, 1985

On Friday, June 14, four experts in graphology presented their conclusions based on the examinations they had conducted of samples of Mengele's handwriting. A Brazilian, a German, and two US experts analyzed Mengele's handwritten application to join the SS in 1937, when he was twenty-six years old, and compared it to the letters and notes found in the Bosserts' house. "There is no doubt that the handwriting belongs to the same person," said David Crown, a former CIA expert sent to Brazil by the US government. On Friday afternoon, Superintendent Tuma met journalists for an official statement: "The man who lived in Nova Europa, Serra Negra, and São Paulo, whose life we are investigating, was Josef Mengele," he said. Nevertheless, he still couldn't say with certainty that the body buried in the Embu cemetery was indeed Mengele's.[433]

FRIDAY, JUNE 21, 1985

After a minute examination of the skeleton, the forensic team did not find any features on it that disagreed with those of Mengele's. Muñoz was certain that if the remains belonged to someone else, they would have found some conflicting information. Furthermore, there was an extensive number of common characteristics, some of them very distinct, such as the fractured pelvis and the osteomyelitis.

The Brazilian forensic team conducted the analysis, but foreign scientists were also allowed to inspect the remains. The skeleton was set up in a central room at the Forensic Medical Institute, and each team had its own room adjacent to it, so they all had access to the bones and could analyze, measure, or photograph them. In a friendly atmosphere, Brazilians, Americans, and Germans exchanged opinions and shared techniques. One such technique they all considered

---

433 "A Vida na Sombra: Mengele teve a proteção de uma rede de amigos em seus dezenove anos de Brasil." *Veja*, June 19, 1985.

fundamental was that of German professor of forensic anthropology Richard Helmer. He used his own method in which he projected a photograph of Mengele onto the exhumed skull, in the exact same position and proportion. Helmer concluded that the fit was perfect. Wilmes Teixeira, who coordinated the foreign team, marveled at how his German colleague was years ahead of the rest, noting that in Germany, forensic scientists could devote themselves exclusively to that type of research.

That Friday, June 21, it seemed that the Mengele case was reaching its high point since the exhumation. At eight in the morning, journalists began arriving at the Federal Police Superintendence building. Due to a lack of space, the press conference was moved to the twentieth floor, where the restaurant and recreation room were located. When the interview began, Tuma was surrounded by more than twenty microphones and television cameras, from Brazil and abroad, eager to record his presentation of the forensic results. According to the Brazilian team, it was very "improbable" that the skeleton belonged to anyone other than Josef Mengele. The US experts then released a preliminary report that stated: "The skeleton is that of Josef Mengele within reasonable scientific certainty."[434] Even after the long-awaited announcement, the Israeli government remained doubtful, and the Ministry of Justice's spokesperson stated that Israel would continue its efforts to locate the Nazi criminal and bring him to justice.[435]

---

[434] *In the Matter of Josef Mengele: A Report to the Attorney General of the United States,* op. cit. p. 152.

[435] Moshe Brilliant, "Mengele's Death Doubted in Israel." *New York Times,* June 10, 1985. Available at: <www.nytimes.com/1985/06/10/world /mengele-s-death-doubted-in-israel.html>. Accessed on: July 19, 2023.

MARCH 1986

Eight months later, when the media interest had declined, Tuma presented what he called the "last proof" that the corpse exhumed in Embu was really Mengele's: dental X-rays.[436] The absence of these records had opened the way for conspiracy theories, which claimed that Mengele had set up a hoax and was still at large. Tuma previously stated that the body had been identified with 99 percent certainty. Nevertheless, the missing 1 percent left room for speculation and, as Stephen Dachi, the American consul in São Paulo, said, "The smoking gun had to be found."

With that in mind, Dachi began his own detective work. Mengele mentioned in his diary, found in the Bossert house, that he had seen a dentist, Dr. Gama, in "Sama," twice. As has already been discussed, Mengele used codes to refer to people and places. The consul had no idea what "Sama" meant but, as a last resort, he exhaustively scoured the phone book until finally finding the dentist Hercy Gonzaga Gama Angelo, in Sànto Amaro. "Sama" was the neighborhood of Santo Amaro! His secretary made an appointment, and Dachi visited the dentist, accompanied by a policeman.

Looking through his files, the dentist found Pedro Hochbichler's, with an address at 5555 Alvarenga Road. It was a great find, but the dentist didn't have any X-rays. He said that the patient had been referred for root-canal treatment by a colleague, Dr. Kasumasa Tutiya, who also worked in Santo Amaro, two blocks away. Dachi gasped, for that information coincided with a clue that the Bosserts had provided: Mengele used to see a Japanese-Brazilian dentist because he thought that would make it harder for the dentist to remember his Western face.

A small door in the heart of Santo Amaro, a very popular shopping area, led to Dr. Tutiya's office. The American consul asked about the patient Pedro Hochbichler. Contrary to Mengele's thesis, the dentist

---

[436] "The teeth prove: It was really Mengele," *O Estado de S. Paulo*, March 28, 1986.

quickly recognized the photos and said that he had eight dental X-ray films of the patient. Dachi thought he had won the lottery. The X-rays perfectly matched those taken from the skull exhumed at the Rosário Cemetery. A statement signed by experts Lowell Levine from the US and Brazilian Carlos Valério stated that now there was absolute scientific proof: the body found in Embu was Mengele's.[437]

On July 23, 1986, Veronezzi closed the investigation into the Mengele case. In addition to taking statements from a series of witnesses at the Federal Police headquarters, the sheriff and Calandra made inquiries in the cities of Nova Europa, Araraquara, and Serra Negra, with the purpose of listening to people who had known Mengele closely. To this extensive work, he added all the technical reports. Finally, he indicted Geza, Gitta, Wolfram, and Liselotte for hiding a clandestine alien in the country. The teacher was also indicted for the crime of burying Mengele's body with false documents and for having inserted a false statement in a public document.

In the end, however, covering up and helping a Nazi criminal in Brazil for so many years resulted in a slap on the wrist. In October 1986, the Attorney General's Office indicted only Liselotte before the judge of the 12th Federal Court in São Paulo. And she was only charged with one crime: ideological falsehood for the false documents. The penalty was one to five years in prison, plus a fine.[438]

The trial would be long. At the hearing in April of the following year, Liselotte admitted that she had not received any threats from Mengele. She also said that she was never attracted by the rewards offered for his capture, which amounted to millions of dollars. Finally,

[437] Alan Riding, "Sleuths Uncover Dental Records, Clinching Mengele Identification." *New York Times*, March 28, 1986. Available at: <www.nytimes.com/1986/03/28/world/sleuths-uncover-dental-records-clinching-mengele-identification.html?searchResultPosition=1>. Accessed on: July 16, 2023.

[438] "Depoimento abre polêmica sobre caso Mengele." *Folha de S. Paulo*, April 9, 1987; "Caso Mengele: Processo já se aproxima do fim." *O Estado de S. Paulo*, May 17, 1987.

Liselotte told the judge that, during that month, she had been receiving anonymous threats by telephone and mail.[439]

The sentence was not handed down until August 1994. She was sentenced to two years in prison and a fine, but her lawyer appealed. In December 1997, the First Panel of the Federal Regional Court ruled that the statute of limitations on the crime of ideological falsehood, committed almost two decades earlier, had already expired. Liselotte would not receive any punishment, nor would any other person who had given Mengele protection in Brazil.[440]

Almost seven years after the discovery of the body in Embu, Germany's attorney general Hans-Eberhard Klein finally announced the case had been closed. "For me, Mengele is dead," he told the press in Frankfurt on April 8, 1992. The German government had asked British geneticist Alec Jeffreys for a DNA test of the remains. Jeffreys, a professor at the University of Leicester, was the leading authority on the subject, having invented the genetic fingerprinting technique. He matched the DNA from the exhumed bones with a sample of Rolf's blood. There was no longer any room for doubt: the skeleton was 99.997 percent sure to be Josef Mengele.

Following the results of the examination, the governments of Germany and Israel finally accepted this conclusion.[441] In October 1992, the OSI concluded its report, and the United States formally closed the Mengele case after almost eight years of investigations.

The doctor who carried out inhumane experiments on children and women in order to have a brilliant academic career ended his life without diplomas, which had been rescinded by the universities of Munich

439 "Liselotte: 'Por que protegi Mengele.'" *O Estado de S. Paulo*, April 10, 1987.

440 4th Federal Court of the São Paulo Section, criminal case no. 8250804.

441 "Genetic Testing Closes the Mengele Inquiry." *New York Times*, April 9, 1992. Available at: <www.nytimes.com/1992/04/09/world/genetic-testing-closes -the-mengele-inquiry.html>. Accessed on: July 16, 2023. "Germans Release Data Said to Prove Bones Exhumed in 1985 Are Mengele's." Jewish Telegraphic Agency, April 9, 1992. Available at: <www.jta.org/archive/germans-release-data-said-to -prove-bones-exhumed-in-1985-are-mengeles>. Accessed on: July 17, 2023.

and Frankfurt in the 1960s. In the opinion of the latter institution, Mengele was no longer worthy of his academic titles because he had run away from the responsibility of facing the serious accusations against him in court.[442]

Almost forty years after his death, Mengele returned to medical school, this time as an object of study. For decades, his skeleton remained forgotten in the Forensic Medical Institute in São Paulo. In 2017, Dr. Muñoz, now sporting a white beard, thought the bones might be useful to his students and asked for permission to use them in forensic medicine classes.[443] And so Mengele's story ended as he had wished: at a university and internationally famous, but in a way he could never have imagined.

[442] David G. Marwell, op. cit., p. 192.

[443] "Ossos de médico do Holocausto são usados em aula de medicina da USP." *O Estado de S. Paulo*, January 11, 2017. Available at: <www.estadao.com.br/ciencia /ossos-de-medico-do-holocausto-sao-usados-em-classe-de-medicina-forense/>. Accessed on: July 17, 2023.

LISELOTTE'S LAST WORDS

After six years of researching and writing this story, I thought the time had come to meet Tante Liselotte face-to-face one more time before bringing this book to an end. I needed some answers but also wanted to share with her what I had found out, especially facts she had chosen not to tell me. Furthermore, something she did say to me had always resonated in my head: "There was a lot of money. A lot of money." Naïvely, I thought she was referring to "a lot of money" paid by the Mengele family, who had always dug into their pockets to help those who covered up for him. The Brazilian Federal Police never investigated any financial plot; as Veronezzi had made it very clear to me, the focus of his investigation was always to determine whether or not Mengele had lived in Brazil, an objective he successfully achieved.

Even without the backing of a police investigation, I gradually came to understand that money was an important, if not fundamental, part of the relationship between Mengele and the people who protected him. Seeing the deed to the Alvarenga Road property, I found out that he never had legal ownership of the house where he spent the last years of his life. First, it belonged to Gitta and Geza, and then it was transferred to Liselotte's name as if it were a gift to her from a friend. Mengele also wrote in a letter that he had helped to buy the house in Serra Negra. Years later, he reported a transaction concerning another property: Geza sold an apartment Mengele owned in São Paulo, although the deed was never in his name. His maid Elsa Gulpian also recalled that Geza made monthly visits to Mengele after which he paid his employees. In other words, it was Geza who brought the money to Mengele.

In addition, Liselotte told international experts in 1985 that she had found ten thousand US dollars among Mengele's belongings after he died. She used about a thousand dollars to pay for the burial expenses and pocketed the rest, following Rolf's instructions.[444] Money is often mentioned in various situations involving Mengele, and at least once it became a bone of contention between him and Wolfgang, when the latter approached the Mengele family in Bavaria, which angered the old Nazi. In 2011, the diaries written by Mengele in Brazil were sold by an auction house in the United States for $245,000. The auctioneers did not disclose the identity of the buyer or the seller.[445] Liselotte was right: "There was a lot of money 'rolling in.'" But it wasn't just from Mengele or his family. There was more, and from the most surprising source of all.

It was late at night on a weekday when I was reading a Mossad study on the persecution of Nazi criminals. A former agent and Holocaust survivor, Yossi Chen, wrote the multi-volume work based on confidential documents, and dedicated a whole volume exclusively to Mengele. The work, published in 2007, remained under wraps for more than a decade, and only recently did the public have access to it. I was very interested to read about the agency's behind-the-scenes

---

444 *In the Matter of Josef Mengele: A Report to the Attorney General of the United States*, op. cit., p. 410.

445 Available at: <https://www.alexautographs.com/auction-lot/the-hidden-journals -of-dr.-josef-mengele-curren_43348AC2A6>. Accessed on: August 28, 2023.

work; but when I got to the last pages, I almost fell off my chair: there was a secret Mossad story involving Liselotte herself.[446]

The story was related to Israel's vigorous resistance to accept that the body buried in Embu was indeed Mengele's. Menachem Russak, the head of the Nazi-hunting unit, insisted that everything was just a fraud and that Liselotte had invented the story of the drowning in Bertioga.[447] This mistrust had deep roots, and the Israeli government believed it owed a moral debt to Mengele's thousands of victims, especially the twins. Therefore, Israel would never declare the Mengele case officially closed, unless there was absolutely no doubt about his death. But the Israeli authorities disputed some points in the forensic report—as, for example, the osteomyelitis found in the remains—and preferred to seek the certainty they so desperately wanted in another way.

Of course, a DNA test would have solved everything quickly. However, at that time, it was not yet available. So, in July 1985, Mossad chief Nahum Admoni decided that the main witnesses to Mengele's life in Brazil should undergo a polygraph test. A lie detector was supposed to confirm whether the Nazi doctor's protectors had been telling the truth when they recounted his fantastic death on the beach and burial under a false name. The Brazilian police agreed to Israel's request for the test and promised to help. Two Israeli agents were to conduct the tests: Victor Cohen, the polygraph operator, and Menachem Russak, from the Nazi-hunting unit. The two embarked for São Paulo to carry out a task that seemed simple and straightforward. And indeed it was, at least initially. Gitta and Geza readily cooperated, but Liselotte refused to do it, and the Brazilian police stated that without consent, there would be no examination. What was supposed to finally end any uncertainty turned out to raise even more suspicion. The Hungarian couple passed the lie detector test,

446 Available at: <https://www.yadvashem.org/archive/about/our-collections/mossad-documents.html>. Accessed on: August 2, 2023.
447 Yossi Chen, op. cit., p. 294.

confirming their previous statements. Nevertheless, that didn't solve the issue, since they weren't present at the drowning in Bertioga or at the burial in Embu. Therefore, the key person to resolve the question was Liselotte, and the Israelis pinned all their hopes on her.[448] Yet she was unyielding, at least for the moment.

Almost four years passed before Liselotte changed her mind. And then came my great surprise: she agreed to take the polygraph test, but imposed a hefty price on the Israelis: $100,000. After a long negotiation mediated by her lawyer, they agreed to $45,000. When she finally went through the lie detector test, Liselotte was very nervous. The first question they asked her was: "Was the man who drowned in Bertioga Josef Mengele?" to which she answered yes. The second question: "Was the man you brought to the Forensic Medical Institute in Santos Josef Mengele?" The answer was also yes. And the last question: "Is Josef Mengele still alive?" She said no. The result was unequivocal: Liselotte had been telling the truth since the discovery of the body in Embu.

In fact, my old teacher had been honest in the polygraph test, with the Federal Police, and with me, even if what she said didn't make sense at the time we met. She had disclosed that she had been offered a lot of money to talk and that she had an agreement with the Jews. She specifically mentioned the name of Menachem Russak. But the way she had told me the story made it sound like the "deal" had been just an act of intimidation to keep her quiet. I could never have imagined that Tante Liselotte had earned $45,000 in a deal with the Israelis, precisely the people Mengele feared most during the entire time he lived in hiding in Brazil. It was quite surprising to me.

Even after this discovery, one point remained unclear. If "a lot of money had rolled in," as Liselotte herself had said using Brazilian slang, why hadn't she accepted the reward of more than three million US dollars when it was announced many years earlier? I turned to the notes I had made shortly after our initial conversation, when I was starting the research for this book. And then I understood why she

448 Yossi Chen, op. cit, pp. 217–20.

didn't cave in to the multimillion-dollar reward. Besides the many phone calls she received from strangers who threatened her, there were others who said, "Some people are not sellouts." She was flattered by these comments. "I feel a certain pride, you know? Am I right?" she asked me. In her heart, Liselotte believed that she was a loyal person, and, according to her logic, asking the Israelis for money made sense; handing her friend over to the authorities did not.

Other questions remained, and I hoped to get answers for them. During our conversation, always using the same slang, she had told me, "A lot of money is still rolling in today."

"But today? He's dead," I wondered.

She replied: "Even today."

"Do you mean there are things that people don't know about? Is that it?" I insisted.

She confirmed: "I know, but I'm not going to talk. The deal I have with them . . . it's serious."

Obviously, she chose not to share all her secrets with me back then, but now I had just discovered one of them by chance, reading the report on the Mossad's secret files. What else was she hiding?

I confess that, after our first conversation about Mengele, I never wanted to speak to her again. Only those who have repeatedly received sinister threats can understand how I felt. I created a kind of emotional shield for myself and decided to carry on with my research without ever approaching Liselotte again. But it wasn't so simple. I had unanswered questions and couldn't overcome my curiosity. Her evasive sentences kept coming back to my mind: "There's a lot, a lot that nobody knows yet . . . I know."

In 2022, I decided to get in touch with her again and called her number many times, but no one would answer. I began to read the Lutheran church's newsletter assiduously to see if her name appeared in the obituaries. After all, she was already in her nineties when we first talked about the case. I asked a friend to help me by calling her at different times, but still nothing. The solution, once again, was to visit her at her home in Brooklin, even though I put it off as long as possible. Finally, I plucked up the courage and went to her house on a Saturday morning. I was apprehensive, because I didn't know what I was about to find, and it's never pleasant to confront someone with thorny issues.

Before I even got out of the car, I noticed that the house façade looked completely different: the 1970s townhouse had been transformed into a typical example of contemporary architecture. I rang the doorbell, and someone quickly answered the door, unlike what had happened the first time I'd been there. I inquired about Liselotte, and a woman who sounded young asked who I was. I answered that I was an acquaintance of Liselotte's, to which the woman replied that she was sorry, but Liselotte had died a few years before. I asked her if she knew when, and she said: "I think in 2018." It was quite a shock for me to hear that Liselotte had died only months after our conversation.

I then decided to reach out to Liselotte's children, Sabine and Andreas, who were accustomed to Mengele's presence in the Bosserts' family life and called him "uncle." Maybe they would have some answers for me. Sabine kindly replied to my request for an interview but declined to talk. While she understood my interest in the subject, neither she nor her brother was going to say anything, because they believed that her parents had already given the police all the necessary information. But as Liselotte admitted before, she hadn't told all of it. Unless new secret documents appear, her knowledge about the Mengele case is ultimately buried with her.

WHEN I WAS A CHILD and had to take the bus home from school, my sisters and I were often greeted with a "Heil, Hitler!" by people we met on the way to the bus station. They weren't neo-Nazis, least of all us. They just found it amusing to associate anyone who had some connection with Germany to Nazism. As a descendant of Germans, I have heard this kind of inane banter all my life. Because of these false associations, some acquaintances in the German community asked me why I would write a book about a subject that could incite even more prejudice. The fact is, prejudice comes from one place: ignorance.

There was indeed a lot of ignorance about Mengele. His name fueled speculation, conspiracy theories, and fake news. No wonder the hunt for him faced so many obstacles. Over the years, many people claimed to have seen him in various parts of the world, even after his death. Mengele was even blamed for the high birth rate of twins in Cândido Godói, a German-settled town in the state of Rio Grande do Sul. Rumors circulated about him going to the town in the 1960s to carry out experiments on women. It took a genetic and historical study of the population to find out that he had had nothing to do with the phenomenon, which had been registered in Cândido Godói at least since the 1930s, when Mengele hadn't even set foot in Brazil.[449]

These fantasies and exaggerations take away from issues and considerations that really matter: ethics in medical research and practice; the dangers of extreme right-wing ideology; the fallacy of biological racism; the importance of punishing criminals who commit war crimes and crimes against humanity; victim reparations; and the idea of good and evil. The most important and poignant lesson of all has come from the people—ordinary people in flesh and blood—who suffered at Mengele's hands as human guinea pigs. Even when it became clear that justice was no longer possible, as Mengele was already dead, they continued the struggle in order to understand what had been done to them.

A representative of Mengele's twins in Israel, the Polish Jona Laks, told me that she secretly sought out Rolf in the early 2000s and exchanged letters with him. She was the only survivor to meet Mengele's son in person. Rolf told her that he wanted a quiet life. But Jona wanted to get some information about what had happened to her and other victims in Auschwitz. She believed that Rolf was the only person who could possibly know anything and hoped that he

---

449 Alexei Barrionuevo, "In a Brazilian Town, a Rogue Gene and a Boom in Twins." *New York Times*, March 24, 2011. Available at: <www.nytimes.com/2011/03/25/world/americas/25brazil.html?searchResultPosition=1>. Accessed on: July 28, 2023.

might have received some documents from his father. But her hope was in vain; he had nothing to offer her. And like the other twins, Jona faced health problems with unknown causes, a direct consequence of Mengele's experiments.[450] While his victims suffered physical and mental torment throughout their lives, the "Angel of Death" ended his days with friends, writing, reading, walking his dogs, tending to his garden, barbecuing, bathing in waterfalls and in the sea of his tropical Bavaria.

---

450 Interview with Jona Laks by telephone, December 12, 2019.

A NOTE ON SOURCES

This book is not a novel. I wrote this story based on years of research into official documents, such as the police investigation into the case and the Federal Police dossier. I also found almost a hundred letters written by Mengele or sent to him, which were originally seized from Liselotte and Wolfram Bossert's family home and later forgotten in a messy room at the National Police Academy Museum in Brasília. I researched in magazines, newspapers, and TV news shows of the period to understand how the witnesses and other characters in this story expressed themselves. I conducted countless interviews with people who knew Mengele in Brazil, doctors from the team that identified his skeleton, Auschwitz survivors, researchers in the United States and Europe, and even Mossad secret agent Rafi Eitan, who, at the age of ninety, gave one of the last interviews of his life for this book.

In his office in Tel Aviv, where we talked personally on a sunny afternoon, Eitan told me how he got very close to catching Mengele in Brazil and how the Mossad co-opted a Brazilian agent for this mission. I asked him how no one had ever talked about it. In his agreeable manner, he shrugged his shoulders and simply said: "That's not my fault." In other words, it wasn't his fault that no journalist had raised the story yet. Like Rafi Eitan, other interviewees were elderly and died before this book was finished. This was the case of Eva Mozes Kor, one of the greatest activists among the twins who were victims of Mengele. She answered my questions by email from the US state of Indiana, where she lived and ran a Holocaust education center. She died shortly afterwards, aged eighty-five, while leading a group on a trip to Auschwitz, as she liked to do every summer.

The result of this intense research is not a biography of Mengele. There are already some of those, and I didn't want to give a platform to a criminal by scrutinizing details of his personal life that don't matter to anyone. My goal is to bring to light a surprising story, a real-life thriller, using the same words that were spoken and recorded in interviews and documents.

The crimes Mengele committed, his victims, how medicine was practiced in the Third Reich, the sentences other Nazi doctors received for their crimes, and the people who supported Mengele's escape—all these aspects form the common thread of this book. Finally, the big question we must face is: How could a criminal of this magnitude and his supporters go completely unpunished in Brazil?

ACKNOWLEDGMENTS

As the old proverb says, "It takes a village to raise a child." The saying, which inspired the title of a 1995 book by Hillary Clinton, may sound hackneyed, but no idea better defines how I feel about this book: it took a community to create it. I would like, therefore, to thank all the people who have generously helped me over the past six years. First of all, my husband, Pablo Sgarbi, who encouraged me from the book's conception to the end. He was the first person to read each chapter and, with his intelligence and sensitivity, made important observations on the fluidity and clarity of the text. I thank my daughter, Helena, who grew up while I was writing this book, for her patience and understanding of the importance of my work. I would also like to thank Elaine Cristina Barboza, our dear Nani, for allowing me to take the time to write, as well as my mother-in-law, Ana Cristina Muniz Sgarbi, Tininha, and my friends Marcelo do Lago, Kelly Andreoli, Santiago Fernández, and Haline Medeiros, all of whom gave me the logistical support I needed to dedicate myself to this work.

Other people helped me with their expertise. Writer Luize Valente offered me her advice and teachings that were fundamental, especially at the beginning. Journalist and writer Rodrigo Alvarez gave me valuable tips on how to format a book project. Several renowned experts in various fields shared their knowledge with me, such as professor and historian Maria Luiza Tucci Carneiro, who generously gave me private history lessons over the phone and recommended readings. International law professor Paulo Borba Casella explained complex concepts and clarified my doubts about war crimes and crimes against humanity. Jewish culture professor Nancy Rozenchan helped me understand a riddle about the Talmud, raised by Liselotte Bossert. Michel Michaelovitch de Mahiques, a University of São Paulo professor at the Oceanographic Institute, elucidated why the Bertioga Sea is so dark, helping me to create a more accurate picture of Mengele's place of death. Coroner Luis Ignacio Pettoruti explained to me the difficulty of determining the age of the body of someone who has drowned, which allowed Mengele's false documents to go unnoticed at the Forensic Medical Institute. Correspondent Ariel Palacios taught me a lot about Buenos Aires and its history. Journalist César Tralli gave me a very important contact in the Federal Police. German historian Carola Sachse, editor of a symposium on the link between the Kaiser Wilhelm Institute and Auschwitz, lent her vast experience on the subject to answer my questions and provide me with research tips. The US historian David G. Marwell became a long-distance friend after the many exchanges we had about the Mengele case.

I'm also grateful to those who helped me resolve practical issues, such as Sinésio Beghini, the former mayor of Serra Negra, who provided documents about the Santa Luzia farm where Mengele lived. Documentary filmmaker Marcelo Felipe Sampaio provided valuable information and contacts, as well as historian Pedro Burini. I would also like to thank my brother-in-law Pedro Ximenes, who took digitized copies of Mengele's letters from the National Police Academy Museum in Brasília. Thanks to my sister Marina Anton, who took me there, and to my dear assistant, who patiently transcribed dozens of letters in German, but prefers to remain unidentified. My sister Carolina Anton, who is a pharmacist and lawyer, went to great lengths to find the lawsuit against Liselotte Bossert, in addition to enlightening my understanding of clinical research practices. My brother-in-law Fabio Horner, a prosecutor, answered my questions about lawsuits and Brazilian legislation. My sister Cristina Anton provided me with the code of medical ethics adopted in Brazil. Kurt Holzapfel, a great reference in my life, was kind enough to obtain for me in Germany a copy of Carola Sachse's book, which was fundamental to this research. I am very grateful to all the interviewees and their relatives who helped make the interviews possible. My friend Guil Nowick played a special role in finding Rafi Eitan, and only rested after we were able to get in touch with Eitan, with the help of a famous Israeli radio presenter.

I would also like to thank my friends Washington Calegari, Fernanda Sindlinger, Eva Gutjahr, Heloísa Becker Albertani, Antonio Stotz, and my father-in-law, José Cesar Garcia Sgarbi, who agreed to be part of the test group for this book and read the first few chapters right from the start. Thanks to their comments and observations, I was able to correct some of the turns the narrative was taking and make this a better book. I would also like to thank Flávio Moura and Luisa Tieppo for their care with the text, and Aline Valli and Gabriella Gonçalles for their tireless efforts in finding the best images to illustrate this book. And to Márcio Alberto Gomes Silva, head of the Research and Publications Service of the National Police Academy's Teaching Directorate, who provided great assistance in finding photos and documents from the Mengele case. I would like to thank my literary agents, Luciana Villas-Boas and Anna Luiza Cardoso, who were wonderful from the very beginning, believing in the book and making suggestions with intelligence and elegance. Finally, I thank my mother, Edla Anton, and my father, Renato Ralf Anton (in memoriam), for giving me life and the best education, inspiration, and love.

BIBLIOGRAPHY

BOOKS, THESES, AND REPORTS

Abal, Felipe Cittolin. *Nazistas no Brasil e extradição: os pedidos de extradição de Franz Stangl e Gustav Wagner em uma análise histórico-jurídica*. Curitiba: Juruá Press, 2014.

Arendt, Hannah. *Eichmann em Jerusalém: Um relato sobre a banalidade do mal*. 19. Reprint. Trans. José Rubens Siqueira. São Paulo: Companhia das Letras Press, 1999.

Beevor, Antony. *A Segunda Guerra Mundial*. Trans. Cristina Cavalcanti. Rio de Janeiro: Record Press, 2015.

Bergman, Ronen. *Rise and Kill First: The Secret History of Israel's Targeted Assassinations*. New York: Random House Press, 2018.

Bethell, Leslie (Org.). *A América Latina após 1930: Argentina, Uruguai, Paraguai e Brasil*. Trans. Gilson César Cardoso de Souza. São Paulo: Edusp Press, 2018. (História da América Latina, Vol. x)

—. *A América Latina de 1870 a 1930*. Trans. Geraldo Gerson de Souza. São Paulo: Edusp Press, 2018. (História da América Latina, Vol. v)

Bethencourt, Francisco. *Racismos: Das Cruzadas ao século xx*. Trans. Luís Oliveira Santos e João Quina Edições. São Paulo: Companhia das Letras Press, 2018.

Büchner, Georg. *Woyzeck*. Berlin: Insel Press, 2007.

Burini, Noedir Pedro Carvalho. *O Anjo da Morte em Serra Negra*. [S.l.: s.n., 19--].

Crasnianski, Tania. *Filhos de nazistas: Os impressionantes retratos de família da elite do nazismo*. Trans. Fernando Scheibe. São Paulo: Vestígio Press, 2018.

Didi-Huberman, Georges. *Imagens apesar de tudo*. Trans. Vanessa Brito and João Pedro Cachopo. São Paulo: 34 Press, 2020.

Eger, Eva Edith. *A bailarina de Auschwitz*. Trans. Débora Chaves. Rio de Janeiro: Sextante Press, 2019.

Ehrenfreund, Norbert. *The Nuremberg Legacy: How the Nazi War Crimes Trials Changed the Course of History*. New York: Palgrave Macmillan Press, 2007.

Eitan, Rafi. *Capturing Eichmann: The Memoirs of a Mossad Spymaster*. Newbury, UK: Greenhill Press, 2002.

Elias, Ruth. *Triumph of Hope: From Theresienstadt and Auschwitz to Israel*. New York: Wiley Press, 1999.

Goñi, Uki. *Perón y Los Alemanes: El espionaje nazi en Argentina*. Buenos Aires: Sudamericana Press, 1998.

—. *The Real Odessa: How Peron Brought the Nazi War Criminals to Argentina*. London: Granta, 2003.

—. *A verdadeira Odessa: O contrabando de nazistas para a Argentina de Perón*. Trans. Berilo Vargas. Rio de Janeiro: Record Press, 2004.

Guez, Olivier. *O desaparecimento de Josef Mengele*. Trans. André Telles. Rio de Janeiro: Intrínseca Press, 2019.

Hitler, Adolf. *Mein Kampf*. New Delhi: Diamond Press, 2021.

Judt, Tony. *Pós-guerra: Uma história da Europa desde 1945*. Trans. José Roberto O'Shea. São Paulo: Objetiva Press, 2008.

Keller, Sven. *Günzburg und der Fall Josef Mengele: Die Heimatstadt und die Jagd nach dem NS-Verbrecher*. Munich: R. Oldenbourg Press, 2003.

Koehl, Robert Lewis. *História revelada da SS*. 2. ed. Trans. Felipe José Lindoso. São Paulo: Crítica Press, 2021.

Kor, Eva Mozes, and Buccieri Lisa Rojany. *Surviving the Angel of Death: The True Story of a Mengele Twin in Auschwitz*. Vancouver: Tanglewood Press, 2009.

Koren, Yehuda, and Eilat Negev. *In Our Hearts We Were Giants, The Remarkable Story of the Lilliput Troupe: A Dwarf Family's Survival of the Holocaust*. New York: Carroll & Graf, 2004.

Kubica, Helena. "Dr. Mengele und seine Verbrechen im Konzentrationslager Auschwitz-Birkenau." *Hefte von Auschwitz*, v. 20, 369–455, 1997.

Langbein, Hermann. *People in Auschwitz*. Chapel Hill: University of North Carolina Press, 2005.

Lara, Fernão Lopez Ginez de. *Modernização e desenvolvimentismo: Formação das primeiras favelas de São Paulo e a favela do Vergueiro*. São Paulo: Faculty of Philosophy, Languages, and Human Sciences-University of São Paulo, 2012. MA Thesis in Human Geography.

Levi, Primo. *É isto um homem?* Trans. Luigi Del Re. Rio de Janeiro: Rocco Press, 2013.

Lifton, Robert Jay. *Los médicos nazis: La ciencia de matar*. 1. Reprint. Buenos Aires: El Ateneo Press, 2021.

Marwell, David G. *Mengele: Unmasking the Angel of Death*. New York: W. W. Norton Press, 2020.

McDonough, Frank, and John Cochrane. *The Holocaust*. London: Bloomsbury Press, 2008.

Mukherjee, Siddhartha. *O gene: Uma história íntima*. Trans. Laura Teixeira Motta. São Paulo: Companhia das Letras Press, 2016.

Müller-Hill, Benno. *Murderous Science: Elimination by Scientific Selection of Jews, Gypsies, and Others, Germany 1933–1945*. New York: Oxford University Press, 1988.

Nyiszli, Miklós. *Auschwitz: A Doctor's Eyewitness Account*. London: Penguin Press, 2012.

Office of Special Investigations (OSI)—Criminal Division. *In the Matter of Josef Mengele: A Report to the Attorney General of the United States—Exhibits*. October 1992. <www.justice.gov/sites/default/files/criminal-hrsp/legacy/2011/06/06/10 -30-92mengele-exhibits.pdf>. Accessed August 4, 2023.

"Operation Reinhard (Einsatz Reinhard)." United States Museum of Holocaust. <encyclopedia.ushmm.org/content/en/article/operation-reinhard-einsatz-reinhard>. Accessed February 20, 2023.

Perl, Gisella. *I Was a Doctor in Auschwitz*. Lanham, MD: Lexington Press, 2019.

Pinsky, Jaime, and Carla Bassanezi Pinsky (Orgs.). *Faces do fanatismo*. São Paulo: Contexto Press, 2004.

Posner, Gerald L., and John Ware. *Mengele: The Complete Story*. New York: Cooper Square Press, 2000.

Rees, Laurence. *The Holocaust: A New History*. London: Penguin Press, 2017.

Ronsefeld, Gavriel D. *O Quarto Reich: Da Segunda Guerra Mundial aos dias de hoje, a ameaça do fantasma do nazismo e o avanço da extrema direita autoritária*. São Paulo: Cultrix Press, 2022.

Sachse, Carola. *Die Verbindung nach Auschwitz: Biowissenschaften und Menschenversuche an Kaiser-Wilhelm-Instituten; Dokumentation eines Symposiums.* Göttingen: Wallstein Press, 2004.

"Sinti and Roma (Gypsies) in Auschwitz." Auschwitz-Birkenau State Museum. <auschwitz.org/en/history/categories-of-prisoners/sinti-and-roma -in-auschwitz>. Accessed June 1, 2021.

"Sixty-first Anniversary of the Liquidation of the Gypsy Camp in Birkenau." Auschwitz-Birkenau State Museum, August 1, 2015. <https://www.auschwitz.org /en/museum/news/sixty-first-anniversary-of-the-liquidation-of-the-gypsy -camp-in-birkenau,427.html>. Accessed July 12, 2023.

Spitz, Vivien. *Doctors from Hell: The Horrific Account of Nazi Experiments on Humans.* Boulder: Sentient Press, 2005.

Stangneth, Bettina. *Eichmann Before Jerusalem: The Unexamined Life of a Mass Murder.* London: The Bodley Head Press, 2004.

Stauber, Roni, and Raphael Vago. *The Roma: A Minority in Europe, Historical, Political and Social Perspectives.* Budapest: Central European University Press, 2007.

Steinke, Ronen. *Fritz Bauer: The Jewish Prosecutor Who Brought Eichmann and Auschwitz to Trial.* Bloomington: Indiana University Press, 2020.

Völklein, Ulrich. *Josef Mengele: Der Arzt von Auschwitz.* Göttingen: Steidl Press, 1999.

Wachsmann, Nikolaus. *KL: A History of the Nazi Concentration Camps.* Boston: Little, Brown Press, 2015.

Wilson, Philip K. "Eugenics." *Encyclopædia Britannica*: <www.britannica.com/ science/eugenics-genetics>. Accessed February 5, 2021.

Yad Vashem. EichmannTrialEn. *Eichmann Trial—Session No. 1.* <www.youtube. com/watch?v=Fv6xbeVozhU>. Accessed October 27, 2022.

ESSAYS AND NEWS ARTICLES

"3 Nations Joining to Hunt Mengele." *New York Times*, May 11, 1985. <www. nytimes.com/1985/05/11/world/3-nations-joining-to-hunt-mengele.html>. Accessed June 13, 2023.

"6 de Junho de 1985." *O Estado de S. Paulo*, June 7, 1985.

"60 Years after Liberation 'It Was Skin and Bones': Soldiers Remember Auschwitz." Jewish Telegraphic Agency. <www.jta.org/archive/60-years-after-liberation-it

-was-skin-and-bones-soldiers-remember-auschwitz>. Accessed November 2, 2021.

"A áustria quer nazista de volta." *O Estado de S. Paulo*, March 3, 1967.

"A exumação do enigma: O mistério do caso Mengele pode estar chegando ao fim." *Veja*, June 12, 1985.

"A prisão do nazista." *Jornal da Tarde*, March 3, 1967.

"A vida na Sombra: Mengele teve a proteção de uma rede de amigos em seus dezenove anos de Brasil." *Veja*, June 19, 1985.

"About the Eichmann Trial." Yad Vashem. <www.yadvashem.org/holocaust /eichmann-trial/about.html>. Accessed October 27, 2022.

Aderet, Ofer. "Ultra-Orthodox Man Buys Diaries of Nazi Doctor Mengele for $245,000." *Haaretz*, July 22, 2011. <www.haaretz.com/jewish/1.5032917>. Accessed July 6, 2023.

Anistia Internacional. *Eichmann Supreme Court Judgment: 50 Years On, Its Significance Today*. London: Amnesty International Publications, 2012. <www.amnesty.org /en/wp-content/uploads/2021/06/ior530132012en.pdf>. Accessed July 17, 2023.

"Antes da morte, a depressão." *O Estado de S. Paulo*, June 11, 1985. "Aparecido Laertes Calandra." Memorial da Resistência de São Paulo. <memorialdaresistenciasp.org .br/pessoas/aparecido-laertes-calandra/>. Accessed June 24, 2023.

"Assustado, agressivo, vivia com medo." *O Estado de S. Paulo*, June 7, 1985. <acervo .estadao.com.br/pagina/#!/19850607-33823-nac-0026-999-26-not>. Accessed July 20, 2023.

Barrionuevo, Alexei. "In a Brazilian Town, a Rogue Gene and a Boom in Twins." *New York Times*, March 24, 2011. <www.nytimes.com/2011/03/25/world/americas /25brazil.html?searchResultPosition=1>. Accessed July 28, 2023.

Bergman, Ronen. "Mengeles Glück." *Zeit*, September 17, 2017. <https://www.zeit. de/2017/37/josef-mengele-auschwitz-arzt-mossad-akten>. Accessed August 28, 2023.

Bernardo, André. "Herberts Cukurs: O nazista que viveu por 20 anos no Brasil e foi executado no Uruguai por agentes do Mossad." BBC, March 6, 2022. <www.bbc .com/portuguese/geral-60481793>. Accessed July 13, 2023.

Brilliant, Moshe. "Mengele's Death Doubted in Israel." *New York Times*, June 10, 1985. <www.nytimes.com/1985/06/10/world/mengele-s-death-doubted-in-israel .html>. Accessed July 19, 2023.

Byham, Inge. "So entkam mein Vater. Die Geheimnisse des Josef Mengele: Seine Flucht. Seine Verstecke. Seine Jahre im Untergrund." *Bunte Illustrierte*, June 20, 1986.

"Carrasco empregava cobaias humanas em suas experiências." *Folha de S.Paulo*, June 16, 1985.

"Casa em Serra Negra, agora atração turística." *O Estado de S. Paulo*, June 14, 1985.

"Caso Mengele: Processo já se aproxima do fim." *O Estado de S. Paulo*, May 17, 1987.

"Centenas de pessoas deixam a favela da Vergueiro e começam outra em El-dorado." *Folha de S.Paulo*, April 16, 1968.

"Controversy over Alleged Tribute to Dead Nazi War Hero." Jewish Telegraphic Agency, December 30, 1982. <www.jta.org/archive/controversy-over-alleged-tribute-to-dead-nazi-war-hero>. Accessed June 13, 2023.

"Depoimento abre polêmica sobre caso Mengele." *Folha de S.Paulo*, April 9, 1987.

"Derulmer Prozess." Stadt Ulm. <www.ulm.de/tourismus/stadtgeschichte /schicksalstage-und-orte/der-ulmer-prozess>. Accessed July 13, 2023.

"Descoberto em sp corpo que pode ser de Mengele." *Folha de S.Paulo*, June 7, 1985.

Fangerau, Heiner, and Irmgard Müller. "Das Standardwerk der Rassen-hygiene von Erwin Baur, Eugen Fischer und Fritz Lenz im Urteil der Psychiatrie und Neurologie 1921–1940." *Der Nervenarzt*, v. 73, p. 1039–46, November 2002. <www .academia.edu/25603311>. Accessed Apr 18, 2021.

"Filho de Gerhard acusa os Bossert." *O Estado de S. Paulo*, June 12, 1985.

"Filho pode ter ido a Bertioga." *O Estado de S. Paulo*, June 8, 1985, p. 15.

Flor, Ana, and Andrea Michael. "Mengele trabalhou dez anos no Brasil." *Folha de S.Paulo*, November 24, 2004. <www1.folha.uol.com.br/folha/brasil/ult96u65893. shtml>. Accessed July 20, 2023.

Friedman, Thomas L. "Jerusalem Listens to the Victims of Mengele." *New York Times*, February 7, 1985.

Galle, Helmut. "Os escritos autobiográficos de Josef Mengele." *Estudos Avançados*, São Paulo, v. 25, n. 71, 2011.

García-moro, María, et al. "La enfermedad de Noma/cancrum oris: Una enfermedad olvidada." *Revista Española de Quimioterapia*, v. 28, n. 5, 225–34, 2015. <seq.es /seq/0214-3429/28/5/moro.pdf>. Accessed July 10, 2023.

"Genetic Testing Closes the Mengele Inquiry." *New York Times*, April 9, 1992. <www .nytimes.com/1992/04/09/world/genetic-testing-closes-the-mengele-inquiry .html>. Accessed July 16, 2023.

"Germans Release Data Said to Prove Bones Exhumed in 1985 Are Mengele's." Jewish Telegraphic Agency, April 9, 1992. <www.jta.org/archive/germans-release -data-said-to-prove-bones-exhumed-in-1985-are-mengeles>. Accessed July 17, 2023.

Grodin, Michael A., Eva Mozes Kor, and Susan Benedict. "The Trial That Never Happened: Josef Mengele and the Twins of Auschwitz." *War Crimes, Genocide & Crimes Against Humanity*, v. 5, 2011. <heinonline.org/HOL /LandingPage?handle=hein.journals/warcrim5&div=4&id=&page=>. Accessed July 6, 2023.

"Gross-rosen." United States Holocaust Memorial Museum. <encyclopedia.ushmm .org/content/en/article/gross-rosen>. Accessed July 12, 2023.

Heller, Aron. "Mossad Opens Archives on Eichmann Capture." *The Times of Israel*, 8 February 2012. <www.timesofisrael.com/mossad-opens-archives-on-eichmann -capture>. Accessed October 24, 2022.

"Histórico." Prefeitura Municipal de Nova Europa. <novaeuropa.sp.gov.br/?pa g=T1RjPU9EZz1PVFU9T0dVPU9HST1PVEE9T0dFPU9HRT0=&id menu=214>. Accessed December 8, 2022.

"Holocaust." *Merriam-Webster Dictionary*. <www.merriam-webster.com/dictionary /holocaust>. Accessed June 3, 2023.

Hudson, Nicholas. "From 'Nation' to 'Race': The Origin of Racial Classification in Eighteenth-Century Thought." *Eighteenth-Century Studies*, Johns Hopkins University Press, v. 29, n. 3, 247–64, primavera de 1996.

"IG Farben." *Encyclopædia Britannica*. <www.britannica.com/topic/IG-Farben>. Accessed July 10, 2023.

"Introduction to the Holocaust." United States Holocaust Memorial Museum. <encyclopedia.ushmm.org/content/pt-br/article/introduction-to-the-holocaust>. Accessed July 13, 2023.

Israel State Archives. *Special Publication: Behind the Scenes at the Eichmann Trial*. <catalog.archives.gov.il/en/chapter/behind-scenes-eichmann-trial>. Accessed July 17, 2023.

"Jewish Survivor Stephanie Heller Testimony." USC Shoah Foundation. <youtube .com/watch?v=0qRp5-D0r0c>. Accessed July 6, 2023.

"José Antônio de Mello." Memorial da Resistência de São Paulo. <memorialdaresisten ciasp.org.br/pessoas/jose-antonio-de-mello/>. Accessed July 2, 2023.

"Judeus fazem julgamento simulado de Josef Mengele." *Jornal Nacional*, February 6, 1985.

Kamm, Henry. "Wiesenthal Lists Mengele Sightings." *New York Times*, May 15, 1985.

"Liselotte: 'Por que protegi Mengele.'" *O Estado de S. Paulo*, April 10, 1987.

Markham, James M. "Mengele 'Double' Called Fervid Nazi." *New York Times*, June 13, 1985. <www.nytimes.com/1985/06/13/world/mengele-double-called-fervid-nazi .html>. Accessed July 20, 2023.

Mengele, Rolf. *The Today Show*. NBC, June 16, 1986.

"Mengele Trail: Clues of Paper, Then of People." *New York Times*, June 23, 1985. <www .nytimes.com/1985/06/23/world/mengele-trail-clues-of-paper-then-of -people.html>. Accessed June 14, 2023.

"Mistério, Mito. Onde está Mengele?" *O Estado de S. Paulo*, March 10, 1985.

"Nazi Hunter, in a Protest in Paraguay, Demands Mengele's Arrest." *New York Times*, 25 May 1985. <www.nytimes.com/1985/05/25/world/nazi-hunter-in-a-protest-in -paraguay-demands-mengele-s-arrest.html>. Accessed June 8, 2023.

"Nazista Teria Proteção." *O Estado de S. Paulo*, 7 March 1967, p. 36. <acervo.estadao .com.br/pagina/#!/19670307-28187-nac-0036-999-36-not/busca/Stangl>. Accessed February 18, 2023.

"O poder das séries contra a violência institucionalizada." *Folha de S.Paulo*, July 21, 2019.

"Ossos de médico do Holocausto são usados em aula de medicina da usp." *O Estado de S. Paulo*, January 11, 2017. <www.estadao.com.br/ciencia/ossos-de -medico-do-holocausto-sao-usados-em-classe-de-medicina-forense>. Accessed July 17, 2023.

Philpot, Robert. "How the Mossad Hunted the 'Butcher of Riga,' Who Murdered Up to 30,000 Jews." *The Times of Israel*, August 1, 2020. <www.timesofisrael .com/how-the-mossad-hunted-the-butcher-of-riga-who-murdered-up-to-300 00-jews>. Accessed July 14, 2023.

"Pista revela: Filho de Mengele em SP." *O Estado de S. Paulo*, June 8, 1985.

Pohl, Dieter. Interview. [Interview given to] Sonia Phalnikar. Deutsche Welle, 20 May 2008. <www.dw.com/en/landmark-trial-pushed-germany-to-tackle -nazi-past/a-3349537>. Accessed July 13, 2023.

"Polícia prende chefe nazista." *O Estado de S. Paulo*, March 2, 1967.

"Read About Eva's Road to Forgiveness." CANDLES Holocaust Museum and Education Center. <candlesholocaustmuseum.org/our-survivors/eva-kor/her-story/her -story.html/title/read-about-eva-s-road-to-forgiveness>. Accessed June 8, 2020.

Reilly, Andrés Lópes. "Josef Mengele: Los ocho días que el 'ángel de la muerte' vivió en Uruguay." *La Nación*, April 2, 2021. <www.lanacion.com.ar/el-mundo/josef-mengele-los-ocho-dias-que-el-angel-de-la-muerte-vivio-en-uruguay-nid02042021/>. Accessed July 13, 2023.

Riding, Alan. "Key Man in Mengele Case: Romeu Tuma." *New York Times*, June 16, 1985.

—. "Sleuths Uncover Dental Records, Clinching Mengele Identification." *New York Times*, March 28, 1986. <www.nytimes.com/1986/03/28/world/sleuths-uncover-dental-records-clinching-mengele-identification.html?-searchResultPosition=1>. Accessed July 16, 2023.

"Sepultado em posição de sentido." *O Estado de S. Paulo*, June 7, 1985, p. 26.

"Sete dentes, chave da resposta." *O Estado de S. Paulo*, June 7, 1985.

Stabei, Pedro. "A última empregada: Ele gostava do Brasil." *O Estado de S. Paulo*, June 8, 1985.

"Task/Preliminary Investigations." Zentrale Stelle der Ländesjustizverwaltungen zur Auflarung nationalsozialistischer Verbrechen. <zentrale-stelle-ludwigsburg.justiz-bw.de/pb/,Len/Startpage/Arbeitsweise-Translate/Task+_+Preliminary+Investigations>. Accessed July 13, 2023.

"The Doctors Trial: The Medical Case of the Subsequent Nuremberg Proceedings." United States Holocaust Memorial Museum. <encyclopedia.ushmm.org/content/en/article/the-doctors-trial-the-medical-case-of-the-subsequent-nuremberg-proceedings>. Accessed July 12, 2023.

"The Fate of the Children." Auschwitz-Birkenau State Museum. <www.auschwitz.org/en/history/fate-of-children/the-fate-of-the-children>. Accessed July 12, 2023.

"The Final Evacuation and Liquidation of the Camp." Auschwitz-Birkenau State Museum. <www.auschwitz.org/en/history/evacuation/the-final-evacuation-and-liquidation-of-the-camp>. Accessed November 4, 2021.

"The Hunt for the Nazi 'Angel of Death': How Israel Tried—and Failed—to Capture Dr. Josef Mengele." *Haaretz*, 9 September 2017. <www.haaretz.com/israel-news/2017-09-09/ty-article/premium/how-israel-tried-and-failed-to-capture-dr-josef-mengele/0000017f-db30-df9c-a17f-ff3809da0000>. Accessed June 12, 2023.

"The Mengele Letters." CANDLES Holocaust Museum and Education Center. <candlesholocaustmuseum.org/educational-resources/mengele-letters.html>. Accessed July 6, 2022.

"The Stories of Six Righteous Among the Nations in Auschwitz." Yad Vashem. https://www.yadvashem.org/yv/en/exhibitions/righteous-auschwitz/index.asp. Accessed July 6, 2023.

"Tuma, Romeu." FGV-CPDOC. <www.fgv.br/CPDOC/acervo/dicionários /verbete-biografico/tuma-romeu>. Accessed August 4, 2023.

"Um Comandante Nazista na Volkswagen do Brasil." Deutsche Welle, July 20, 2017. <www.dw.com/pt-br/um-comandante-nazista-na-volkswagen-do-brasil /a-39853635>. Accessed February 20, 2023.

"Veja a lista dos 377 apontados como responsáveis por crimes na ditadura." G1, 10 Dec. 2014. <g1.globo.com/politica/noticia/2014/12/veja-lista-dos-377-apontados -como-responsaveis-por-crimes-na-ditadura.html>. Accessed July 2, 2023.

"What Is the Origin of the Term Holocaust?" *Encyclopaedia Britannica.* <www .britannica.com/story/what-is-the-origin-of-the-term-holocaust>. Accessed June 3, 2020.

"Why Did Israel Let Mengele Go?" *New York Times*, September 6, 2017. <www. nytimes.com/2017/09/06/sunday-review/israel-mengele-auschwitz-holocaust. html>. Accessed June 13, 2023.

"Wiesenthal, o caçador contesta." *O Estado de S. Paulo*, June 7, 1985.

PRIMARY SOURCES

Brasil. Ministério da Justiça. Polícia Federal. *Inquérito policial n. 1-0097/86*, Vol. 6.

Bundeskriminalamt. *Dossiê Mengele*. Wiesbaden, June 28, 1985, p. 7, arq. 15.

Chen, Yossi. *Looking for a Needle in a Haystack: In Search of the Auschwitz "Doctor of Death."* Jerusalem: Yad Vashem Press, 2007. <https://www.yadvashem.org /yv/pdf-drupal/he/archive/mossad-documents/mengele.pdf>. Accessed August 22, 2023.

—. 4ª Vara Criminal Federal. *Processo-crime n. 8250804, Ré: Liselotte Bossert.*

Mengele, Josef. *Correspondência entre 1969 e 1979.* Museu da Academia Nacional de Polícia, Brasília.

Office of Special Investigations (OSI)—criminal division. *In the Matter of Josef Mengele: A Report to the Attorney General of the United States.* October 1992. <https:// www.justice.gov/sites/default/files/criminal-hrsp/legacy/2011/02/04/10-01-92 mengele-rpt.pdf>. Accessed July 20, 2023.

São Paulo, 11th Property Registry Office. Registration 2762, book 2, record 1.

USC Shoah Foundation. Testimonies from Holocaust Survivors. <https://vha.usc .edu/search>.

WEBSITES

CANDLES Holocaust Museum
https://candlesholocaustmuseum.org/

Centro de Pesquisa e Documentação de História Contemporânea do Brasil
https://cpdoc.fgv.br/

Israel State Archives
https://www.archives.gov.il/en/

Memorial and Museum Auschwitz-Birkenau
http://www.auschwitz.org

United States Holocaust Memorial Museum
https://www.ushmm.org/

NEWSPAPER ARCHIVES

BBC

Bunte

Deutsche Welle

Folha de S.Paulo Haaretz

La Nación

New York Times

O Estado de S. Paulo

Spiegel

Times of Israel

TV Globo

Veja

DOCUMENTARIES

Eldorado: Mengele Vivo ou Morto. Director: Marcelo Felipe Sampaio. São Paulo: Laguna Films, MS Pictures, 2019 (71 min.).

"The Hunt for Doctor Mengele." *World in Action*, Season 15, Episode 5. Producer: Michael Beckham and Brian Lapping. Editor: Ray Fitzwalter. Music: Shawm Phillips. United Kingdom: Granada Television, November 20, 1978 (58 min.). <www .youtube.com/watch?v=W2UjdyZLBrs>. Accessed August 23, 2023.

The Search for Mengele. Director: Brian Moser. Producers: Brian Moser, William Bemister, David Frost, and Roger James. London: Central Television, Home Office Production, 1985 (58 min.).

INTERVIEWS

Adolfo Krause, director of the school where Liselotte worked when the Mengele case broke in 1985.

Alfeo Silotto, resident of Serra Negra, was a teenager when Mengele lived in the city and remembers several stories about "su Pedro."

Carola Sachse, German historian who researched the connection between the Kaiser Wilhelm Institute in Dahlem, Berlin, and the Auschwitz concentration camp.

Cyrla Gewertz, Polish victim of Mengele's medical experiments in Auschwitz. By a huge coincidence, he spent his holidays in Serra Negra, the same city where Mengele lived.

Daniel Romero Muñoz, coroner at the Instituto Médico Legal de SP responsible for the team of Brazilian experts who identified Mengele's skeleton.

David G. Marwell, American historian who participated in the Mengele investigation for the United States Department of Justice.

Espedito Dias Romão, police officer who recorded Mengele's death on Bertioga beach in 1979.

Eva Mozes Kor, victim of Mengele and activist who created the CANDLES association in the United States to reunite the surviving twins.

Evelyn (did not want to disclose her surname), whose children were students of Liselotte Bossert and whose mother was a victim of Mengele in Auschwitz.

Joana Laks, victim of Mengele in Auschwitz and founder of a twins association in Israel.

Liselotte Bossert, a kindergarten teacher and Mengele's protector, who buried him under a false name in the cemetery in Embu.

Marco Antônio Veronezzi, chief delegate of the Federal Police in 1985, responsible for investigating the Mengele case.

Maria Luiza Tucci Carneiro, professor of history at the Faculty of Philosophy, Letters, and Human Sciences at the University of São Paulo.

Members of the German community in São Paulo, who preferred not to be identified.

Michel Michaelovitch de Mahiques, professor at the Oceanographic Institute of the University of São Paulo.

Nancy Rozenchan, professor of Hebrew and Jewish language and literature and Jewish culture at the Faculty of Philosophy, Letters, and Human Sciences at the University of São Paulo.

Paulo Borba Casella, professor of international law at the Faculty of Law of the University of São Paulo.

Rafi Eitan, commander of Mossad operations to kidnap Eichmann and Mengele.

Sinésio Beghini, former mayor of Serra Negra.

Thomas Will, chief prosecutor of the Central Office for Investigating Nazi Crimes, Ludwigsburg, Germany.

Wilmes Teixeira, coroner and former director of the Legal Medical Institute of Mogi das Cruzes, in the state of São Paulo. He coordinated the team of foreign scientists during the examination of Mengele's skeleton.

Yigal Haychuk, Brazilian Mossad agent who participated in the operation to kidnap Mengele.